Derwentwater: in the Lap of the Gods

A brief history of the lives of those who have preserved the beauty of this valley for the last 250 years

Ian Hall

Orchard House Books

Published by Orchard House Books 2019

Orchard House Books
Raven Lane
Applethwaite
Keswick
CA12 4PN

A CIP catalogue record is available from the British Library

ISBN-13: 978-0-9928156-5-3
www.orchardhousebooks.co.uk

To Jennifer, my constant companion on all our walks in the lap of the Gods and canoe trips on the waters of Derwent.

CONTENTS

DERWENTWATER: IN THE LAP OF THE GODS

The title is deliberately ambiguous. On the one hand the lake and its accompanying valley feel to both visitors and locals like the lap of the Gods – the Vale of Elysium as one of the earliest writers, Camden, put it four and a half centuries ago. On the other hand its beauty has at times hung in the balance, in the lap of the Gods. 450 years ago its woods were ravaged to provide fuel to power the smelters at Brigham Forge when the German miners were extracting copper by the ton from the mines in Borrowdale and Newlands, and there was scarcely a mature tree to be seen. 270 years ago the trees had recovered and were again harvested by the new owners: Greenwich Hospital for Distressed Sailors – the nautical equivalent of the present Chelsea Pensioners.

2019 sees the 250th anniversary of what is arguably the first guide written of the area, and the beginnings of tourism. Thomas Gray, the poet who wrote the 'Elegy written in a country churchyard', visited in early October 1769 and published a journal of his travels. Echoing Camden he too dubbed the valley as the 'Vale of Elysium'. He stayed in the Queen's Head in Keswick from 3 – 7 October, travelling up Borrowdale and around the lake. He wrote appreciatively of its beauty though it was only a brief decade since the eastern shoreline had been clear-felled by Greenwich Hospital. Included in that felling were the then-famous oaks on Crow Park, and it was the loss of these and the ravaged stumps all along the shore that first mobilised public opinion to resist the requirements of industry over the demands of the picturesque.

Gray was the first of the poets who might qualify as the Gods of my title, but he was far from the last. Thirty years on from Gray at the beginning of the 19th century Wordsworth came to Grasmere and Coleridge and Southey to Keswick. Wordsworth used his influence with John Marshall, a wealthy industrialist from Leeds, to assist in the purchase and hence protection of the former Greenwich Hospital lands, after Southey had spent many years scheming with his friend Edward Hawke Locker, who was superintendent of the Derwentwater Estate for Greenwich Hospital, to keep the woodland for its amenity rather than timber value.

The other Gods in whose laps the preservation of the beauty around us has lain have been largely absentee landlords, wealthy men who have owned large tracts which they could afford to maintain, while at the same time preventing others from building on every lovely promontory, bay and hillside. The Marshall family at various times from 1832 owned and managed the eastern shores, all four islands, and, on the western shore, Hawes End. Their influence on Keswick town itself was huge, building and maintaining an interest in St. John's Church and School. The western shore from 1784 was owned and developed along picturesque lines by Lord William Gordon and later by his nephew Lt. Colonel Sir John Woodford, till his death in 1879.

The irrepressible Joseph Pocklington perhaps left more of an architectural mark with his mansions on Derwent Island, Barrow Bay and at Portinscale: the country house originally called Finkle Street, now more melodiously Derwent Bank. He alone amongst the Gods showed what might have happened to Derwentwater without the restraining hand of the others.

The last of these largely philanthropic owners was Herbert Wilson Walker with a family business as tanners in Whitehaven and many other towns and also the last private owner of the eastern shoreline. He was responsible for the controlled expansion of the town in the early 20th century and ultimately for the handing over of his estates to the National Trust.

Now, fittingly in this more egalitarian age, we are all Gods if we take seriously the National Trust's strapline to be here 'For ever, for everyone'. For the first time since the days of Alice de Rumilly in 1200 AD almost all the valley is in its single hands – perhaps symbolised by the millennium sculpture by the lakeside in Victoria Bay, Brandlehow, of a pair of cupped hands. The same pressures of enterprise versus preservation are still at play. Over 200 years ago the entrepreneurs were the likes of Peter Crosthwaite with his museum and the various guides leading the early 'tourists' up hill and down the dale, conducting loud and raucous regattas on the lake. Now they seek to string vast cables to act as zip-wires or cable cars for the delight of the many millions who are drawn to the lap of the Gods to worship, to be refreshed in body and in spirit. Derwentwater's fate still lies in the lap of the Gods, and now we are all Gods.

PROLOGUE

DERWENTWATER – THE LAKE ITSELF

Maybe everyone has a favourite lake. Tranquil Grasmere, busy Windermere, mighty Ullswater – or perhaps brooding Wastwater or Ennerdale. Mine is Derwentwater, and that mainly for its islands. No matter from where you view the lake – close by on the many paths around it, or from a nearby fell top, perhaps Catbells or Walla Crag, or even from distant Glaramara or the heights of Skiddaw or the more lowly Latrigg – the main islands draw the eye, their teardrop shape appealing to our sense of harmony. And whichever lake is your favourite, it certainly can't be denied that Derwentwater is the clear winner for its islands.

How many would you suppose there are? Not an easy question, it turns out. The main ones are easy, of course: Derwent Island, with the house on it; St Herbert's Island with its Celtic connections; Lord's Island, close to Stable Hills with its colony of herons; and the less-visited Rampsholme Island, little brother to St Herbert's. But then there are the smaller isles, each with its tree or two. There's a group of four, if the lake is at its normal level, just opposite Lingholm. But if the lake is low at least two of them join as the causeway between them emerges from the water. At the same time the little isle beside Friar's Crag has its own dry path to the mainland – so that's two fewer islands! Ah, but, if the lake is low up to four stony outcrops emerge – two between Derwent Island and St Herbert's; one South of St Herbert's, actually named as Scarf Stones on the OS map, from the old Norse name for Cormorant; and another at the head of the lake.

Touring round the lake anticlockwise from Lingholm we see a lovely verdant isle in Hawes End Bay, Otterbield, and another in Abbot's Bay called Otter Island. Clearly otters were once common on the lake, but none have been sighted since 1970. At the very head of the lake is a cheat of an island, separated from the shore by a narrow channel just wide enough to canoe through – but an island, nevertheless. Continuing along the Eastern shore brings us – preferably by boat, for the margin here is marshy and difficult on foot – to the group of six (at least) where the River Derwent has piled up silt and stone over the millennia separated by meandering and ever-shifting channels. Last, and perhaps strangest of all these smaller islets, appearing only in very special conditions, is the 'floating' island in Lodore Bay. Very rarely seen, this is actually masses of lake-floor vegetation and indeed the soil it grows in (the lake here is shallow) which are propelled to the surface on the rare occasions the water is warm enough to cause the methane trapped under the vegetable layer to make it light enough to bring it to the surface. Not a true contender for an island, then.

Totting all these pearls together, there are at least sixteen isles, islets and islands, and sometimes as many as twenty. Three of them, Derwent Island, St Herbert's and Lords' have long and fascinating histories – part of the subject of this book.

For reasons buried in the mists of time these three principal islands have been in different ownership right up to the time they were separately donated to the National Trust; the last in 1951. St. Herbert's Island belonged to the Earls of Northumberland ever since it was granted them by William Rufus around 1080, until they sold it to Sir Wilfrid Lawson in 1614 as part of his bid to become Lord of the Manor of Borrowdale. Lord's Island and Rampsholme belonged to the de Derwentwater family at least from the time of Adam de Derwentwater in the early 1100s, and then to their successors the Radcliffes until their eventual sale to Greenwich Hospital in 1735. Derwent Island is perhaps the strangest of them all, being argued over in the 12th century before becoming Vicar's Island, belonging to Fountains Abbey but leased to their Vicar of Crosthwaite.

Not only have the islands never historically had but a single owner, the lake itself throughout history and indeed even now has been split into two, always along the same notional line, as shown in the map opposite. Each half of the lake has had a variety of owners, but no-one, not even the National Trust, has ever owned both halves. It is strange that the line is not simply from the river's exit to its entrance near Lodore, but it has always had the bend opposite Barrow House.

THE EARLIEST TOURERS

In the early days of visitors to the Lake District Derwentwater was the Mecca, the pole to which all were drawn. Windermere would have been easier to access, but lacked the grandeur of the Jaws of Borrowdale, the magnificence of the panorama, and frankly the sheer beauty of the lake itself. People came to admire the beauty but also to be frightened (from afar) by the ruggedness of Walla Crag, Castle Crag, and the fells of Borrowdale. Artists could be relied upon to accentuate the awesome, providing terrifying engravings for tourers to take back home to enliven their stories of the rigours and hardships they had faced.

Indeed there were hardships, for travel around the lake in those earliest days was hazardous. There was no accepted track capable of accommodating a carriage, so the only way was either on foot or on horseback. Many preferred to hire a boatman and travel on the lake itself,

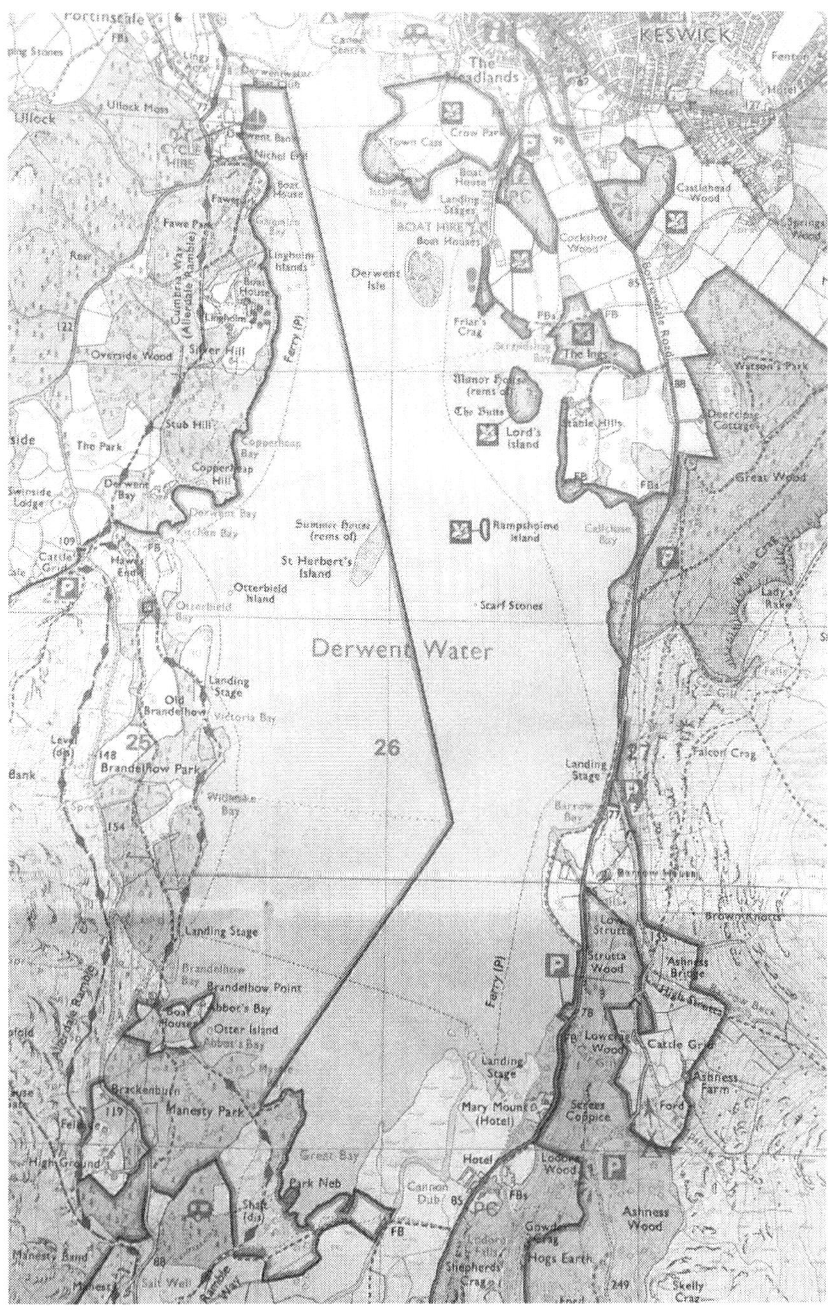

calling in at various 'stations' on the way. The first recorded circuit by a tourer was by Arthur Young in 1770 and his description of the shoreline near Lodore gives a flavour of the enthralled language which was so seductive, drawing in eager followers. He is on his boat below Surprise View, nearing Lodore Falls:

'You look up a wall of rock, perpendicular to the top, scattered with wood, that seems to hang in the air; a large stream rushes from a cliff near the top and falls, in the most romantic manner, several hundred feet.' An accomplished artist, he made this sketch of the falls.

Boating for pleasure soon caught on, and Greenwich Hospital, as owners of the Eastern shoreline and half of the lake issued annual licences to various individuals – some for work, some for pleasure, and several for boatmen ferrying passengers around the lake.

Amount of One Years Rent due on the 5th Day of April 1852 from the following Persons for liberty of having and using Boats upon that part of the Lake of Derwentwater belonging to the Commissioners of Greenwich Hospital, and who have way Leave and Passage over the Grounds of the said Commissioners to and from the Shores of the said Lake.

	Owners Names	Description	No. of Boats	Amount £	s	d
	William Peachy Esqr.		1	.	10	6
	Joseph Pocklington Esqr.		1	.	10	6
	Robert Southey Esqr.		1	.	10	6
	George Ansell	Solicitor	1	.	10	6
	George Rotkin	Black Lead Pencil Manufr.	1	.	10	6
	Thomas Hutton	Late Guide to the Royal Oak	1	.	10	6
	Joseph Jansom	Pleasure and Fishing	1	.	10	6
	John Grave	Guide to the Queen's Head	1	.	10	6
	Joseph Tolson	Fisherman	1	.	10	6
✓	John Pearson	Fisherman	1	.	10	6
✓	John Moor	Guide and Fisherman	2	1	1	.
✓	William Grave	Guide	1	.	10	6
	Harryman Walker	Guide and Fisherman	1	.	10	6
	William Messenger	Racing Boat	1	.	10	6
	William Bowe	Guide and Fisherman	1	.	10	6
	Thomas Fallows	Wherry Boat	1	.	10	6
✓	John Richardson	Pleasure and Fishing	1	.	10	6
×	Joseph James	Pleasure Boat	1	.	10	6
	Joseph Brown	Guide and Fisherman	1	.	10	6
✓	William Atkinson	Pleasure Boat	1	.	10	6
×	Thomas Iveson	Pleasure and Fishing	1	.	10	6
✓	Nicholas Copperthwaite	Fisherman	1	.	10	6
	James Lowther	Overlooker of St. Herberts Isle	1	.	10	6
×	Henry Proley	Pleasure Boat	1	.	10	6
✓	John Walker	Guide and Fisherman	1	.	10	6
✓	Joseph Graham	Pleasure Boat	1	.	10	6
		21.	27	14	3	6

Photo courtesy of Derek Denman

The account sheet on the previous page is from 1832 and includes some famous names, and some less so, whose stories we will explore: William Peachy; Joseph Pocklington; Robert Southey; Thomas Hutton (guide and museum owner) and James Lowther (in charge of the Summer House on St. Herbert's Island). Notice how many are already involved in the tourist trade. The standard charge is ten shillings and sixpence.

Writing in 1770 Arthur Young was perhaps the first of 'the tourers' to publish a sort of guide for others to follow as they came to wonder at the majesty of the fells and serenity of the lake, but he was certainly far from the last. Thomas Gray, the poet most famous for his 'Elegy in a country churchyard' visited a year earlier than Young and wrote to his friend Dr. Wharton about his five days at Keswick but his journal wasn't published till 1775. Thomas West's guide, first published in 1778, ran to five editions. William Gilpin, prebendary of Salisbury Cathedral, had the temerity to address his guide of 1786 based on observations made in 1772, to George III's Queen Charlotte – but then, he was also a great artist, credited with being 'the father of the picturesque'. And he was writing about the lake where the art of the picturesque was carried to its limits, and perhaps beyond.

Here, around Derwentwater, Thomas West first proposed 'viewing stations' where the visitor would get the most picturesque view of the lake. Artists brought 'Claude Glasses' the better to compose a picture they could draw or paint. These rather quaint objects were slightly convex mirrors made of blackened glass: standing with their back to the view the artist could see in his glass a somewhat compressed and darkened version of the view – perfect for committing to paper to bring out the major features. West's eight stations were shown on Peter Crosthwaite's map of *'The matchless Lake of Derwent, (situate in the most delightful Vale which perhaps Human Eye beheld)'* of 1783. Crosthwaite wasn't one to undersell his products. Going clockwise round the lake West starts at Crow Park, moves on to the summit of Cockshot Wood, then to high up under Falcon Crag and so on to station 4 which is on top of Castle Crag, a mile south of Grange. The fifth is on top of Swinside Hill and the sixth on the summit of the wooded hill behind Nichol End and Fawe Park. The seventh is on top of Vicarage Hill near Crosthwaite Church. The eighth I cannot find on the map! Several of these stations are now overgrown with woodland and no longer good viewpoints. At first glance it is surprising he didn't include a station on the terrace road below Catbells – but it was yet to be built.

Drawing and painting is all well and good, but how to make money by it? Joseph Farington RA was the first to capitalise on his artistic skills in the Lakes by commissioning engravings of his watercolours, allowing him to print off unlimited black and white – or rather greyscale – copies. These found a ready market among the new breed of tourist, deprived of the Grand Tour of Italy and the Alps by the continental wars. The first of these were available in 1785, and went on being produced for the next thirty years. Here's a late engraving of his watercolour of Derwentwater from Brow Top.

Derwentwater by Joseph Farington RA, engraved by F R Hay in 1816

In almost at the start of the tourist explosion which changed the face of both Keswick and Lake Derwentwater was that larger-than-life figure Joseph Pocklington who bought Derwent Island in 1778 and merits a chapter to himself later. The lake can never before have seen (or heard) the like of the regattas he and his fellow entrepreneur Peter Crosthwaite put on to enthral with spectacle the growing numbers of tourists coming to this new-found nirvana. Galleons sallied forth to 'capture' Pocklington's Island, cannon thundering with many an echo from the surrounding fells. Muskets and pistols belched flame (but no shot) and budding actors fell before them till at last Pocklington's cellar was liberated and feasting and merriment became the order of the night.

Ever since then the lake has been the highway for boating for pleasure, as well as the continued business transport that has always gone on. Occasionally there have been fatal accidents – though, as in most cases the boats have been overloaded accident may be too generous a word. At least two cases of boats overloaded with cargo are recorded: in 1657

William Munkhouse drowned when his boat, loaded to the gunwales with stone from Lord's Island, was swamped and sank near Friar's Crag[1]; in the early 1800s the same fate befell John Nixon, the boatman ferrying slates from Hawes End Bay to St. Herbert's Island to roof the new boathouse. Worst of all was the drowning of five young ladies out for a pleasure cruise in a large rowing boat in 1898. Again the boat was overloaded because at thc last moment a gentleman joined them in the stern, and when a storm blew up and the waves became choppy near St. Herbert's Island the boat shipped water and began to sink. The oarsman and the unwanted gentleman escaped but the ladies, weighed down by the heavy garments of the time and probably unable to swim anyway, were all drowned.[2]

OWNERSHIP OF THE LAKE ITSELF

If there ever was a time when one person owned the entire lake it was back in the 1100s, though it is doubtful even then. Those were the days when a particular family for three generations had only daughters surviving – three in two cases – which is why areas of land and water got split up so comprehensively. The family are the de Rumillys, originating for our purposes in a French nobleman, Robert de Rumilly who was given large tracts of land by William Rufus, the Conqueror's son, including the 'Honour of Skipton'. The title just means an area around a castle. Opposite is Robert's family tree, stripped to its essentials to help follow the thread.

In each generation, there being no male inheritor, the properties were split among the daughters, leading to acrimonious lawsuits and a much diminished estate. The only time Derwentwater may have been in one family's hands is during the marriage of Cecily de Rumilly the first, and in her widowhood. Her share of old Robert's vast holdings included Skipton and Allerdale north of the River Derwent, later called Allerdale below Derwent; including the East half of Derwentwater. Her husband William Meschin owned Copeland, based on Egremont Castle which he had built on the simple Motte and Bailey principle, and at that time included the West side and shores of Derwentwater. So between them they owned the entire lake, and for the twenty years of her widowhood Cecily administered both Allerdale and Copeland.[3]

---

[1] Crosthwaite Parish Registers

[2] Ray Greenhow, *The Derwentwater Disaster, 12th August 1898.*

[3] William Farrer and Charles Travis Clay. Editors, *Early Yorkshire Charters*, Vol 7, p. 3

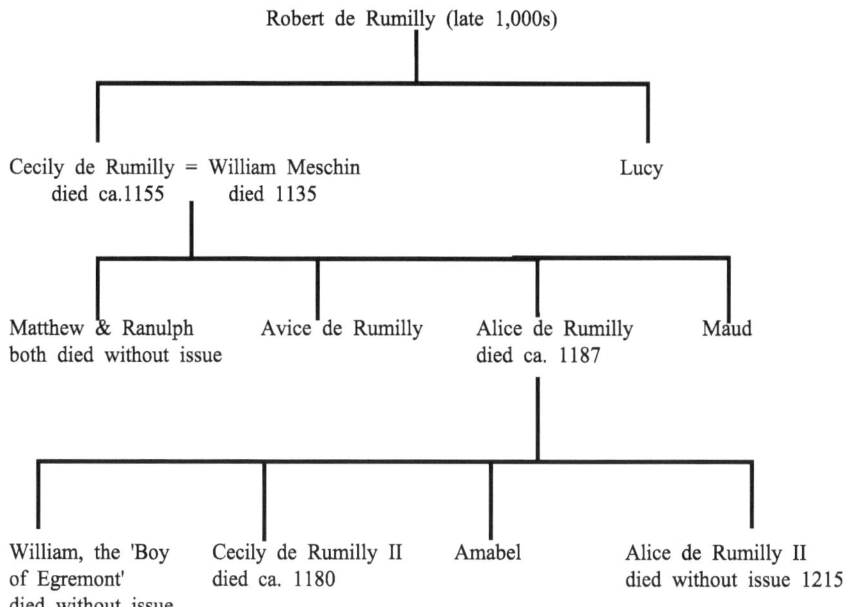

Her daughter Alice I was forced to marry a very unsavoury character, a Scot and nephew of the King of Scotland, one William Fitz Duncan, who married her mainly to get his hands on Cecily's lands, and in practice it was he who pulled the strings. They had the three daughters and one son shown in line four of the family tree. The son, William, should of course have inherited Allerdale and Copeland, including Derwentwater, but he died in a hunting accident, falling into the River Wharfe when jumping the narrow cleft known still as The Strid. This tragedy provided Wordsworth with one of his best-known poems, *The white doe of Ryedale*, but it robbed Alice of her only son, leaving her to split her lands amongst her three daughters, Cecily II, Amabel and Alice de Rumilly II.

And that's where the Lake got divided again, after its short unification. Cecily took Copeland and Egremont Castle while Alice II received Allerdale below Derwent which included what was to become Keswick, the hamlet of Crosthwaite and all Borrowdale South of the lake.[4] Although she married twice Alice II had no children and gave herself to helping the newly founded monasteries of Fountains Abbey, Bolton Abbey and, in Lancashire North of the Sands, Furness Abbey. In particular she gave lands at Crosthwaite, Keswick and Bassenthwaite to Fountains Abbey and re-furbished Saint Kentigern's Church at Crosthwaite in 1181.

[4] *Early Yorkshire Charters*, p.19

After her first husband died she gave the East side of the Borrowdale valley, including that part of Derwentwater, to Fountains Abbey around 1195. Except that she had already given Derwent Island to the parish of Crosthwaite as glebe land for the Vicar of Crosthwaite – so it changed name from Hestholm (Stallion Island) to Vicar's Island. After her second husband died she sold the West side of Borrowdale to Furness Abbey around 1208. That is in as far as she owned it: its boundaries were the Copeland Honour now belonging to her sister Cecily II, which came to halfway across the lake.

Not long after this the Honour of Copeland and Egremont Castle came into the Percy hands. The Percys were a noble family in the North-East who were soon knighted to become the Earls of Northumberland. As with de Rumilly, the first Percy on English soil came over with William the Conqueror and was given estates as a reward: and like de Rumilly he took his name from the town in Northern France he came from – Percy, in Normandy. The Percy family, Earls of Northumberland, held Copeland and Egremont for centuries till the line fizzled out in 1750. Sir William Wyndham, a brother-in-law of the last female Percy, inherited Egremont and Copeland and was created First Earl of Egremont and became Lord of the Manor, including the West side of the lake.

All was well for the next two Earls, except that the third earl left no legitimate male heir. He did father a number of illegitimate ones however, and the eldest, George Wyndham, inherited most of the land but was barred from the title. For twenty years he was plain Colonel George Wyndham, till in 1859 Queen Victoria gave him the title Lord Leconfield. The West side of the lake remained a Leconfield possession till it was bought by the National Trust in 1958 with money subscribed by the Friends of the Lake District and other supporters.

What follows is the story of the intricate cat's cradle of owners, poets, entrepreneurs, recluses, quangos, business-men, and plain workers who have aspired to keep this lake as the lap of the Gods: a place where all who would come to wonder, to paint, to experience adventure were and are still, welcome.

PART ONE
ST. HERBERT'S ISLAND

CHAPTER ONE

ST. HERBERT AND HIS ISLAND

My personal favourite of all the islands, St. Herbert's rises almost perfectly in the middle of the lake, two kilometres from the Northern shore where the river drains out near Derwentwater Marina and two kilometres from where the river comes in at Lodore Bay. It lies slightly nearer the Western edge, three-quarters of a kilometre from Hawse End bay, while it is a full kilometre over to Calf Close bay on the Eastern fringe. I like to think this is a courtesy on its part, allowing little Rampsholme Island space to breathe between St Herbert's and the bay.

This makes it a natural destination for anyone hiring a boat from Keswick's Landing Stages, from Derwentwater Marina, from Nichol End or indeed from Platty+ at Lodore. It's a decent row with a worthwhile quest at the end of it, for St Herbert's Island repays the effort many times over. It has a history going back to the 7th Century hermit monk who gives it its name. There are goose nests in spring with their speckled eggs and fiercely proud matriarchs hissing their warning to any who venture too close. There are plenty of sites for making a den, if you want to copy St. Herbert – and plenty of evidence of fires even though the National Trust, which owns all the islands, frowns upon them. A grassy bay faces over to Hawse End – perfect for a picnic and a lie in the afternoon sun. Lie there a while pretending to count as your children get lost playing hide and seek. Be sure to look up as you eventually search, there are many inviting trees to climb, and where better to hide away?

Anyone exploring the four to five acres (depending on the height of the lake) soon comes across what he imagines to be the ruins of St Herbert's hermitage, a fine circle of broken down walls some thirty feet across, with the remains of a fire invariably in the middle. It is easy to sit here awhile musing on the life he must have led – the privations of winter, with the lake all around frozen solid. Easy then to slip off to the delights of Keswick, except that he freely chose his solitude, and in any case, Keswick in the 7th Century was no more than a tiny hamlet with little to offer even to a hermit. You will have rowed over on a fine day, with the lake calm, the sun perhaps warming your back as you ply the oars. What must it be like when the rain lashes the lake and the wind whips up white horses all around? What visions of glory sustained this hermit saint, making his self-inflicted solitude worthwhile?

Alas, the ruins around you are not those which sheltered the saint, though it is possible they occupy the same site. More than one building has

Our grand-children cooking sausages in the ruins of the summer house.

been here, and other ruins spoke the same to William Wordsworth who penned these lines on this very place:

> If thou in the dear love of some one Friend
> Hast been so happy that thou know'st what thoughts
> Will sometimes in the happiness of love
> Make the heart sink, then wilt thou reverence
> This quiet spot; and, Stranger! not unmoved
> Wilt thou behold this shapeless heap of stones,
> The desolate ruins of St. Herbert's Cell.
> Here stood his threshold; here was spread the roof
> That sheltered him, a self-secluded Man.

This poem appeared in Vol II of 'The Lyrical Ballads' published in 1800. It probably began life in April1794 when William and his sister Dorothy rowed across to the island, whilst staying in Windy Brow Cottage, Keswick. They were there as the guests of William and Raisley Calvert, school friends from Wordsworth's Hawkshead days, and it was the first time since they were children they had spent time together. Those few weeks in Keswick were life-changing for them: they made the momentous decision to spend their lives together; Raisley Calvert, who was dying of tuberculosis, offered William a bequest of £600 – later increased to £900 – which would give them the means; and a delight with the Lake District was born in their souls. William was himself 'a self-secluded man' having left his French mistress Annette Vallon pregnant with their daughter Caroline in France just a couple of years previously.

THE FIRST KNOWN RECORD OF ST. HERBERT'S ISLAND: AROUND 700 AD.

We would know nothing of St. Herbert had he not formed a post-script in the Venerable Bede's account of the far more famous St. Cuthbert. Bede was a monk in the 7th and 8th Century (672 -735 AD) in Jarrow Abbey, then called the Monastery of St Peter, and a great writer, linguist and translator. His most famous work is 'The Ecclesiastical History of the English People' and in his stories of St. Cuthbert he is recording almost contemporaneous history, as Cuthbert died in 687 AD. Whilst to modern readers his mix of miracle and historical fact raises questions regarding his dependability the life of St. Cuthbert is sufficiently recorded independently to allow us to accept the more factual stories as true. Among these is his account of the friendship between St. Cuthbert and St. Herbert, which forms chapter 29 of Book IV in the work above. The same story with a few small changes appears also in Bede's 'Book of the life and miracles of St. Cuthbert'.

Herbert appears as the person to whom Cuthbert most openly revealed that he was dying, and Bede tells us he did so because the two saints were close friends. Although Cuthbert clearly was a man of the world, becoming Bishop of Lindisfarne for the last two years of his life, he shared with Herbert a desire for the life of a reclusive hermit and spent the preceding decade alone, firstly on the little island just off Lindisfarne, known now as St. Cuthbert's Island, and later on the wild and desolate Inner Farne Island, six miles out in the North Sea.

It was in these last two years of Cuthbert's life that the meeting with Herbert as told in Bede's 'History' took place. As bishop of Lindisfarne Cuthbert travelled across northern England, and was due to visit Carlisle. Here is the tale as told by Bede.

> There was a priest of praiseworthy life named Herbert, who had for a long time been linked in a spiritual friendship with the man of God. He lived the life of a hermit on an island in the great lake which is the source of the river Derwent, and used to visit Cuthbert each year to seek his advice on matters of eternal salvation. Hearing that Cuthbert had come to the city of Lugubalia (Carlisle), he went to visit him as usual, wishing to be ever more fervently inspired to heavenly desires by his salutary guidance. As each in turn regaled the other with exhilarating draughts of heavenly life, Cuthbert said

> among other things: 'Brother Herbert, remember that, whatever you wish to ask or tell me you must do before we part, because you will not see me again in this world. For I know that the day of my death is approaching, and I shall soon be put off this earthly tabernacle.

As an aside, the second of Bede's books, above, mentions that Cuthbert was in Carlisle 'not only to consecrate priests, but also to bless the queen herself with his holy conversation.' This queen is reckoned to be the widow of the English king Egfrid who had been slain in battle two years before in a raid against the Picts and Britons of the west[5].

Bede then tells us of Herbert's distress at this news, and his slightly strange request that if Cuthbert is to die very soon, he, Herbert, might die at the same time so that 'we may pass away together to the vision of heavenly grace.' Bede records that Herbert was granted his wish, and that the two saints both died on their respective islands of seclusion on 20th March 687 AD. Bede goes on to record, of St. Herbert, that:

> Herbert was first tried by a long illness. And one may believe that God's mercy decreed this in order that, if his merits were inferior to those of the blessed Cuthbert, the chastening of a long illness might supply what was lacking; in this way he would be made equal in grace with his intercessor and in departing this life at the same time would merit to enter into the same state of eternal blessedness.

Is it fanciful to deduce from this snippet some idea of the reasons behind Herbert's and other hermits' motives for their voluntary seclusion from the world? There was clearly an explicit belief in a life after death – a life where one would get one's just deserts. Was this why so many felt the need to eschew all contact with other people, that they might not be tempted into what they saw as sin? Was self-exclusion seen by some as penance, a voluntary self-chastisement to hasten one's entry into Heaven? It seems so, and certainly life on the tiny island in the middle of Derwentwater through all the seasons must have been gruelling – especially when ill. St Herbert's Island is a good place to ponder these philosophies.

Who might have been Herbert's neighbours in what is now Keswick, but then an unnamed small collection of hovels? Christianity had taken hold, and there was a church on the site of the present-day Crosthwaite Church. Its dedication is to St. Kentigern, whom legend says founded it in

---

[5] Rev. Thomas Lees MA, Article XXXII of the *Transactions of the Cumberland and Westmorland Antiquarian & Archaeological Society [hereafter TCWAAS]*

553 AD, around a hundred years before Herbert's time there. So we may imagine a small community of Christians who may have kept a watchful eye on the island (from Friars' Crag) and responded when it was apparent Herbert had died. Presumably it was this community who kept alive his memory and somehow informed Bede of the coincidence of his and Cuthbert's death – a coincidence that would be worth preserving in memory.

THE NEXT REFERENCE, IN 1374, BY BISHOP THOMAS APPLEBY.

Thomas Appleby was bishop of Carlisle from 1363 -1395, and Carlisle Record Office holds an incomplete set of his registers, in Latin, which have been translated and published by R.L.Storey. *(Vol 96 of the Canterbury and York Society, 2006).* Entry 323 is the mandate to the vicar of Crosthwaite in 1374, and reads as follows:

> The bishop has read in the book of the Venerable Bede on the history of the English people that Herbert, a priest, was a disciple of St. Cuthbert. He lived on an island in Derwentwater but visited Cuthbert annually to receive his guidance. When Cuthbert happened to come to Carlisle, Herbert went to Cuthbert who told him he expected to die soon. Herbert tearfully begged that Cuthbert would pray that he might die first. After a pause Cuthbert replied that this prayer was answered. On 13 April following [687], Cuthbert died on Farne Island, and Herbert died on his island. The bishop believes that few know about this miracle and orders the vicar to go to Herbert's Island on the said thirteenth day and celebrate the mass for St. Cuthbert cum nota; with a grant of indulgence for 40 days to those who attend. Dated at Rose (Castle, the bishop's palace).

This record raises as many questions as it answers: in particular, how is it that the bishop, having read Bede's accounts, mistakes the dates of Cuthbert's and Herbert's deaths? Bede is clear that they died on 20th March, but here Thomas Appleby is quoting 13th April. The answer is most probably that he mistook the date quoted by Bede for their deaths. Bede of course wrote in Anglo-Saxon, but translated into the Latin Bishop Appleby would be reading it is written as 'xiii Kal. Aprilis' which indeed is as it appears in the Calendarium of the York Missal as St. Cuthbert's Day. This was how they wrote the 20th March in the Latin of his day, meaning the 13th day <u>before</u> the Kalends (1st) of April. Counting both the beginning and end days, this is indeed 20th March. Thomas probably took that to mean 13th day <u>after</u> 1st April. Incidentally, I can't resist pointing out that the year

Bishop Thomas chose, 1374, is exactly twice as much as the year of Herbert's death, 687. Expect further revelations in 2061.

Bishop Appleby paid for a chapel to be built on St. Herbert's Island – presumably particularly for use on the 13th April when the annual pilgrimage took place, but no doubt for occasional use by other holy men. It was still visible in 1586 when William Camden wrote his *Britannia, or A Chorographical Description of the Flourishing Kingdoms of England, Scotland, and Ireland.* This was written in Latin and is the first published guide to Britain, approached county by county. In it he says of St. Herbert's Island and Derwentwater:

> Divers springs cometh out of Borodale, and so make a great lough that we call a pool, and therein be three isles. In the one is the head places of the M. Radclyf, another is called St. Hereberts isle, **where is a chapel**, (My emphasis) the 3d is Vicar isle full of trees like a wilderness. Keswic is placed in a narrow bottom under vast mountains full of mines. There is carried on a manufactory of flannels, linseys, and yarn. It has a school. Its vale a circle between land and water of about 20 miles is the Elysium of the north. The form of the lake is irregular, extending about three miles and an half from north to south and about one mile and an half broad; its greatest depth 20 feet. The river Derwent passes through and gives name to it. The southern extremity is a composition of all that is horrible. An immense chasm opens up in the midst, whose entrance is divided by a rude conic hill, once topt by a castle, beyond a chain of craggs, patched with snow, and containing various minerals, overshading the dark winding deeps of Borrowdale. The north view is a beautiful contrast.[6]

So now we have two buildings on the island: St. Herbert's cell and Bishop Appleby's chapel. It may well be that St. Herbert's cell had entirely disappeared and Appleby built on a different site, or that the ruins of the cell were still visible and Appleby re-used the stone and built on the same site. Is this the site still so visible near the lake-shore? (Grid reference NY25966132). Jamie Lund, the National Trust's archaeologist surveyed the islands in 1999 and concluded there had been an ancient building in the middle of the island (grid reference NY25946130) which he identified as the chapel ruins. What then are the much more extensive ruins by the lakeshore, the ones most visitors assume are Herbert's cell?

---

[6] Translated from the 1607 Latin edition by Richard Gough, published London, 1789.

These are in fact much more recent, being but 220 years old, or thereabouts. They are the ruins of a 'pleasure house' or Summer House, built by the then owner of the Island, Sir Wilfrid Lawson, sometime around 1795-1800 – more of him later. The summer house was much in use in Jonathon Otley's time, and he writes of it in his '*Guidebook, a Concise Description of the English Lakes'*. On page 18 we read:

> One [island], nearer the middle of the lake, is called St. Herbert's Isle, from being the residence of that holy man; who, according to the Venerable Bede, was contemporary with St. Cuthbert, and died about A.D. 687. It appears that several centuries afterwards, the anniversary of his death was, by the Bishop of the diocese, enjoined to be celebrated upon this spot in religious offices. Some remains of what is said to have been his cell are still to be seen among the trees with which the island is covered. Near thirty years ago, a small grotto or fishing cot was built by the late Sir Wilfred Lawson, of Brayton House, to whose successor the island now belongs[7].

This is a critical reference, making it clear that there are at least two sites – the new summer house and the site described by Lund in 1999. What is still unclear is which site, if either, was the site of the original cell. It is probably just wishful thinking to imagine for a moment that Herbert's cell could have been on the site of the summer house, but there are a couple of hints that it might have been.

There is one reference in Hutchinson's History which says 'The remains of St. Herbert's hermitage appear to this day, one apartment twenty feet long and sixteen broad, probably his chapel; the other, narrower, his cell.'[8] This is an unreliable reference, not appearing in any earlier account, but these remains may have been what Camden referred to as the chapel. Since these ruins are no longer visible anywhere else on the island it is tempting to think they may have been on the site of the summer house which Lawson built, and the stones re-used. The plan, a chapel and a cell side by side, is the same as that which Bede describes as St. Cuthbert's building on Inner Farne.

> The building is almost of a round form, from wall to wall about four or five poles in extent. The wall on the outside is higher than a man, but within by excavating the rock, he made it much deeper, to prevent the eyes and thoughts from wandering, that the mind might be bent on heavenly things, and the pious inhabitant might behold

[7] Jonathan Otley, *A Description of the English Lakes*, 1823

[8] Hutchinson, William *A history of the county of Cumberland* 1794

nothing from his residence but the heavens above him. The walls were constructed, not of hewn stones or of brick and mortar, but of rough stones and turf which had been taken out from the ground within.... There were two chambers in the house, one an oratory and one for domestic purposes. He finished the walls of them by digging round and cutting away the natural soil within and without, and formed the roof of rough poles and straw.'[9]

As the two men were friends Herbert's cell may well have been similar, but smaller, and Hutchinson may be justified.

There is a temptation to imagine him as a simple hermit, never leaving the island, living on fish and perhaps the few vegetables he could grow: the ultimate ascetic. But the scant picture in Bede is very different. It's clear Herbert left his island at least annually to visit his friend and mentor, Cuthbert; sometimes in Carlisle, as at their last meeting, but presumably more often on the east coast, even perhaps at Cuthbert's cell on Inner Farne. Might he not well have constructed a smaller replica of his guide's cell? We know pilgrims made their way to the Farne Islands to receive spiritual blessing from Cuthbert: might the same not be true of Herbert?

To sum up, then: clearly the ruins we pore over on the island are those of the summer house built by Sir Wilfrid Lawson around 1800 AD. It is a remote possibility that they are on the site of St. Herbert's original cell, and also possible that Bishop Appleby's chapel was built on this site too. The stones may have been used three times over. There is also the almost invisible site in the middle of the island which might be the original cell site and/or the chapel site.

The print overleaf is taken from an engraving of the summer house by Theodore H A Fielding, published by Thomas McLean, 26 Haymarket, London, et al, 1822. Once again, the ruins now visible are certainly of this summer house – which would probably re-use the original stones of the chapel, which in its turn may have re-used stones from St. Herbert cell.

This, presumably, is an accurate portrayal, which is more than can be said for the one beneath it: the great JMW Turner's watercolour purporting to be of St Herbert's chapel painted in 1834!

[9] Bede's *Vita Cuthberti*, pp. 214 – 17

The Summer House on St Herbert's Island, Theodore H A Fielding

St Herbert's Island for Rogers's poems, ca. 1830: JMW Turner

CHAPTER TWO

THE LAWSON YEARS 1614-1850

Sir Wilfrid Lawson bought St. Herbert's Island from the Right Honourable Henry, Earl of Northumberland on 8th June, 1614 and so began nearly a quarter of a millennium of ownership, almost always by a Sir Wilfrid or a Sir Gilfrid Lawson – even if it meant a change of name.[10] This first indenture as usual retains all 'mines, fishing, liberties, franchises and royalties' to the Earl and his heirs, and levies an annual rent or lease of ten shillings 'with a power of distress for non-payment'. This particular Sir Wilfrid Lawson was intent on widening his portfolio of property in Borrowdale in preparation for a bid to become Lord of the Manor there. He had bought up all of Watendlath and Stonethwaite from Walter Graham earlier in the century, and thereby hangs a tale...

The Sir Wilfrid Lawson of the beginning of the 17th century and advent of King James I was a prominent man in the history of the Borders at that time. These were the last throes of the Border Reivers, with the Graham family the chief thorn in the side of the new King James. On his way south to his coronation in London to unite England and Scotland, while James was at Berwick on the east coast border the Grahams led a destructive foray deep into Cumberland, penetrating as far as Penrith. King James instituted a regime to control the Borders as a Crown colony – under the jurisdiction of a royal commission led by Sir Wilfrid Lawson. This was in 1603. The commission, and Sir Wilfrid, were determined to be rid of the Graham family. A hundred and fifty Graham men were forcibly enlisted in the army, and when that failed to work they were exiled to Ireland, with some of the most extreme being hanged. This was in 1606 – the very year when Sir Wilfrid was able to buy all of Walter Graham's Borrowdale holdings. Walter's grandfather, Richard Graemes (Graham) of Eske in Netherby had bought the forfeited Fountains Abbey holdings in Borrowdale for £134 14s 2d in 1546, when Henry VIII dissolved the abbeys and sold off their property. One might wonder why Henry VIII would sell to such a lawless Reiver, but he did.[11] The deeds of conveyance make it clear Sir Wilfrid paid properly for his acquisitions, but one cannot help but wonder whether Walter Graham had a choice as to selling.[12] Sir Wilfrid held the power of life or death over Walter's son, the notorious

---

[10] Carlisle Record Office, bundle D/NT/6

[11] Bouch & Jones: *A short economic and social history of the Lake Counties 1500 – 1830,* Manchester.

[12] Molly Lefebure *'Cumberland Heritage' pp. 49,50*

Richard Graham, 'worst of the reivers', and chose only to exile him briefly to Ireland instead of hanging him.

Sir Wilfrid's chance to become Lord of the Manor came soon after his purchase of St. Herbert's Island, in November 1614. A pair of asset-strippers from London, William Whitmore and Jonas Verdon, bought all King James' rights in Borrowdale, including several farms along with the mineral, fishing, timber etc. rights, and were keen to sell them on piecemeal to make a profit. Among their 38 farms sold were two to Sir Wilfrid, a freehold tenement in Stonethwaite and another in Rosthwaite, on 23rd November 1614 – just five days before the Great Deed of Borrowdale was signed.[13]

The Great Deed purports to grant

> 'all the woods... wastes, commons, stinted pastures ... ways and entries, these being things which cannot conveniently be apportioned and divided' to all 38 commoners 'for the apportionable benefit of themselves and of the rest of the tenants of the Manor ... ratably and apportionably according to the several rents which they respectively have paid for the several tenements'[14].

That was the rub: Lawson owned more properties than the rest of the commoners put together, and he very soon arrogated to himself the title of 'Lord of the Manor' and levied fines and rents for common rights on the fells around, and claimed all the timber.

At the time Sir Wilfrid lived at Isel Hall, just to the North-West of Bassenthwaite Lake. He had no male heirs, so on his death in 1632 his estate passed to his brother's grandson – another Wilfrid of course. Old Sir Wilfrid's brother William and William's son, another William, had both conveniently died, leaving the field open for this second Wilfrid, who turned out to be a force to be reckoned with. He was the first to institute the Manorial Court at Rosthwaite, cementing the Lawson claim to be Lords of the Manor, and the minutes of that first meeting are in D/Law/6 in Carlisle Record Office. (Next page)

This second Sir Wilfrid, who took over in 1632, began the Civil War years (1642-1651) as a Royalist, but quickly changed sides when he detected the likely outcome, though his son Sir William Lawson remained a staunch supporter of King Charles I. Sir Wilfrid recognised the impregnability of St. Herbert's Island and quickly established a garrison there.[15]

---

[13] Carlisle Record Office, bundle D/Law/1/160

[14] CRO, *Great deed of Borrowdale*

[15] J. Fisher Crosthwaite *Old Borrowdale* CWAAS 1875-6

Part of the original minutes of the first manorial court meeting in Rosthwaite, held in 1632

Transcription:

The names of the tenants within Borrowdale who were formerly tenants of Sir Wilfrid Lawson, Knight, and the sum of every man's whole years rent sett. domine (= settled to the lord?) the 6th day of June anno domini 1632

Watendlath	*£*	*s*	*d*
*'Imprimis' *Myles Wilson of Eshness*	*0*	*6*	*2*
Peter Winder	*1*	*2*	*8*
Edward Birket junior	*1*	*0*	*0*
Edward Birket senior	*0*	*10*	*0*
John Birket	*0*	*10*	*0*
Gawine Norman	*0*	*14*	*0*
John Wilson	*0*	*13*	*4*
John Langthwaite senior	*0*	*8*	*4*
John Langthwaite junior	*0*	*13*	*4*
Myles Birket	*0*	*5*	*8*

*(Imprimis means 'in the first place' and is used before the first name of, here, the Watendlath tenants, and later the Stonethwaite tenants.)

We will see, later, Cornet Philipson's abortive attempt to capture the garrison for the Royalists, and how it was intended as an arsenal for the Royalist guns captured in Carlisle.

Throughout these years Lawson was based at Isel Hall, a fine mansion on the banks of the River Derwent just north of Bassenthwaite Lake, but he managed to get his acquisitive hands on Brayton Mansion and lands, near Aspatria, in 1658. Brayton had belonged to one Thomas Salkeld who left it to his three daughters, who agreed to sell in order to be able to split the proceeds. Sir Wilfrid bought it for £1,000. One of the husbands signing away their inheritance was a Thomas Wybergh: we shall meet his eponymous descendant who managed to square the account a little later.

Sir Wilfrid purchased a baronetcy in 1688 for £2,000 from King James II, becoming the first of ten baronets of Isel, eight of whom were called either Wilfrid or Gilfrid, and six of these served as members of Parliament. He died later that year. Ordinarily the title and the estate would have passed to his son William, who as we saw opposed his father in the Civil War, but William pre-deceased him, having previously lost his eyesight. So he left Isel and the title of Second Baronet of Isel to William's son – inevitably named Wilfrid! To his own second son, named, guess what, Wilfrid, he left the Brayton estate. And so the twin families of Isel Lawsons and Brayton Lawsons came into being, their subsequent histories inter-twining.

Sir Wilfrid and his wife are buried in Isel church and an epitaph to them is in the chancel:

> Here lies Sir Wilfrid Lawson, baronet, and his Lady Jane
> He departed this life 13th day of December 1688 aged 79
> And she the 8th June 1677 aged 65. Having married four
> sons and eight daughters. Vivit post funera virtue.

The Latin translates as 'Virtue outlives death' and is the motto of the city of Nottingham. I don't think there is any connection.

Although the Baronetcy was 'of Isel' in fact most of the baronets lived at Brayton. This was because the Isel line died out fairly soon, so that the title passed to Sir Gilfrid Lawson who was one of the Brayton branch. The Isel branch named the 5th baronet 'Mordaunt Lawson' breaking the tradition of Wilfrids; no doubt sealing their fate! Mordaunt died aged ten, having been the baronet a mere four years. Most of the documents in the Lawson file are from Brayton. The baronets seem to have been an abstemious bunch, no fewer than four of the ten dying without issue, which accounts for the continuous passing of the title to brothers and cousins.

The next Sir Wilfrid of interest to St. Herbert's Island turned out to be the last. He was the tenth baronet of Isel, from 1794 -1806. His portrait is below.

Sir Wilfrid Lawson, 10th Baronet of Isel.

Sometime in his short tenure of the island this Sir Wilfrid Lawson had a 'summer-house' built on the island. This raises the question: just when? William Wordsworth published the poem in chapter one in 1800, but probably after a visit in 1794, so presumably the summer-house didn't exist then, since Wordsworth was gazing on visible ruins (of the chapel). Probably then the summer-house was built around 1795 as Jonathan Otley described it as being nearly thirty years old in 1823. The baronet died without issue in 1806, but his will, written in 1802, takes care of the inheritance. His estate is left to the second son of one Thomas Wybergh – and so we come full circle from 150 years previously when an ancestral Thomas Wybergh was a party in the sale to the Lawsons. The reason is that Wybergh's wife and Lawson's wife were sisters: why the inheritor should be the second son is unclear, though the Wyberghs were substantial landowners in their own right so the first may already have been taken care of. Or maybe Thomas was the only one prepared to change his name as required by the will – to Thomas Lawson, and to take upon himself the Lawson coat of arms.[16]

When Sir Wilfrid died in 1806 the baronetcy died with him. Young Thomas Wybergh as was, Lawson as he became, was only 18 and so could not inherit in his own right till he became 21. He celebrated his 21st birthday in style with a great party on St. Herbert's Island in and around the summer-house followed by a ball in Keswick to which the great and the good of all the surrounding area were invited and came. There is a letter in the D/NT/6 bundle in Carlisle Record office in which a James Lowther of Keswick confirms he was a waiter at the island that day, and that there were 'boat races, one of which was for a silver cup given by Mr. Thomas Lawson which was won by one Edward Birkett in his boat "The Lively"'. Lowther goes on to affirm that on 10th June 1824 he was taken on to be the caretaker of the 'cottage or Hermitage' and has been so ever since, with the key in his possession. Lowther further states that Sir Wilfrid Lawson entertained his brothers and friends there every summer, and had a boat-house built there too. He remembers that a slate merchant, John Nixon, was drowned when his boat full of slates for the boathouse was swamped and sank.[17]

Alas, young Thomas did not live long to enjoy his inheritance. According to the plaque in Isel Church he died 'of a consumption on his passage from the island of Madeira on 2nd May 1812', a bachelor and without issue, whereupon Wilfrid Wybergh, the fifth son of Thomas Wybergh the elder inherited the estates including the island.[18] It almost seems that the curse on any Lawson not called Wilfrid or Gilfrid had struck again. The new Sir Wilfrid – Wybergh as was, Lawson as he became – had a new baronetcy created for him, as that of Isel had died with Old Sir Wilfrid in 1806. He was created Sir Wilfrid Lawson, 1st Baronet of Brayton on 1st September 1831 by King William IV, and lived to a ripe old age. Very sensibly he named his first-born son Wilfrid, as did that son, so there were three more Sir Wilfrid Lawsons, but of Brayton, not Isel. This last Wilfrid had no heirs, so the title passed to his nephew Hilton: he died unmarried and without issue in 1959, and the Brayton Baronetcy died with him.

This new owner of St. Herbert's Island, Wilfrid Lawson – Wybergh as was – made a reasonable income from the island, for in the records D/NT/6 are three different accounts of sales of timber from the island. The

---

[16] Will of Sir Wilfrid Lawson, 10th Baronet of Isel held at CRO

[17] Letter of 8th October 1850 from Lawson's solicitors to Henry Marshall's solicitors, prior to his purchase in D/NT/6 documents in CRO

[18] Declaration by Thomas Wybergh in 1850 confirming Sir Wilfrid Lawson's right to sell the island to Henry Marshall, in D/NT/6 documents in CRO.

cottage guardian, James Lowther, remembers at least three sales: 'one Joseph Clark of Embleton, a woodmonger, cut down trees about eight or nine years ago and one John Glasson, another woodmonger, purchased trees cut down on the island by Sir Wilfrid about four or five years ago.' However, in 1850 he decided to sell this small piece of his estate. The buyer was Henry Cowper Marshall, who had already owned Derwent Isle since buying it from Susannah Peachy in 1844. For the first time since 1200 or thereabout these two islands were in the same ownership.

CHAPTER THREE

THE CIVIL WAR AND CORNET ROBERT PHILIPSON.

(1642-1651)

There are a few (very few) hints in the literature of two remarkable incidents regarding the Island in the English Civil War, taking place around 1645 and 1648. As we have seen the current Sir Wilfrid Lawson became a Parliamentarian and used St. Herbert's Island as a safe store for weapons and artillery, guarded there by a small garrison of soldiers. There is a tale – little more than a tale – that a Cornet Robert Philipson attempted to take the island by surprise, and to liberate for the Royalists the stock of armaments. (Cornet was originally the third and lowest grade of commissioned officer in a British cavalry troop, after captain and lieutenant. It was abolished in the Cardwell Reforms of 1871 and replaced by sub-lieutenant.)

The event is baldly told in Susan Johnson's essay in C&W Transactions, 1981, Article VII, where she says 'With Sir Wilfrid Lawson busy outside Carlisle, in April 1645 Cornet Robert Philipson "adventured" to surprise Lawson's own island on Derwentwater, which we call St. Herbert's.'

Mrs Johnson gives no reference to suggest where this story comes from, but there is some corroboration in the writings of J. Fisher Crosthwaite in a paper read to the Keswick Literary Society, February 2nd, 1874. He says:

> That St. Herbert's Island was for the Parliamentarians I showed in a former paper. Sir Gilfrid (sic, wrongly) Lawson, the owner, (ancestor of the present Sir Wilfred Lawson), had great stores of ammunition there for Parliament. Robert Phillipson, of Belle Island, Windermere, a Royalist and one of the defenders of Carlisle Castle, sallied forth one night, cut his way through the lines besieging the Castle with a party and rode up to Cat-Bells, expecting to find the custodier of the island a traitor, as he had feigned to be. But he found every boat upon the lake drawn up on the island, and his demand for the surrender of it was received with shouts of derisive laughter. Phillipson found that he had been hoaxed. He immediately turned his horse's head towards Carlisle and galloped with his party over Binsa again, after a bootless ride of 60 miles.[19]

[19] J. Fisher Crosthwaite *'The last of the Derwentwaters'* 1874

Robert was the younger brother of Hudleston Philipson, a captain in the Royalist army in 1645, so, as younger brother he may well have been a lowly cornet at the beginning of the war. They were both garrisoned in Carlisle Castle defending the city during the long siege laid by the Parliamentarians (1644-5). Isaac Tullie, in whose name Tullie House Museum now stands in Carlisle, was an eighteen-year-old at the time, and kept a journal of the siege in which he commends the Philipson brothers for their courage and fighting abilities (and prodigious drinking). He recounts a story that the Parliamentarians were frightened by the ghost of a Royalist officer who threatens that if they do not defect to the Royalists he will bring them before Captain Philipson, who is therefore clearly a figure to be feared. Robert Philipson was shot in the back in a skirmish outside Carlisle's defensive walls and retired to the family home – Belle Island on Windermere. Here, he was besieged by a Colonel Briggs, the Roundhead mayor of Kendal, among many other qualifications; though his island withstood the siege which was lifted when brother Hudleston returned from Carlisle.

A further twist to the tale is an allusion in Sir Walter Scott's poem 'Rokeby' where one line reads 'A horseman arm'd, at headlong speed' gallops into a church seeking his quarry. In the 1813 second edition a footnote attributes this line's lineage (!) to the actions of none other than Robert Philipson, who by that time has risen to Major.

> Note II, 'A horseman arm'd, at headlong speed' Stanza XXXII,
>
> This, and what follows, is taken from a real achievement by Major Robert Philipson, called, from his desperate and adventurous courage, Robin the Devil; which, as being very inaccurately noticed upon this note in the first edition, shall now be given in a more authentic form. The chief place of his retreat was not Lord's Island in Derwentwater, but Curwen's Island in the lake of Windermere.
>
> This island formerly belonged to the Philipsons, a family of note in Westmoreland. During the Civil Wars two of them, an elder and a younger brother, served the king. The former, who was the proprietor of it, commanded a regiment; the latter was a major…

To cut a long story short, the chief Parliamentarian in the Kendal area was the above-mentioned Colonel Briggs, 'a steady friend to usurption'[20], who sought, ineffectively, to lay hold of Robert, who was popularly known as Robin the Devil, in an eight-month siege, which was

[20] Walter Scott, *The Poetical Works: With a Sketch of His Life*. p.250

terminated by the return of Robert's brother Hudleston. Robert sought revenge on Colonel Briggs whom he suspected was in Kendal Church, since it was a Sunday, and galloped there and without dismounting rode in and up and down the aisles looking for his quarry: without success, for Briggs was elsewhere. The congregation, outraged by his actions, pulled him from his horse and in the skirmish which followed he left his helmet and sword, which relics are still proudly on show above the vestry door in Kendal Parish Church.[21]

The second reference to St. Herbert's Island in the Civil War comes from another article in the CWAAS Transactions, – that of D.R. Perriam, Article XIII, on *'The demolition of the priory of St. Mary, Carlisle'. (TCWAAS 1988).*

In this long article on the destruction of the nave of Carlisle Cathedral, along with many other buildings of the even older Priory of St. Mary, Perriam notes that:

'Such was the fear that the guns from Carlisle would fall into enemy (i.e. Royalist) hands that they were taken to St. Herbert's Isle on Derwentwater and kept under strong guard.'

I have found no other reference to this squirrelling away of Carlisle guns, but see no reason to doubt Perriam's account. He quotes C.S.P.D, 1648-9, 59, 5th May 1648, showing that things did not go according to plan "we are informed there are some ordnance which were lately at Carlisle and were with the arms and ammunition belonging to Cumberland, appointed by the Commons' Order of 17 June [1647] to be secured in St. Herbert's Isle… but lie by the way between Carlisle and St. Herbert's Isle, liable to be seized by the malignants and used against the Parliament." [22]

Clearly these are two separate incidents, one in 1645 the other in 1648, and they reinforce the conclusion that St. Herbert's Island was at that time seen as a suitable, easily defended garrison for the safe storage of armaments for the Parliamentarians.[23]

In 1850, as we have seen, St. Herbert's Island was sold to Henry Cowper Marshall. As his story belongs much more to Derwent Island we will leave St. Herbert's in 1850, returning to it only tangentially later.

---

[21], J. W. Lake '*Sir Walter Scott*' 1838

[22] Calendar of State Papers Domestic

[23] Lysons *Magna Britannia* p. 86

PART TWO
LORD'S ISLAND

CHAPTER FOUR

1200-1600

Lord's Island lies just ninety yards out from the eastern shore of Derwentwater at Stable Hills, now a National Trust private farmhouse. As with all the islands the NT owns Lord's Island, and on its website asks that we neither land on it nor boat round the eastern shoreline. This is understandable since in springtime it is a veritable maternity unit for the three types of geese which patrol the lake and the valley: Grey-lag, Barnacle and Canada. However, it is also a shame, because the ruins on Lord's Island are much more extensive than those on St Herbert's and have a much more extensively recorded provenance. That said, unless you are an archaeologist you would see very little to excite you: but those who are and have been have left fascinating records of what is there, and the written record of the family who built and owned this large house around 1460. They were the Derwentwaters; Earls, Lords, Baronets and so on, and in later years the Ratcliffes when the male line died out. Their recorded history is very long and frequently distinguished – and not infrequently infamous too.

Inevitably any account of the history of the island itself must include at least a record of the more famous members of that family, who for centuries held Lord's Island as their family seat. I am deeply indebted to two articles in the Transactions of the Cumberland & Westmorland Antiquarian and Archaeological Society, both in the 1904 Volume. Article XXII by the redoubtable W.G.Collingwood is entitled *'The home of the Derwentwater family'* and Article XXIII by W.N.Thompson is *'The Derwentwaters and Ratcliffes'*. Together they gathered virtually all the source material available, and this history can only aspire to be a re-telling for the modern reader of their scholarly essays. It would be tedious continually to acknowledge them as source: suffice to say their work underpins all that follows.

Let's start with the house on the island. The National Trust claims a date of 1460 for its foundation. This is the date suggested by John Fisher Crosthwaite, a noted antiquarian in 19th Century Keswick, and if true would apply to what is now the central part of the ruins, which is certainly older than the more recent (but still ancient) additions. The first record of the island is as a gift from Alice de Rumilly II to Adam de Derwentwater around 1200 AD. The Derwentwaters held it for a couple of hundred years till John de Derwentwater died around 1400 AD, when his only child was female: Elizabeth de Derwentwater known rather superfluously as 'the heiress of the isle'. She married Sir Nicholas Ratcliffe in 1417 and started the long line of Ratcliffes who owned Lord's Isle till 1735. Their son, Sir Thomas Ratcliffe, married Margaret Parr, the aunt of Katherine Parr, the sixth wife of Henry VIII.. These two built the original house on the island, more or less as the first 'holiday home' in the Keswick area, while actually living near Appleby at Ormeshead (now the village of Ormside).[24] Nicholson and Burn in their *History and antiquities of the counties of Cumberland and Westmorland* Vol. II have this to say about the couple and their new house: 'Castlerigg (was) the ancient seat of the lords of the manor of Derwentwater. But after the heiress of that family was married into the Ratcliffs, the family seat was removed into Northumberland, and the castle went to ruin, and with the stones thereof the Ratcliffs built an house of pleasure in one of the islands of Derwentwater.'[25]

This source (Nicolson and Burn) is frequently quoted in Cumbrian history. 'Nicolson' was Joseph Nicolson, grandson of Bishop William Nicolson of Carlisle, who had collected most of the original material for the two volumes published in 1777. Richard Burn was Chancellor of the diocese of Carlisle and vicar of Orton (near Carlisle).

It seems, then, that the first, central part of the house on Lord's Island was built around 1460, using the stones from the ruins of Castlerigg, which is said to have been at the top of the hill above Keswick on the Ambleside road, a fine site, overlooking the lake. This is confirmed by another great source of Cumbrian history: 'Cumberland', 1816, compiled by the Lyson brothers Daniel and Samuel, one of a series county by county under the title Magna Britannia. Usually simply referred to as 'The Lysons', it has the great merit of frequently quoting much older sources. For instance, with regard to our Lord's Island house they say (p.85):

'The Derwentwater family are said to have had a seat at Castlerigg, overlooking the fine lake from which they took their name. Their successors, the Radcliffes, built a house for their residence on the island called Lord's Island, now belonging to Greenwich Hospital. Leland, who was in Cumberland in 1539, calls this 'the Head Place' of the Radcliffes.'[26]

The John Leland referred to by the Lysons (and virtually every antiquarian ever since the 16th Century) was a truly amazing gatherer of books, facts, artefacts and knowledge of the whole of Britain in Henry VIII's day – knowledge he recorded and presented to the king as a 'New Year's gift' around 1544. He originated the template followed by the

[24] Nicolson and Burn, i., p. 515
[25] Nicolson and Burn ii., p. 80
[26] The Lysons, *Magna Britannia: Cumberland.*

Lysons of approaching the task county by county. His (then unpublished) works formed the basis of Camden's 'Britannia' published in 1586, and have informed British history ever since.

Meanwhile, back at the Ratcliffe family, Thomas and Margaret's son **Richard Ratcliffe** made a great name for himself in government, being in the inner circle of King Richard III's court, along with William Catesby and Francis Lovell. The three were lampooned in a couplet nailed to the door of St Paul's Cathedral which read

'The Cat, the Rat and Lovell our dog
rulyth all England under a hog.'

(Lovell's coat of arms featured a dog: Richard III's a pig, or hog). William Colyngbourne, the author of this scurrilous doggerel was hanged, drawn and quartered for his pains, but his rhyme demonstrates the heights a Ratcliffe from lowly Keswick could ascend. Sadly Richard died alongside his king at the Battle of Bosworth. (Colyngbourne is said to have died muttering to himself 'Oh Lord, yet more troubles').

For the sake of clarity, here is a small section of the family tree of the descendants of Thomas and Margaret Radcliffe, the four generations who were primarily involved with Lord's Island.

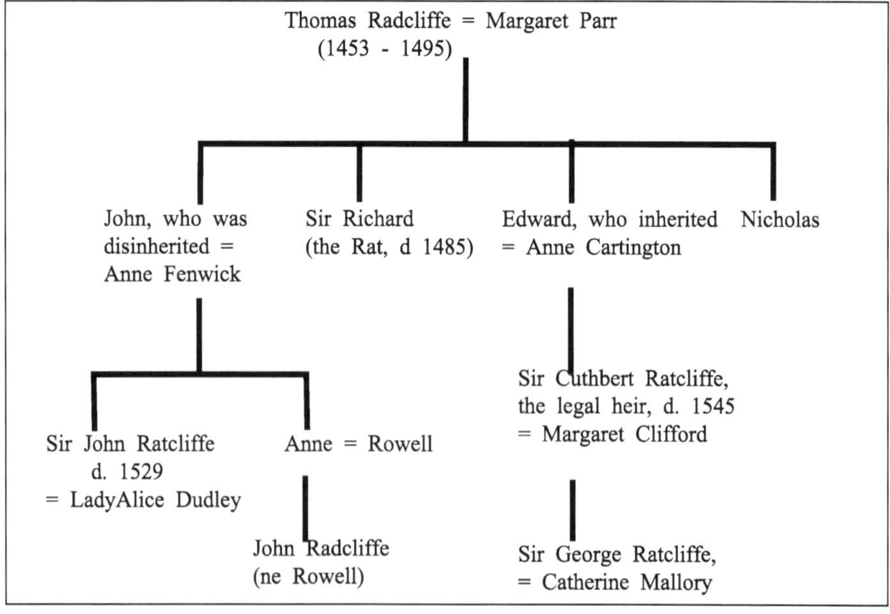

If Leland was correct in 1539 that the Lord's Island house was the 'Head Place' of the Radcliffe's, then that would almost certainly be the house to which **Sir John Ratcliffe** brought his young wife, **Lady Alice**

Dudley. (Left branch of the tree). These two were a tenacious couple who managed to hold on to the house and the demesne that went with it against almost overwhelming odds. For some reason – presumably a monumental family row – his father, also John Ratcliffe, the first-born son of old Thomas and Margaret, and elder brother of the famous Richard, above – was disinherited by his father. However, father John held on to Lord's Island, and the Derwentwater demesne, and succeeded despite this disinheritance in passing it on to his son, who became Sir John Ratcliffe, a respected sheriff of Cumberland for many of the early years of Henry VIII's reign. He is buried in Crosthwaite Church, and a brass on the wall there gives the date of his death as February 2nd. 1527.

The brass to Sir John and Lady Alice Ratcliffe
"Of your charity pray for the soul of Sir John Radcliffe, Knight, and for the state of Dame Alice his Wife, which Sir John died the 2nd February, 1527, on whose soul Jesu have mercy."

Unfortunately this seems an error, as his will is dated 'the first day of Februarii, in the yere of God a thousand five hundred twentye and nyne yeres, and in the xxj.yere of the reigne of our soveraing Lord King Henry the eight'. That is February 1st 1529 (or, as we would now say, 1530, since

New Year's Day was put back from March 25th to 1st January in 1582.when Pope Gregory XIII reformed the old Julian calendar.) Sir John is said to have died the day after.[27]

The redoubtable Lady Alice, Sir John Ratcliffe's widow, held on to the Derwentwater estate till her death in 1554 despite the earlier disinheritance, but on her death it passed to her nephew **Sir George Ratcliffe**, the legal heir according to the disputed disinheritance. Sir George was an interesting man in his own right, being Warden of the East Marches, but it is his wife, the formidable **Lady Catherine Ratcliffe** (née Mallory) who is of prime interest in the ongoing saga of Derwentwater and Keswick. The Ratcliffes seem to have had a knack of marrying extremely capable but obstinate women, and Lady Catherine is no exception. The story of her dealings with the German miners who came to Keswick in 1564 and mined copper here for the next forty years or so belongs partly to the third of our islands – Derwent Island – but it is appropriate here to visit some of the dealings they had. The Germans came at the express invitation of Queen Elizabeth who was in sore need of copper for many uses, but primarily to 'copper-bottom' her fleet of ships. She granted them licence to mine in Newlands (Goldscope Mine) and Borrowdale (Copperplate Mine) among others, and granted them the name 'The Company of Mines Royal'. Lady Catherine was a constant thorn in the side of the Company.

THE GERMAN MINERS

Daniel Ulstat came from Germany to take on the role of assistant governor of the new company. His report to Sir William Cecil, Queen Elizabeth's Secretary of State, is largely a diatribe against Lady Catherine. To quote: 'I find that we cannot occupy these mines quietly so long as my Lady has possession and rule of this town (Keswick). For she does so delay as from day to day and in such sort, that it is very troublesome. And nevertheless does raise the prices from time to time (of timber) by the good help of her friends, that in manner it were so good, if it were possible, to fetch it out of Dutchland'[28]

In short, Lady Catherine did all she could to extort a fortune from the German miners. Cleverly, she leased them, at a pittance, the area which became their main smelting house and forge at Brigham (the area still known as 'The Forge'), but then sold them timber to fire the furnaces at exorbitant prices, making sure all other landowners around the area didn't

[27] The Radclyffe Tracts i., p.4. These Tracts appear in the papers at Greenwich Hospital, entitled *Archaeologia Æliana.*

[28] M. B. Donald, *'Elizabethan Copper'* p152

undercut her. In despair the Germans bought from Ireland and created a harbour at Workington for the unloading of ships. Things got to such a pass that the company of Mines Royal obtained from Queen Elizabeth a 'large and ample commission' against Lady Ratcliffe, and a special letter threatening that if she did not abide by the commission she must appear before the Queen in London. All to no avail, for Lady Catherine had powerful friends in Cumberland.

Ulstat goes on in his letter to Sir William Cecil (Lord Burghley) to make the astonishing request that Burghley should use his influence with Queen Elizabeth to *'make some exchange with the Lady Ratcliffe for this Lordship of Keswick'*, or, failing that, to allow the Company of Mines Royal to buy the said Lordship. He is worried that the lease they have on Brigham Forge is only twenty-one years, meaning that in the all-too-foreseeable future it, and all the buildings they have constructed at great expense, will revert to her Ladyship. Burghley forbore to bother Her Majesty.

For us this raises the tantalising question: why is it Lady Catherine and not Sir George who is chief negotiator in the dealings with the miners? Ulstat makes it clear that it was Sir George who signed the original lease of the Forge and we know Sir George was still alive in 1577 when he entailed the manors of 'Castell Rigg and Darwynwater and lands and messuages in Castellrygg, Darwynwater and Keswyck, and free fishery in the waters of Darwynwater' on his son and heir Francis, who had married the previous year.[29] And yet all the dealings the Company made are with Lady Catherine. Not only so, but when one of their number, a Leonard Shtultz, was murdered in Keswick by a man surnamed Fisher and his accomplices, Lady Catherine used her influence to protect the perpetrators.[30] I assume the reason is that Sir George spent most of his time in Northumberland, in charge of the East Marches, while Catherine lived on Lord's Island and was, de facto, the only one to deal with. Ulstat recognises the practical reality, calling her 'my Lady Ratcliffe in whose Lordship we dwell.' It is clear that in this latter half of the 16th Century Lady Ratcliffe lives on Lord's Island, in the enlarged house, while her husband, Sir George, is far away in Northumberland. To reinforce this interpretation we have, on October 18, 1571, an 'Agreement between Richard Dudley, esq., on behalf of the Queen, <u>and Lady Ratcliffe</u> of the Isle of Derwentwater for the lease of a courthouse in the marketplace of Keswick'.[31] (My emphasis)

---

29 *Common Roll*, Easter, 19 Eliz., *memb.*643

30 *Calendar of State Papers, Domestic,* 1547-80, p.279

31 W.N.Thompson, *The Derwentwaters and Ratcliffes*, p..313

CHAPTER FIVE

THE HOUSE ON LORD'S ISLAND

W.G.Collingwood in the article cited above hazards that the original house was a simple hall, shown on his plan of the excavations as the black walled oblong building: one room only. Clearly this would not serve as the 'Head Place' Leland refers to in 1539, so we may safely assume that the extensive enlargement and additions to make a genuine home, rather than a simple getaway took place before then; most likely by the disinherited John Ratcliffe, in an effort to establish himself on the island – an effort which paid off, for his line continued there. This was not so long after the original founding in 1460. Collingwood's careful plan shows a thorough-going large house, suitable for what was still the leading family in the area. Collingwood drew up this plan in the course of a careful archaeological dig he conducted in 1902 at the behest of the CWAAS, along with Mr. T.H. Hodgson FSA and Mrs. Hodgson.

Here is Collingwood's 1902 plan of the house and surrounds.

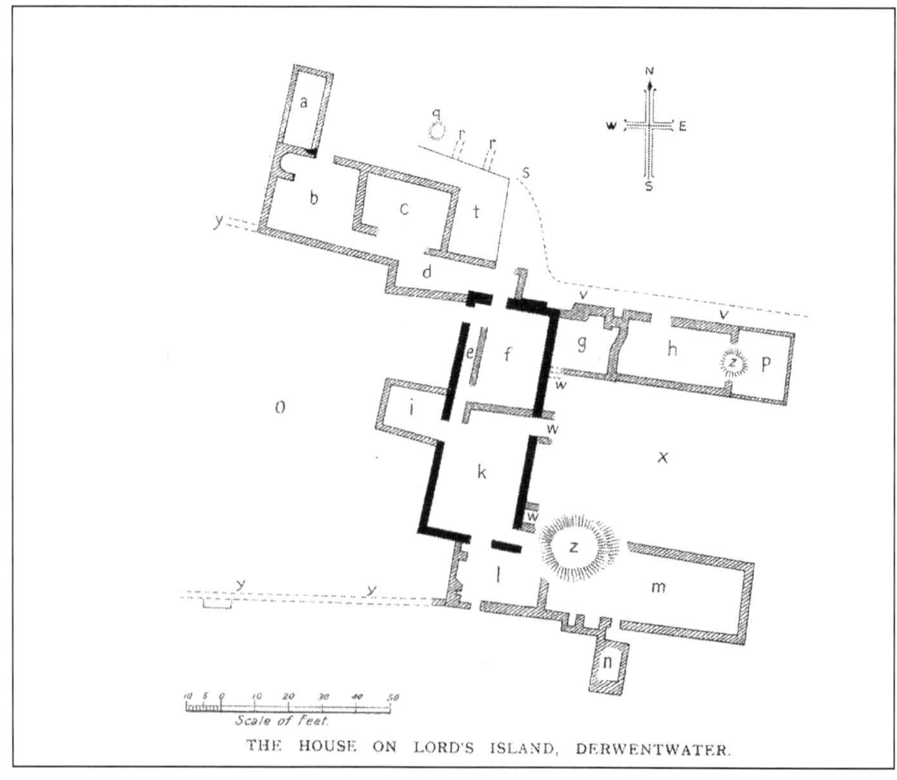

THE HOUSE ON LORD'S ISLAND, DERWENTWATER.

The key to the lettering is as follows :—
a—Outbuilding.
b—Kitchen.
c—Pantry.
d, e—Passages.
f, g, h, i, k, 1, m—Rooms.
n—Turret (or staircase ?).
o—Garden.
p—Paved court with kerb and step.
q—Tank.
r, r—Drains.
s—Rubbish heap.
t—Paved court with kerb.
y, v—Cobble path with kerb.
w, w, w—Steps ?
x—Court.
y, y, y—Fragments of dry-built walls.
z, z—Trees and roots preventing excavation.

Collingwood comments rather scathingly on a previous plan – an 'ichnography' – drawn up in 1796 by the irrepressible Joseph Pocklington – King Pocky as he was known to generations of Keswickians. Indeed, he declines even to print it in his booklet. Nevertheless, I feel Pocklington's plan does have some merit. For one thing it was drawn more than a century before Collingwood's, in 1796, when there were doubtless better remains. For another it shows a staircase leading up to a room above the great hall. If there were indeed some stairs left, as Pocklington's plan shows overleaf, then at least part of the house was double-storeyed, making it a very substantial dwelling.

Other than this there is no way of determining whether the house was single or double-storey, for it is a matter of record that at a later date the stones were removed to make the current Moot Hall in Keswick. Collingwood queries whether the small oblong ruin marked 'n' on his plan might have been a staircase. Even single-storeyed it is a large house, and we may imagine servants in the Northern rooms, sleeping in room h with outside access to the kitchen and pantry through corridor d. The drains r, tank q, and rubbish heap s are in easy reach for them, through the back door of the kitchen b. There was easy access with food to the dining room at f, and a main room at k looking out West onto the garden and with access down the steps w to the courtyard x. Rooms 1 & m might then have been bedrooms, though m is very long – some 57 feet – possibly with others above, if n was in fact a staircase.

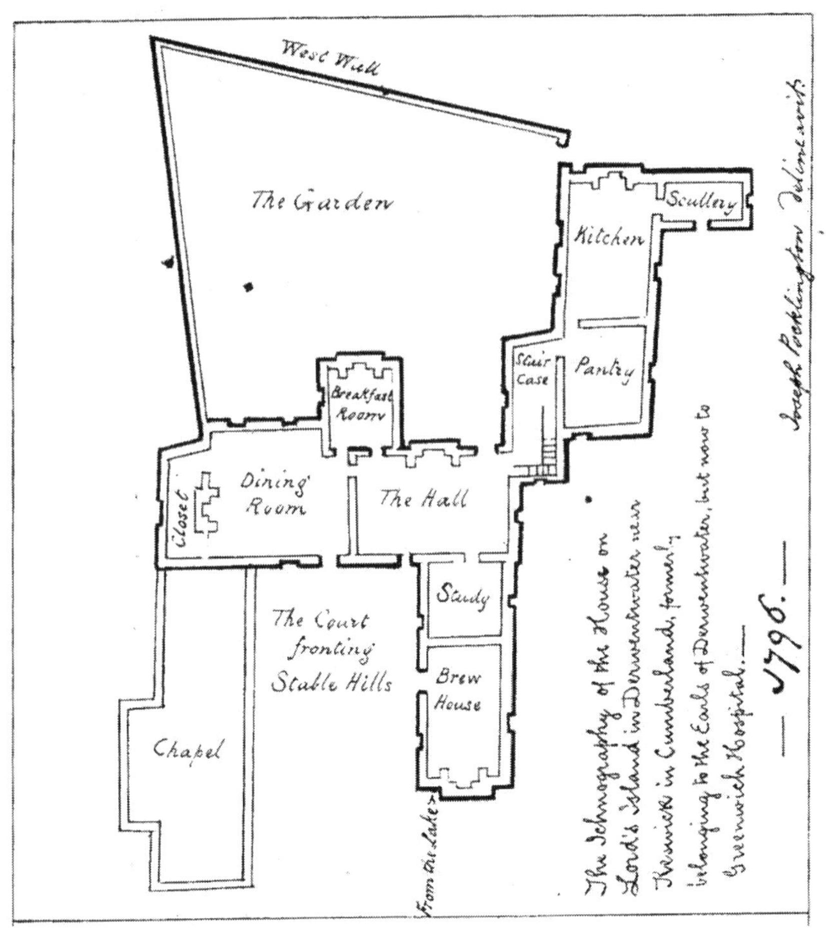

Joseph Pocklington's 'Ichnography'

Those are my guesses: here are the more educated surmises of Collingwood, who had a lot more to go on in 1902, when the ruins were better preserved and he had the benefits of excavation. He starts with room h which Pocklington had suggested was a brew house, and agrees that, as it doesn't open into the rest of the house but did have a fireplace on the east wall it might well have served that purpose. On the subject of fireplaces, they found evidence of hearths in rooms g, f, l & m. These fireplaces were all made from rather poor quality red brick, which may well have come from the old brickfield and kiln behind Castlerigg Manor – then the home of Mr. R.D. Marshall, who owned Lord's Island and authorized and assisted in the dig. The fireplace in room m was very large, in keeping with the room itself: 57 feet long and 20 feet wide. Room m opens to the outside world via a porch in the alcove formed with ‘n’ – the solid base which Collingwood speculates was probably the base of either a staircase or a bell tower. It is of appropriate dimensions: 14’6” x 9’6”.

There is a strong tradition that a bell once hung on Lord’s Island, adding weight to the thesis of the bell-tower. This bell is the subject of a paper by the Rev. H Whitehead in the 1891 Transactions of the CWAAS (No XI, Article XIV, pp. 152 – 157), in which he makes the following points:

- The bell which then hung in Keswick Town Hall was brought from the ruined house on Lord’s Island.
- The Town Hall itself was built largely from masonry from the ruins.
- The bell is inscribed H D 1001 R O. He deduces that the actual date is 1601, the foundry having mistakenly used a 0 instead of a 6. R O he suggests are the initials of Robert Oldfield, a peripatetic member of the York firm who worked from 1586 – 1615. He has no theory as to H D.
- He makes the point that the same number, or date, is on an old seat formerly in the chapel of St. John’s-in-the-vale, without being able to draw any conclusion.

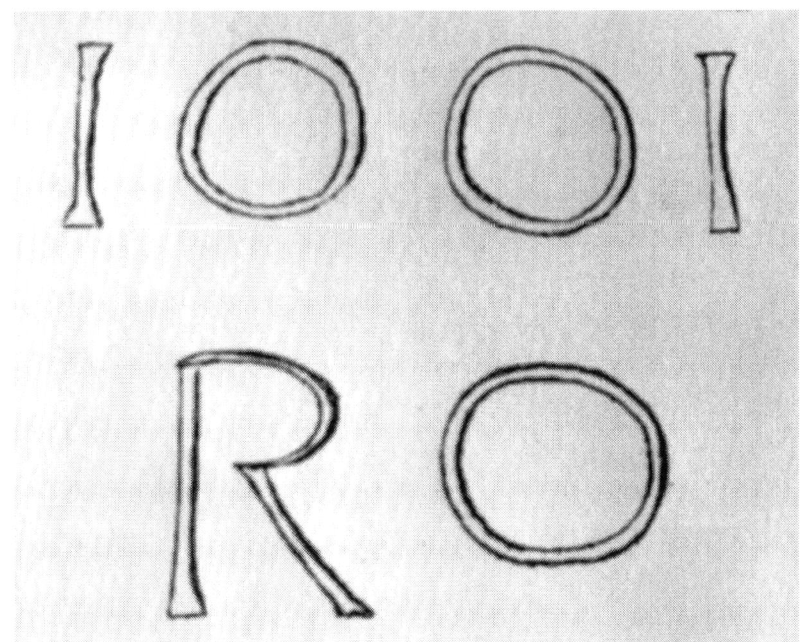

The inscription on the bell.

It is an unresolved question as to how the island was accessed. The most obvious answer is 'by boat', and this is surely true of at least some of the island's history. The point 'B' on the plan of the island was identified by Collingwood as a boat landing place, and there is still clearly a wharf on the Stable Hills side of the channel, ten yards long and two yards wide. The very name Stable Hills presumably derives from the days when the family's horses had to stay on the mainland, stabled, fed and groomed there. So there can be no doubt that boats were used. However, there is a persistent legend that there was once a bridge from Stable Hills to the island, and this is by no means impossible. The water in this channel is shallow, nowhere over six feet deep, and it is not inconceivable that what would in effect be a jetty, built on long wooden piles, much as the present jetties on the lake, could span the ninety yards channel. There are some remains of such piles on the Stable Hills side but they could just be an ancient short jetty. However, modern experience of the vulnerability of the present jetties in winter storms and rising lake levels suggests such a bridge would be expensive to maintain. It seems to me more likely that gentry such as the Ratcliffes would prefer the physical distancing from the Keswick Hoi Polloi: otherwise, why live on an island? With servants at both sides to ferry them at any time the channel would be only a slight irritation, more than made up for by the useful isolation.

WHEN WAS THE HOUSE DISMANTLED, AND WHY?

It seems the house fell into disrepair and was eventually dismantled around the time of the Civil War – the mid-1600s. There is a strong tradition that the stone was re-used to build the courthouse in Keswick on the site of the present Moot Hall, which has been rebuilt more than once. One pointer as to the actual date is an entry in Crosthwaite Church registers noting the death of William Munkhouse in 1657 who, tradition again holds, was drowned rowing a boat overloaded with stone taken from Lord's Island to build the Moot Hall. It is said to have sunk just off Friar's Crag, in shallow water, and to have left there a cairn of stone visible for years later when the lake level was low. A 1664 lease refers to 'One certain house situate and standing in the middle of the said Towne of Keswicke belonging unto the said Sir Francis Radcliffe, commonly known by the name of Courthouse or Moot Hall'. Presumably the bell was transferred at the same time.

As ever, politics and religion appear to be at the heart of the house's fall from grace. The only surviving heir of Sir George and Lady Catherine Radcliffe was Francis, who in 1576 married Isabel, daughter of Sir Ralph

Grey of Chillingham.[32] He and his wife found the diversions of Northumberland more attractive than an island in Derwentwater and spent all their time there, and eventually leased the Island Hall to a younger branch of the family, and 'both hall and branch went to decay together.'[33] Sir Francis was a strong Roman Catholic at a period of history when such faith was known as 'recusancy' and was punishable by confiscation of land and property. He is mentioned in letters from the Bishop of Durham in 1597 and again in 1601, and it is probable that he transferred his Cumberland estates, including Derwentwater, to his son-in-law so that they would not be forfeited. This was Roger Widdrington, who had married Francis and Isabel's first daughter, Mary, born 1st June 1582. However, Roger also was a Roman Catholic – but of the party prepared to swear the Oath of Allegiance imposed by James I. The dereliction of the house on Lord's Island was probably due to the fact that Roger and Mary much preferred Cartington Tower, the castle in Northumberland which Francis also settled on the couple in 1601.

This of course raises questions about the provenance of the bell. If its date really is 1601 is it likely to have been installed on the island at the very time that the Radcliffe family was growing tired of living there? Roger Widdrington took on the lease in 1600, before he and Mary were given Cartington Tower so it may be that the installation of the bell (and possibly the bell tower, if indeed it existed) was a wedding present.

By 1619 recusancy was less of an impediment to preferment and Francis Radcliffe was made a baronet, with the title 'Francis Radcliff of Darwentwater, Co. Cumberland, Esq.'[34] He died in 1622, succeeded by his eldest son Edward who 'enfranchised' for the sum of £1441 his sixty Keswick tenants, among whom was Joseph Hechstetter, grandson of Daniel Hechstetter who had been the leading German miner in Lady Catherine's day. A nice irony! Enfranchisement was in its infancy in the early part of the 17th Century, but was gathering steam as parliament sought to rid itself of the perpetual oligarchy who had ruled till then. In practice the squire, Francis Radcliffe in this case, sold the freehold of a tenant's property to the tenant, who generally was then able to vote in parliamentary elections – hence the name enfranchisement. Usually the squire was in need of a large amount of money in the short term, and was prepared to sacrifice the longer term annual rental income in return. The 60 Keswick tenants paid an average of £24 each for their freehold.

---

[32] Radcliffe Tracts ii.

[33] Radcliffe Tracts ii

[34] G.E.Cokayne. *Complete Baronetage*, I. p.134

CHAPTER SIX

OWNERSHIP OF LORD'S ISLAND 1200-1735

It is clear from the above that for a very long time Lord's Isle was owned firstly by the de Derwentwater family and then by their successors by marriage, the Ratcliffes. The first recorded owner is Adam de Derwentwater who is a witness to Alice de Rumilly's sale of the western part of Borrowdale to Furness Abbey in 1210 AD.[35] He also gave the Furness monks wayleave through his land.[36] The next family member of interest is Sir Thomas de Derwentwater (died 1302). He it was who obtained from King Edward I Keswick's charter to hold a market every Saturday. The R.D. Marshall of the archaeological dig fame held a copy of the charter in Latin, which his colleague W.G.Collingwood translated. Apart from the weekly market the charter also allowed for an annual fair of five days duration 'on the vigil, the day and the morrow of the blessed Mary Magdalene and for the following two days unless such market and fair shall be to the annoyance of the neighbouring markets and fairs'[37] (Mary Magdalene's Day is July 22nd).

As we have seen the Island, along with all the other lands, passed to the Ratcliffe family via the marriage of Elizabeth 'the heiress of the Isle' to Sir Nicholas Ratcliffe in 1417 or thereabouts. The Ratcliffes were eventually (1688) elevated to the peerage, with Sir Francis Ratcliffe, the third Baronet, becoming the first Earl of Derwentwater. Alas, the earldom did not last long, for the third earl, James Ratcliffe, was a prominent Jacobite and was executed for high treason in 1716. In his fascinating booklet *'The last of the Derwentwaters'* J. Fisher Crosthwaite tells his story eloquently. J. Fisher Crosthwaite was the grandson of Peter Crosthwaite, the founder (in 1784) of the Keswick Museum, and I assume he inherited a great number of papers and stories of old Keswick from his grandfather. Certainly, in his many papers read in general to 'The Keswick Literary Society' he rarely denotes any sources, so I can only paraphrase what he has written. For those wishing to read the whole story for themselves 'The Last of the Derwentwaters' is available free to download from the excellent British Library collection using the website: https://books.google.co.uk/books/about/TheLastoftheDerwentwaters.html?i

---

[35] Bain's *Calendar of Documents. Scotland, I*, p.554 and Beck's *Ann. Furn.*, p. 175

[36] *Ann. Furn.*, p. 81

[37] *Charter roll of 4 Edward I., (1276)No. 9*

d=DkhJM0vZEXkC&redir_esc=y or just Google J. Fisher Crosthwaite and follow the links.

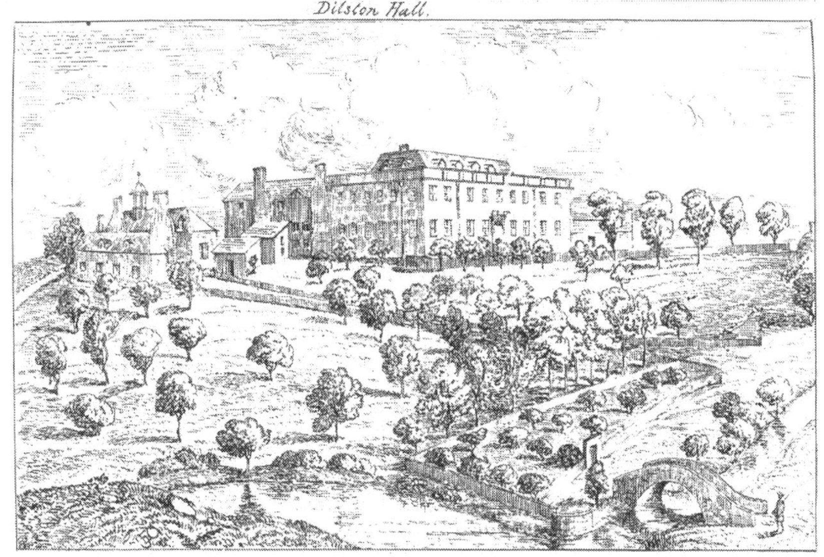

Dilston Hall

Drawn on the spot by Thos. Oliver of Hexham in Northumberland and published according to Act of Parliament July 17. 1766.

James Ratcliffe, Third Earl of Derwentwater, only once visited the area from which he took his name, for he inherited Dilston Tower, or Castle, in Northumberland, a very fine house largely constructed by his grandfather Sir Francis Ratcliffe. He was born in London in 1689, being one year older than the son of King James II – known to us as James, The Old Pretender. He was brought up in Paris, as was Prince James, and they were good friends from early childhood. In Paris he also fell in love with Anna Maria Webb, daughter of Sir John Webb of Dorset, Baronet. They married in 1712 and two years later moved into the new Hall he had built at Dilston.

Not surprisingly the Earl and his Lady preferred this fine hall to the ruined and demolished house on Lord's Island. However, they had but a brief five years of enjoyment of it before the long train of events which led to the Earl's downfall began.

A group of Scottish noblemen led by Lord Mar proclaimed the Old Pretender to be James VIII of Scotland on 16th August 1715 and sought gentry on both sides of the Border to raise an army to defeat the new King

George I of England. The Earl of Derwentwater, a Catholic and a long-term friend of the Prince and a Jacobite at heart was soon embroiled. Inevitably George I issued a warrant for his and his brother Charles' arrest. The Earl vacillated: he had much to lose if the insurrection should fail, and for three months he went into hiding till, sneaking back into Dilston Hall one night Lady Anna Maria threw down her fan upon the bed and told him to take it and give her his sword. Stung, the Earl set his heart to the cause and next morning mustered his troops and, joined by his brother, rode out to join the army gathering in Hexham, where, on 19th October 1715 James was proclaimed to be James III. At first all went well for the rag-tag army marching south, for they met no opposition in Kirkby Lonsdale, Kendal or Lancaster. However, in Preston they were met by General Willes and a force of trained men. There was a brief and one-sided battle before the Scots capitulated and seventy-five noblemen, including The Earl of Derwentwater and his brother Charles were taken prisoner.

The parliament of George I had little stomach for exacting the ultimate penalty on Derwentwater and the other noblemen languishing in the Tower and three times he was offered his life if he would only acknowledge the Hanoverian title and accept the Protestant religion; the last on the scaffold. He refused, and was beheaded on the 24th February 1716.

Other nobles had wives more ardent and more enterprising than the lady Anna Maria. As Crosthwaite puts it:

> The Countess of Nithsdale and Lady Nairn concealed themselves behind a window curtain in an ante-room of the Palace, and waiting until the King passed through, suddenly came forward and threw themselves at his feet, but were rudely repulsed. Lady Nithsdale ascertaining that the King would show clemency to some of the condemned lords, but that her husband would certainly not be of the number, set her wits to work to release her husband, and with consummate skill and devotion she effected his escape in female attire on the night of the 23rd. When the news of Lord Nithsdale's escape was brought to King George he flew into a great passion, and said he was betrayed, for there must have been some confederacy; and he instantly dispatched two trusty persons to the Tower to see that the other prisoners were well secured. The King, however, afterwards observed that "Lord Nithsdale had done the best thing that a man in his situation could do." The House of Lords over-ruled Sir Robert Walpole and the ministry, and carried an address to the King "for a reprieve to such of the condemned lords as should deserve his mercy," by a majority of five. The Ministers alarmed at

their defeat, met in Council and dictated the King's answer as follows:—"that on this and all other occasions he would do what he thought most consistent with the dignity of the Crown and the safety of the people."[38]

The governments of the first two Georges sought to forfeit the Earl's estates to the Crown, but when the case was heard in Westminster Hall the settlement he had made before his marriage was upheld and his widow and family allowed to retain their properties and land. His brother Charles had escaped from prison and lived in exile in France, and when Earl James' only son and heir, the Honourable John Radcliff died in a horse-riding accident – again in France where he too was living – the estates passed to him, Countess Anna Maria having died in 1723. Charles, though, had long been attainted and under sentence of death and was barred from his inheritance, so now the Crown had its way and took possession of all the Earl's estates including, of course, little Lord's Island and all the Derwentwater estate.

There is a story, no more than a legend, that the Countess of Derwentwater fled Keswick in 1715, presumably when her husband, the Third Earl had been captured, and avoided the sentries who had been posted on the roads to apprehend her. The story goes that she made her escape up the very steep path immediately to the south of Walla Crag – still called Lady's Rake – carrying all her plate and jewels, and a quantity of hard cash, hoping to get to London to bribe the Whigs into allowing her husband to go free. There is also a legend that in fact she dropped a chest of plate in the lake, never to be found. There are some glaring inaccuracies in this tale – we know for instance that the Lady Derwentwater of 1715 lived at Dilston and barely knew Keswick. There is the usual stuff of legend – another chest of plate was said to be lost in Lake Windermere at Silverholme. And yet there is an element of truth too, for between 1856 and 1862 one Henry Lightfoot of Keswick found a number of silver coins near the Lady's Rake footpath and sold them to Mr. Jackson of Keswick, whose manuscript note gives the exact spot they were found. It is on the north side of Catbeck Gill, which divides Walla Crag from Falcon Crag; south of the wall of Great Wood and at a few yards from it, a short distance above where the wall takes a sudden bend northwards. The coins were scattered loose among the gravel.[39] Collingwood goes on to say the coins themselves were displayed at 'our meeting' on August 30th 1902, by Mr. Jackson's son, Edward Jackson. There were 34 in all, all silver pennies of

---

[38] J. Fisher Crosthwaite *'The last of the Derwentwaters'* p. 30

[39] W G Collingwood *'The home of the Derwentwaters'* (TCWAAS) 1902 p. 273

Edward I and Edward II, which means they were minted after 1272 and before 1327 – two centuries and more before the demise of the Third Earl.[40] It would seem then that there is a kernel of truth to the legend, in that the location is correct, and that someone a very long time ago lost a small fortune there.

The next three generations continued to use the title, but it had no genuine provenance after the third earl was attainted, and in any case the Jacobite blood continued to run in their veins, making them ever vulnerable to charges of treason. Charles Ratcliffe, who styled himself the Fifth Earl of Derwentwater, was secretary to Bonnie Prince Charlie and was beheaded for his pains in 1746. There were however no lands for him to be Earl of, since the entire Derwentwater Estate was gifted to Greenwich Hospital in 1735.

---

[40] Collingwood

PART THREE
DERWENT ISLAND

CHAPTER SEVEN

DERWENT ISLAND, FORMERLY KNOWN AS VICAR'S ISLAND AND HESTHOLM.

With its position, just 150 yards off-shore from the boat landings and path to Friars Crag, Derwent Island is perhaps the most famous of the four main islands, and it certainly has the most colourful and chequered history of them all. However, Derwent Island really is strictly off limits for landing these days, and has been for most of its usage. The National Trust which owns this and all the islands also owns and rents out the house on the island, and protects its tenant's privacy closely. But rowing or sailing round it you can't help being struck by the Italian influence on the house, and in particular the boathouse and mooring. That influence came in the 18th Century when Joseph Pocklington, the flamboyant 'King Pocky', designed and built the current house, but that was at least five centuries later than its earliest recorded use.

The first time we come across the island in the ancient records is in the *Chronicon Cumbrie* – papers from Wetheral Priory. These state that Gospatric, illegitimate son of Waldeve, was given the island sometime in the period 1145 – 1179. Waldeve was then Lord of Allerdale. At that time it was called Hestholm, which literally means 'horse island'. His tenure must have been tenuous, for the entire Derwentwater estates were also in the hands of Alice de Rumilly II in the 12th Century and she granted the island to Fountains Abbey along with free transit for their boat before 1216. However, Gospatric's inheritors, the de Bassenthwaite family, must have held on to some claim because it wasn't till 1327 that Sir Alexander de Bassenthwaite finally 'quitclaimed' the island to Fountains Abbey. A quitclaim is pretty well what it says: the grantor (de Bassenthwaite) of a quitclaim gives up any rights he may have had in some property in favour of the grantee (Fountains Abbey in this case). Around the same time – and presumably necessitating the quitclaim – the Abbey leased the island, now called Eastholm, to Thomas, son of Duncan de Lasceles for two shillings a year. *(ibid)* The whole process seems to be just a 'tidying-up' exercise, because Thomas turns out to be the husband of Christiana – great-great-great- granddaughter of Old Gospatric.[41]

Actually the whole cat's cradle is a good deal more complicated. Nicholson and Burn in their *History and antiquities of the counties of Cumberland and Westmorland* Vol. II p. 68

[41] *Archaeologia Aeliana, Or, Miscellaneous Tracts Relating to Antiquity* Published by Society of Antiquaries of Newcastle-upon-Tyne, 1904

(https://archive.org/stream/historyantiquiti02nico#page/70/mode/2up) make it clear that both families (Alice de Rumilly and Gospatric de Bassenthwaite) derive from the same 12th Century sire: Ranulph de Meschines. It seems the two branches of the family both held a claim to the island. Actually, Derwent Island was an exception: as we have seen in the chapter on Lord's Island, the Radcliffe family held all the Eastern side of Derwentwater, including Lord's Island and Rampsholme. Their boundary went down the middle of the lake, and should have included Derwent Island – but never did.

So Fountains Abbey held Derwent Island and all the land gifted by Lady Alice de Rumilly from roughly 1200 till the Dissolution of the monasteries under Henry VIII in 1539, when it became Crown property. Some of the property, including Vicar's Island, as Derwent Island was then called, was granted separately to one John Williamson[42], it being described as 'the wood, containing one acre, called the Vicar Isle in the water of Derwent'. This is confirmed by Leland, writing in 1539, who wrote of the islands of Derwentwater that 'the 3d is Vicar Isle full of trees like a wilderness' as quoted by Camden, the Lysons and others since.

The next to buy Vicar's Island was The Company of Mines Royal, the German company set up to mine copper in Newlands and Borrowdale in 1566, and this is where its occupied history begins. Queen Elizabeth and her government were seriously short of copper, the vital ingredient of the smaller coins of the realm, and for years the amount of pure copper in the coins had been diminishing, leading to a devaluation of the currency. These were the days when the value of a coin, copper, silver or gold, was inherent in the actual metal therein. A sovereign contained a pound's worth of gold; a penny a penny's worth of copper and their value lay in the difficulty of mining the mineral. Of course there were other uses for copper too, but it was the devaluation of the currency that was the most pressing, along with the wish to 'copper-bottom' her ships.

There are two excellent books on the Company of Mines Royal: *Elizabethan Keswick* by W.G. Collingwood was originally published by the CWAAS in 1912 and has been reprinted by Forgotten Books www.forgottenbooks.com and *Elizabethan Copper* by M.B. Donald published by Pergamon Press in 1955, and by Red Earth Publications in 1994. The former contains extracts from the original account books, 1564 – 1577, of the German miners in the archives of Augsburg, as transcribed and translated by Collingwood. The latter gives the entire story of the company from the early initiatives by Thomas Thurland from 1562 onwards through the setting up of the company in 1566, to its eventual

[42] Hutchinson's '*Cumberland*' Vol 2, p. 158

demise in 1603. Donald's sources are the many documents and letters preserved from the chief characters involved in the Company, together with Daniel Hochstetter's original journal which gives so much detail. Together they comprise an invaluable insight into 16th Century life in Keswick.

The company bought Vicar's Island from John Williamson in 1569, possibly thinking to have a safer lodging for their workers after a Keswick mob murdered one of them, Leonard Stoultz, in 1566. More likely the island was seen as a good place to store valuable horses, tools and provisions, being that much harder steal from. At any rate we read in Collingwood p.35:

'Vicar's Island. – Three workmen cleaning the island we have bought from John Williamson, rooting up bushes, hedges and weeds, carrying away stones, and preparing it for our riding horses, £1 1s 0d. The price of the island to be £60; paid as first instalment £10.'

The following expense noted is interesting in its own right:

'Rent to Miladi Catharina Radclieff, paid through her bailey Parsovel Radclieff, for the land on which the smelthouses stand, due at Michaelmas, 1/- per year according to the agreement made with Sir George Radclieff; three years' rent from Michaelmas 1566, 3/-.': virtually a peppercorn rental for the land at Brigham.

The next cost attributable to the Island is on p.49:

March 28 (1569). Building – W. Hochholzer has lengthened the pier at the lake, 10/-.

Then on p. 56 we get the completion of the purchase:

Vicar's Island. – Balance of £60 to John Wilmson; the deed now sealed. This is on May 23rd 1569.

However, it is from Donald's book that we learn in detail what the Germans did with the island. On p. 159 he tells us that they built a slate-roofed Brewhouse made of lime and stone, 39 feet long by 20 feet wide. The mash vat, where the malt is mixed with hot water was 3' by 5' and had a straw covering. The copper brewing kettle where the wort was sterilized was set in stone with a roaster – an iron grate – below it. The guile which is used for fermenting the wort was 2.5 by 3 feet. They also built a bakehouse adjoining the brewhouse, this 20' by 12'. It contained moulding boards, a kneading trough and a brake for bread. Then they erected a dovecote, 17 feet high, a small beer cellar, a garden 50 yards square and an orchard 80 by 90 yards, a well 60 feet deep, a timber windmill 11 feet square with a pair of grindstones and an open thatched peat house.

Donald doesn't give any specific references for all this information, and it rather contradicts the initial statement that the island was cleared in preparation for the riding horses. Collingwood confirms that all these buildings – and more – were undertaken on the island, but not till 1571when the smelthouses at Brigham were substantially complete, so the horses may well have been kept there for a couple of years. On p. 102 Collingwood gathers together all the charges for the works on the island, and extends the list of buildings etc. to include a pig-sty, plus the fact that 300 apple and pear trees were brought for the orchard, and an exhaustive account of all the costs incurred, which came to a grand total of £155 17s. 11½ which doesn't seem a lot even when translated into our terms – a factor of say 300 – giving a present day cost of around £45,000.

There were, then, no houses and no-one (except perhaps a guard and worker or two) living on the island, and these utilitarian buildings didn't stand the test of time after the company was wound up in 1603, for the sale document recording the sale of Castlerigg and Derwentwater Manor by the Radcliffes in 1653 mentions 'all that parcel of pasture ground called Vickar Isle with a little ruinous house on it, bounded by the great lake called Darwentwater containing three acres and one roode.' Even by 1600 the windmill was 'sor decayed and ready to fall'.[43] Sic transit Gloria mundi.

It seems there must have been some trees left on the island after the first flush of building in 1570, for Donald also tells us that in 1600 there was 'a house built by Mr. John Smythe at the end of the smelting house (at Brigham), the timber thereof (for the most part) was brought out of the Vicar's Isle and is now a large peat house and will hold 1500 horseloads of peat. Which house was built about 15 years since.'[44]

It is interesting that the Radcliffes should at last have got their hands on Vicar's Island, for it never previously belonged to them. I presume they must have bought it from the defunct Company of Mines Royal sometime after 1603, only to sell it again in 1653. Presumably the buyer was one Ashbridge of Padigill in the parish of Caldbeck, for he sold it on in 1681 for £15 10s to a Mr. Wilson, of Ashness in the parish of Crosthwaite. Sometime in the next century it was inherited by Miles Ponsonby of Haile from his mother, Dorothy née Wilson. He then sold it to Edward Nicholson of Keswick, and by the latter to Joseph Pocklington of Carlton Hall, Notts., for £300 each time, Feb. and March, 1778. And so we come to the great Joseph Pocklington era – a mere eighteen years long in time, but an aeon in development.

[43] M.B. Donald *'Elizabethan Copper'* p. 365

[44] M.B. Donald p. 366

CHAPTER EIGHT

JOSEPH POCKLINGTON ON DERWENT ISLAND: 1778 - 1796

Joseph Pocklington (1736–1817) was not born into a successful Nottinghamshire banking family, as almost all biographies repeat, but into a property-owning prosperous Newark family. That at least is the conclusion of Marjorie Brown's tellingly titled biography 'A Man of no Taste Whatsoever' (2010). He did however inherit a considerable sum passed down from two great-uncles and received sufficient legacy at the age of 26 to allow him a life of leisure and luxury. Nevertheless, he was an astute business-man, buying, building and selling property and increasing his already considerable fortune. An ebullient, extravert character he took Keswick by storm, dividing opinion between those who thought him a brash off-comer set upon ruining the natural peace and beauty and those businessmen and builders who rubbed their hands in pleasure at the amount of money he brought to the town – both himself and from the visitors his exploits began to attract. He found a worthy confederate in the person of Peter Crosthwaite who had opened his Museum in 1781.

Crosthwaite had spent many years at sea working for the East India Company; as an admiral he had been in charge of protecting cargo ships from pirates. This experience was to prove fruitful both in securing exhibits for his museum and in making contacts with other travellers who would provide further exhibits once Crosthwaite was settled in the Lakes. It also came to the fore when Pocklington and he hatched their scheme for mock sea battles when Crosthwaite would attempt to capture Pocklington's island firing cannon from his boats – he of course the admiral of the fleet. He used his seafaring experience to plan the siege to the minutest detail, choreographing gun and cannon fire by a flag raising system. Pocklington had cannon set up around his landing stage and rebuffed the would-be assailants with their mighty roar. All tremendous fun and very good for attracting visitors to the town – Peter Crosthwaite's mission in life. This developed into an annual event, running for ten years, widely publicised as the Derwentwater Regattas. These included mock sea battles, horse swimming races, and live cannon fire from King Pocky's battery on the island. (The name King Pocky was coined by Samuel Taylor Coleridge, a later resident in nearby Greta Hall, who generally exhibited a profound revulsion for Pocklington's renowned lack of taste.)

On Vicar's Island – soon becoming known locally as Pocklington's Island – Joseph spent a fortune, to the delight of the local builders for miles around. On the crown of the island soon arose a splendid double-fronted mansion, and in the grounds a mock fort on the South shore, some 33 feet long, a battery on the East, facing the mainland, 43 feet long, along with Saint Mary's church and a boathouse. To cap it all off he also raised a mock Druid's Circle on the south shore, facing up the lake, and a giant 'Druid's stone' behind the house. He claimed the length of the island to be 251 yards 1 foot and 8 inches; the width to be 169 yards 1 foot 0 inches – remarkable accuracy on an island with variable lake levels! If true then the area of the island is roughly 6½ acres.

A view from the East of Pocklington's Island in Derwentwater near Keswick in Cumberland
Drawn upon the spot by Joseph Pocklington Esq. of Carlton House, Newark, Nottinghamshire, 1786

Samuel Ladyman, a notable philanthropist in Keswick who donated many seats and fountains to the town, also left a book of recollections '*Thoughts and Recollections of Keswick and its Inhabitants during Sixty Years* (1885), Keswick. He claims his father, Thomas Ladyman, was employed by Pocklington to build both Barrow House, on the eastern shores of Derwentwater and, later, the house on Derwent Island. This

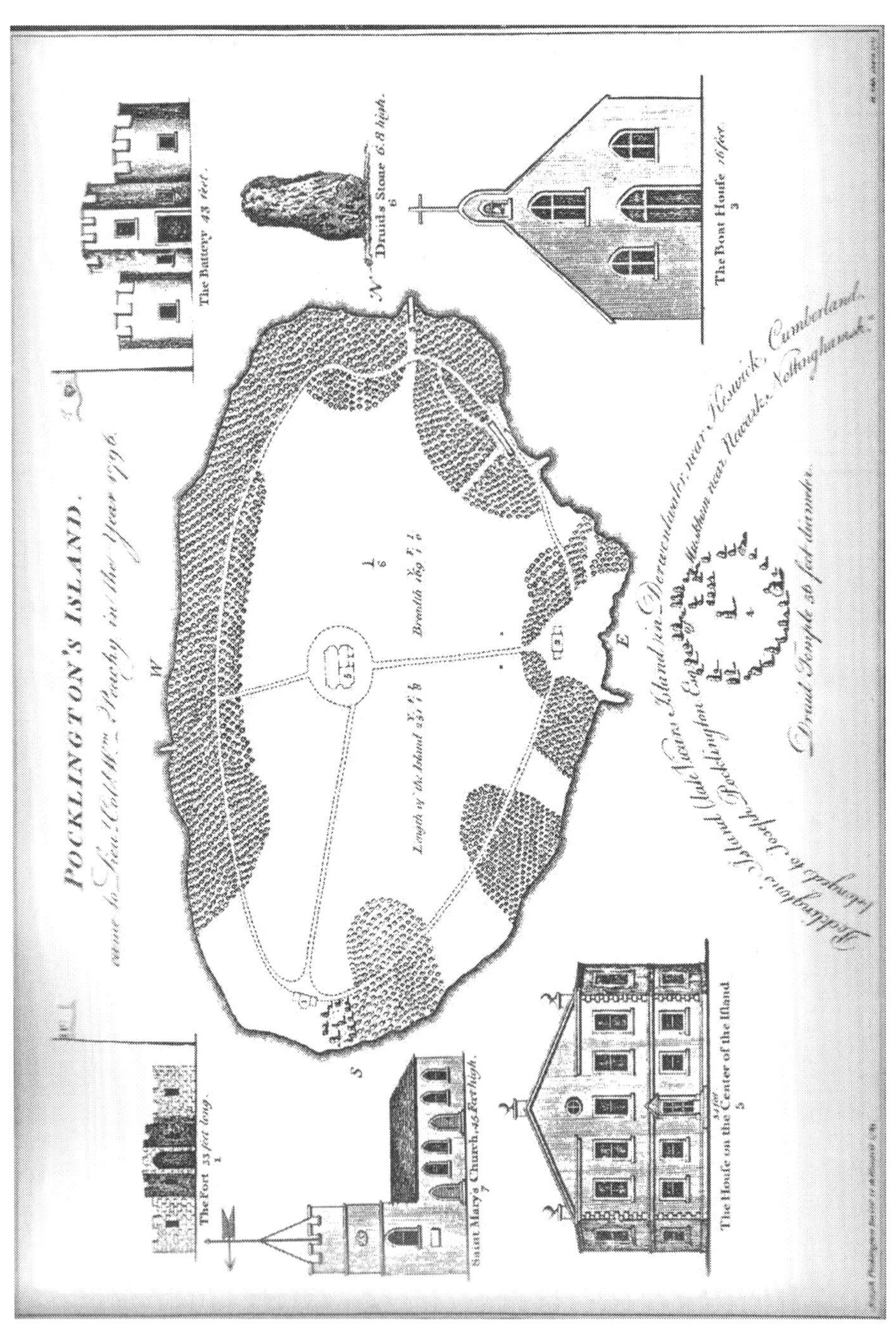

Peter Crosthwaite's plan of the island and all its accoutrements in 1788

seems in contravention of the historical order of events, and I only draw attention because he further claims that his father was also the architect for the house on Derwent Island, and discovered late in the proceedings that he had forgotten to put in a staircase, which they then had to place in an awkward corner.[45]

THE DERWENTWATER REGATTAS

These deserve a section to themselves, for they were the first manifestation of the various festivals, activities and extravaganzas put on particularly to encourage visitors, 'tourers' as Peter Crosthwaite called them, to Keswick in particular.

This print of the closing stages of the 1787 Regatta is by a genuine artist, Robert Smirke RA (1752-1845). Smirke had stationed himself close to the Fort on the Southern shore the better to portray the finale and has captured the astonishing realism of the staged battle, with muskets firing, a barrel of beer being looted from King Pocky's handily placed store, and on the lake itself three gunboats all firing off their cannon. These cannon were the chief draw for visitors, for the echoes achieved from the crags – particularly Walla and Falcon – were spectacular, and generated an

[45] Samuel Ladyman: ''*Thoughts and Recollections of Keswick and its Inhabitants during Sixty Years* (1885), Keswick, available online at http://archive.org/details/thoughtsandreco00ladygoog

atmosphere of noise and excitement similar to the most lavish of firework displays today. I assume the lordly figure on the left, firing his pistol to protect his ladies, is Pocklington himself.

The regattas ran for ten years, from 1781 – 1790, though they had a few hiccups at first. The very first one had to be postponed until late evening because of torrential rain during the day, and so was seen by only a few die-hards who forswore the inns. Fortunately the second was a brilliant success, and was reported in the third edition of West's *Guide to the Lakes* in the following glowing terms:

> 'A terrible cannonade began on both sides... this continued for some time and being echoed from hill to hill in an amazing variety of sound filled the ear with whatever could produce astonishment and awe. All Nature seemed to be in an uproar, which impressed on the awakened imagination the most lively ideas of "the war of elements" and the "crush of worlds".'

Peter Crosthwaite had a serious rival in Keswick, Thomas Hutton, who ran a competing museum and was also a guide, taking 'tourers' up Skiddaw. Hutchinson's 'Cumberland' bemoans the fact that they would not combine to produce one fine museum[46]. At the regatta of 1789, while Crosthwaite was preparing to launch the attack from behind Friar's Crag, Hutton, with two other guides from the inns, rowed over to Pocklington's Island and, having announced the attack was off, offered to row the assembled company back to the mainland at one shilling a head.[47]

Pocklington and Crosthwaite presaged a debate which has rumbled on for 240 years and shows no sign of abating. They are the first of the entrepreneurs, businessmen and financiers who regularly seek to exploit, encourage, titillate and entertain what in their day were the thousands and are now the millions of pleasure and leisure-seekers who visit the Lake District every year. Lined up in battle against them, in their day, were the Poets, the Romantics and the view-seekers, peering into their 'Claude glasses' which would give the most 'picturesque' view from prescribed stations. They were drawn by the writings of Thomas West and Thomas Gray who published their guides to the Lakes just before Pocklington burst on the scene.[48] Their most significant spokesman was William Wordsworth who, many years later in a letter complaining about the coming railways

---

[46] Hutchinson's '*Cumberland Vol II*, p.155

[47] Crosthwaite's Journal, quoted in Thomason and Woof *'Derwentwater, the Vale of Elysium'*

[48] Thomas Gray *'Journal of his Tour in the Lake District'* (1769) and Thomas West '*Guide to the Lake District'* (1780).

described Pocklington as 'a native of Nottinghamshire, who played strange pranks by his buildings and plantations upon Vicar's Island, in Derwentwater, which his admiration, such as it was, of the country, and probably a wish to be a leader in a new fashion, had tempted him to purchase' Wordsworth was equally critical of the newly-affluent mill-owners who built themselves opulent piles on the shores of Windermere.[49]

I'll leave the last word on this discussion to Thomason and Woof, the authors of the guide to the 1986 Dove Cottage exhibition of *'Derwentwater: The Vale of Elysium'* who conclude that:

> 'What emerges out of the story is an interest in the aesthetic conscience of the eighteenth century, ... Could it be that the sense of responsibility shared by the poets, commentators and artists finally impinged upon the landowners who were 'improving' their estates? The building of houses in a way that was sympathetic to the environment, the planting and felling of trees in a way that might enhance the landscape, the creation of roads and pathways so that thereby the visitor might the better enjoy the prospect, are all part of the eighteenth century dynamic.'[50]

LEASE AND RELEASE.... AND RECOVERY

Joseph Pocklington's ownership of Derwent Isle highlights two aspects of transfer of land which were common from the early 17th Century right up to 1845 when a new Act of Parliament made it unnecessary. When Joseph first buys Vicar's Island it is from Edward Nicholson. The system is that on 20th March 1778 Nicholson signs over the tenancy of the Island to Pocklington for the sum of 'five shillings of lawfull money of Great Britain' and for the price of 'one pepper corn if it be lawfully demanded' per year thenceforward. Another indenture signed the next day (21st March) then signs over all rights on the land for the consideration of £300. This seems cumbersome but was the usual method of transfer because to make an actual sale of land, rather than transferring all rights to a sitting tenant, required official 'enrolment' – the creation of a roll, numbered and kept by the state. This was both costly and very public so the Lease and Release was widespread.

If that seems convoluted, the next bit of legality Joseph faced over his island is positively Byzantine. The sale to Nicholson had been from

[49] Wordsworth, "First Letter on the Keswick and Windermere Railway".

[50] David Thomason and Robert Woof, *Derwentwater, the Vale of Elysium,* Grasmere, Trustees of Dove Cottage, 1986, introduction.

Miles Ponsonby, a wealthy landowner from West Cumberland, and it turned out that there had been an overlooked claimant on his estate, his mother Dorothy, daughter and heiress of Miles Wilson of Ashness, through whom Vicar's Island had come into the Ponsonby estate. It was necessary to extinguish this arcane right (called an entail), since it impinged on Joseph's absolute ownership, as the Dowager Lady Ponsonby (Dorothy) had this claim – which she didn't intend to use, being already dead! So in 1780 he, Miles Ponsonby, (who describes himself in flowery terms but makes it clear he is the son and heir of both his father and more especially his mother Dorothy née Wilson, deceased) and Daniel Jopson of Chapel in Borrowdale enter an indenture in the Court of Common Pleas in Keswick. Daniel Jopson seems to have lent £460 to John Ponsonby in 1750 as a mortgage with Dorothy's inheritance – Vicar's Island, Ashness and Watendlath – as collateral. The rate is 3.75 % to be paid every 21st November. The mortgage is redeemed by Anthony Ponsonby (third of John's sons) and John Senhouse in a document dated 12th January 1766.

The indenture is a masterpiece of flummery, but entirely typical of many used at that time. They sign a lease to one Rogers Jortin (who was a genuine lawyer of Lincoln's Inn) and sign over a lease for a year to him. This lease includes many probably fictitious pieces of land of dubious names and negligent acreage (e.g. Thwaite Field Seven acres Sow Field seven acres…. Honkearth forty acres, Strutta twenty acres), and also Vicar's Isle. At this point it looks like an ordinary lease, to be followed by a release. Jortin is described as the 'tenant to the praecipe'. This lease is dated 29th March 1780, and is followed by a Release signed on 30th March as if this were a genuine lease. It is not: Jortin is just that weasel 'tenant to the praecipe'. Next, in the Easter term of the sitting of the Justice of the Common Pleas Ponsonby, Pocklington, Jopson and others unnamed invent a 'defendant' with the name Job Charlton of Brough who 'demands' of Rogers Jortin vast areas of land (including Vicar's Isle, the only genuine article) saying one Hugh Hunt had deceived Charlton in some way connected to the estate. 'Hugh Hunt' is the giveaway. He was often cited as the deceiver, but never existed. Rogers Jortin appeared and 'vouched to warranty' Ponsonby, stating that he received the land from him and called on him to prove his title. Ponsonby warranted a court official, variously named in the document as Thomas Francis Martin, Thomas Francis Tenant and plain Thomas Francis as his 'common vouchee', and Job Charlton demanded the lands back from him.

Thomas Francis duly turned up in court and defended his right to the lands and denied that Hugh Hunt had dispossessed Job Charlton. He then 'put himself on the country' – that is, agreed to abide by the decision of the court. At this point Charlton asked for leave to talk privately with Francis, went out and then returned alone. Judge Christopher Aglionby solemnly summoned Francis to re-appear, but he came not, and was therefore declared to be in contempt of court, and could not defend his claim to the title of the lands. The judge therefore ordered that Job Charlton should recover the land from Rogers Jortin, who would be compensated by Miles Ponsonby and Joseph Pocklington. They in turn should be compensated by poor old Thomas Francis. As a poor employee of the court he could make no recompense and put himself 'in mercy'. Basically, no-one recompensed anyone, because the whole farrago was a sham – but the upshot is that the land is now held in fee simple, any tricky entitlements having been expunged.[51]

I don't really understand the labyrinthine complexity of all this, but that's how it was done many, many times. Everyone was complicit in the sham proceedings, and the system prevailed for a couple of centuries!

All these documents were copied by Pocklington's lawyers in 1796 when demanded by William Peachy, and survive as true copies of the originals in Carlisle Record Office in the box D/NT/6.

I also don't understand Edward Nicholson's part in all this. He was the first buyer of Vicar's Island from Miles Ponsonby, by Lease and Release on 4th and 5th February 1778, paying £300, and then promptly resold to Joseph Pocklington, apparently for the same £300 by Lease and Release on 20th & 21st March the same year. He must have been set up by Pocklington, who must also surely have paid him for the task – but why? Was Ponsonby unwilling to sell to Pocklington?

On a personal note I am interested to see Daniel Jopson, of Chapel in Borrowdale involved as a mortgagor and apparent leaseholder of the island for a time. Daniel Jopson figures in my book 'Thorneythwaite Farm, Borrowdale' as a canny yeoman farmer who bested the Lord of the Manor, Sir Gilfrid Lawson, removing a dozen straight oak trees for his own use and successfully defending himself against Lawson's bailiff, Grainger.[52] Clearly Daniel was a man to be reckoned with.

---

[51] CRO D/NT/6

[52] Ian Hall *Thorneythwaite Farm, Borrowdale*, p 130.

CHAPTER NINE

OWNERSHIP OF DERWENT ISLAND/VICAR'S ISLE/HESTHOLM

As we have seen the earliest known owners of the Island, back in the 12th Century, were the Lords of the Manor of Allerdale north of the Derwent. At that time, and for centuries later, it was an intrusion into the lands on the east of Lake Derwentwater which were owned initially by the de Derwentwater family and in succession to them the Radcliffe family. The dividing line between the manors went up the middle of the lake, but Hestholm, as the island was then known, was the exception. In 1195 or thereabouts it was part of the gift of the Crosthwaite lands by Alice de Rumilly II to Fountains Abbey. She founded the new Crosthwaite Church in 1185 and this was probably when it became Vicar's Isle – part of the glebe allowed to the Vicar of Crosthwaite. It remained in Fountains Abbey hands till Henry VIII dissolved the monasteries and became the property of the Crown in 1539.

Granted to John Williamson by the Crown it remained in his hands till he sold it to the Company of Mines Royal in 1569, for £60. They held it till the company folded around 1603, and I assume became part of the Radcliffes' Derwentwater Estate till they sold it, along with other nearby lands, in 1653 – the Civil War period. Presumably the buyer was one Ashbridge of Padigill in the parish of Caldbeck, for he sold it on in 1681 for £15 10s. to a Mr. Miles Wilson, of Ashness in the parish of Crosthwaite. It came into the Ponsonby family, of Hale Hall, when Wilson's daughter Dorothy married John Ponsonby, who left it to his son Miles Ponsonby of Haile who then sold it to Edward Nicholson of Keswick, and by the latter to Joseph Pocklington of Carlton Hall, Notts., for £300 each time, Feb. and March, 1778. Hutchinson in his account of a visit to the Lakes in 1773 wrote of 'Vicar's Island, containing about six acres of corn land; on the eastern side of which a few sycamores formed a little grove, covering a hovel'.[53]

Wordsworth, bemoaning the changes made by Pocklington, wrote that 'At the bidding of an alien improver, the Hind's Cottage, upon Vicar's Island…with its embowering sycamores and cattle-shed, disappeared from the corner where they stood'.[54]

[53] Hutchinson 1774, pp. 115-7.

[54] Wordsworth *Scenery of the Lakes*, 1822, p. 61

Similarly, West's 1778 guide to the Lakes described Vicar's Isle as 'with a hut upon it, stript of its late ornamental trees by the unfeeling hand of avarice'.[55]

Joseph Pocklington made his heavy-handed mark on the island before selling it on, with all his many new buildings thereon to William Peachy of Shoddesdon and South Park, Hants for £2000 in 1796. Mrs Susannah Peachy (widow of Lt. Gen. William Peachy) of Black Down House, Surrey, sold it in 1844 to H. C. Marshall of Headingley, Leeds, for £3440. Henry Marshall left it to his son John Marshall III in 1884, and John to his widow Ernestine for her lifetime and then to his son Denis who used it as his retreat from his life as a schoolmaster at Sedbergh School. Denis Marshall, grandson of Henry, gifted it to the National Trust in 1951 – 'for ever, for everyone'.[56]

Lieutenant General Sir William Peachy (the army title was almost entirely ceremonial) was, in his way, as ebullient and outrageous a character as Joseph Pocklington, and yet has left virtually no mark on Keswick history. Taking possession of Derwent Isle in 1796 he used it as a summer retreat from his familial home in Gosport, Hampshire – and from his parliamentary duties as MP for Yarmouth in the Isle of Wight (1797 – 1802). He rose eventually to the rank of Major-General and had Gilbert & Sullivan been writing The Pirates of Penzance fifty years earlier would have been a strong contender for the original 'modern major-general'. One of his recorded misadventures was to capsize his skiff in the middle of the lake, having to be unceremoniously rescued by his servants, who towed him in 'like a Triton, waving his hat round his head, and huzzaing as he approached his own shores'.[57]

When Robert Southey took up residence at Greta Hall in 1803 the two families struck up a close friendship, though one in which Southey frequently commented somewhat sardonically on his friend's garrulousness and ebullience. Southey told a friend in 1806 that:

> 'The Colonel has sent me half a collar of brawn and a little barrel of pickled sturgeon. This cost me a letter of thanks, which again produced such an answer! I wish you had seen it: he writes just as he

[55] West 1778, p. 114

[56] Carlisle Record Office, *Reference D NT/6: Vicar's Island*

[57] D.R. Fisher, editor, *The history of Parliament: the House of Commons 1820-1832*

> talks - world without end, Amen! However he is a good-natured homo, if ever there was one.'[58]

The changes Peachy instituted were commended by both Southey and Wordsworth. The former wrote in 1807 of the island,

> 'A few years ago it was hideously disfigured with forts and batteries, a sham church, and a new druidical temple, and except a few fir-trees the whole was bare. The present owner has done all which a man of taste could do in removing these deformities: the church is converted into a tool-house, the forts demolished, the batteries dismantled, the stones of the druidical temple employed in forming a bank, and the whole island planted'.

In 1810 Wordsworth gave a similar judgement:

> 'The taste of a succeeding proprietor rectified the mistakes as far as was practicable, and has ridded the spot of its puerilities. The church, after having been docked of its steeple, is applied both ostensibly and really, to the purpose for which the body of the pile was actually erected, namely a boat-house; the fort is demolished; and, without indignation on the part of the spirits of the ancient Druids who officiated at the circle upon the opposite hill, the mimic arrangement of stones, with its sanctum sanctorum, has been swept away'.

Southey was very fond of Peachy's first wife, Emma Frances Charter who died of consumption early in their time in Keswick and for whom he wrote a poetic epitaph. His third daughter, Emma (February 1808–May 1809), was named after her, but sadly also died, aged only one year, in the same year. Peachy married again in 1812, to a West Indian widow – the Susannah Peachy who sold Derwent Isle and its accoutrements to Henry Marshall in 1844. Susannah's son from her previous marriage, James Henry, and his family were the most frequent inhabitants of the island in the 1830s.

For all the calumny heaped on his head in the thirty or so years after Joseph Pocklington built his three local villas – Derwent Isle house, Barrow House at the south-East end of the lake, and what is now known as Derwent Bank in Portinscale – all three have stood the test of time, though much altered, and all three receive special commendation in the recent

[58] John Wood Warter (ed.), *Selections from the Letters of Robert Southey*, (London, 1856), pp.355–359

successful bid for World Heritage Site inscription to be awarded to the Lake District.

In the 2015 Nomination Document, Part 2, Derwent Isle is listed as one of the key villas in the Borrowdale and Bassenthwaite Valley (Area 9) along with Barrow House and Derwent Bank, also Pocklington houses. The Nomination Document describes the importance of the landscape in the second strand of outstanding universal value (OUV) in this area, celebrated as part of 'a landscape of great Sublime and Picturesque beauty. Villas and designed landscapes proliferated on the shores and islands of Derwent Water and Bassenthwaite...' The area is also important in demonstrating the third OUV as this was where 'the first concerns emerged over the preservation of the scenic qualities and beauty of the Lake District...followed in the late 18th and early 19th centuries by the purchase of key parts of Borrowdale by John Marshall and others keen to preserve the beauty of the area';[59]

Perhaps Joseph Pocklington deserved better from the 'Disgusted, of Keswick' brigade.

It is to that John Marshall and his son Henry Cowper Marshall and their involvement with Derwent Isle in particular and the Lake District in general that we now turn our attention.

[59] Lake District World Heritage Site Nomination Document Part 2, 2015, 319-320

CHAPTER TEN

HENRY COWPER MARSHALL 1808-1884

In one sense we come upon Henry Cowper Marshall out of time, for he was the fourth son of a couple who are integral to the development of the eastern shore of Derwentwater: John Marshall and Jane née Pollard. They will have their own story in Part Four, and a fascinating story it is, intermingled with the lives of William and Dorothy Wordsworth.

Henry married Catherine Spring-Rice in 1837, thereby beginning a connection with that illustrious family which became quite convoluted. His older brother James Garth Marshall, a late starter, married Catherine's sister Mary four years later, at the age of 39. Mary had been, until her marriage, a Maid of Honour to the young Queen Victoria since her accession in 1837. Their father, Thomas Spring-Rice, was Lord Monteagle, a notable Irish-born politician who had been MP for Limerick for many years since 1820, and was now MP for Cambridge. These years between his two daughters' marriages were stressful in the extreme for Spring-Rice. An able Whig politician he was made Chancellor of the Exchequer when his party won the General Election in 1835, under Lord Melbourne (who became Queen Victoria's favourite Prime Minister). It was not a good time to be Chancellor, as the persistent crop failures which were to culminate in the Great Potato Blight were producing a severe recession. Ultimately Spring-Rice was made the scapegoat for the government's poor handling of the deepening crisis, and he was forced out of office in 1839. As is not unusual in politics, then or now, he was immediately elevated to the peerage, being given the title Lord Monteagle of Brandon (in the County of Kerry).

As the potato blight began to cause famine in his native Ireland Lord Monteagle lived up to his liberal ideals, extending so much credit to his tenants and workers on the family estate in Munster that he was almost bankrupt. His first wife, Lady Theodosia Pery, daughter of Edmund Pery, 1st Earl of Limerick and mother of course to Catherine and Mary, died in 1839 – truly an 'annus horribilis' for Spring-Rice, leaving him widowed, out of Parliament, and almost bankrupt. Neither Catherine nor Mary can have brought much of a dowry to the Marshall family, but then money was not a problem in that family, for their father, John Marshall, had made a fortune by perfecting flax spinning machines which produced linen for a fraction of the previous labour intensive methods. What the Marshall family needed were good social connections, and where better to find them than by marriage into court circles?

The families were about to become even more deeply entwined, however, for when Lord Monteagle's wife died he too looked to the Marshall clan for comfort and a successor, finding her in the person of Henry and James' elder sister Marianne (or as sometimes written, Mary-Anne). When they married, a decent two years after Lady Monteagle's death, Marianne was 42, a mere nine years younger than her husband. Monteagle's money problems were solved and the Marshall's social standing thoroughly pedigreed. James Garth Marshall, marrying Mary Spring-Rice in 1841, found himself in the strange position of having Lord Monteagle as both brother-in-law and father-in-law. I wonder how they addressed each other.

One further entanglement between the families came about when Henry's niece, Elizabeth Margaret Marshall, living at Patterdale Hall, married Lord Monteagle's first-born son, Thomas Spring-Rice II. That made four marriage alliances between the families. One of Elizabeth and Thomas's children, Cecil Spring-Rice wrote the hymn beloved of all public schools ever since: 'I vow to thee my country.' The family had a house in Watermillock; Old Church, close to Hallsteads, the Marshall mansion on Ullswater's shores, and here Cecil spent much of his youth. Old Church was given to Elizabeth in John Marshall's will. There is a plaque to Cecil on the lower bridge at Aira Force, shown below, and another to his brothers on the upper bridge. The bridges were built in their memory.

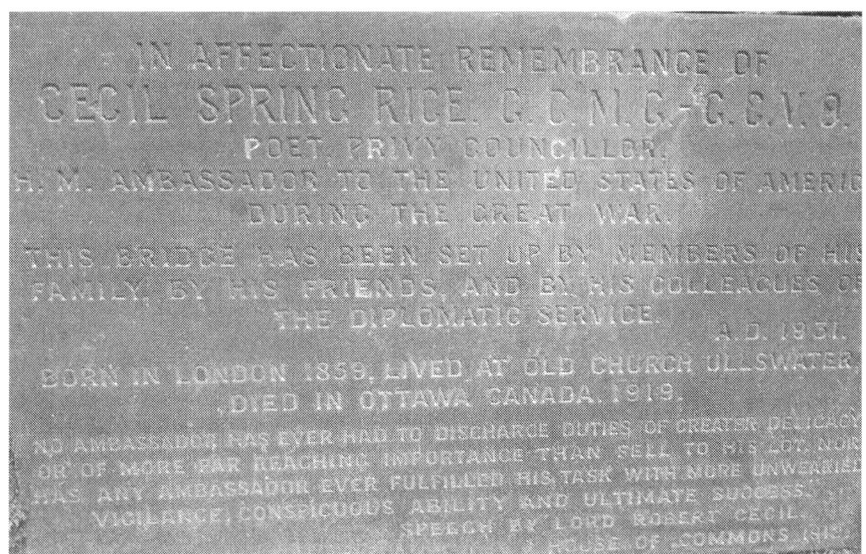

Henry and Catherine bought Derwent Island from Susannah Peachy in 1844, almost the last of the Marshall family purchases in the Lake

District. Over the previous thirty years family members had bought no fewer than forty separate parcels of land, estates and houses totalling 5,830 acres, at a total cost of £200,000 – the equivalent of around £10 million pounds in today's money.[60] In those terms Henry's purchase seems very small: six acres for £3,440. In terms of influence in the Keswick area it was far greater for Henry was chief trustee for his brother John's Castlerigg Estate and he and his family were Keswick stalwarts for over a century.

Henry Cowper Marshall, wearing his mayoral chain

Not that they lived on the island full-time in any sense, at least not in those early days. Henry and his brother James were heavily involved in the family business in Headingley, each with impressive houses there. Henry lived at Weetwood Hall, James at Headingley House. Derwent Island in

---

[60] Denman, Derek *Materialising Cultural Value in the English Lakes, 1735-1845: A Study of the responses of new landowners to representations of place and people,* Lancaster University thesis, 2011. p. 236

those first years was very much Henry and Catherine's 'holiday cottage', a retreat for the summer season from the rigours of industry. John Marshall, founder of the business, was 79 when Henry bought the island and died a short year later, so he and James, together with their younger brother Arthur, should have been full-time directors of a company competing in an increasingly difficult market.

In fact the Marshall business was already in decline and by 1846 there were more years of loss-making than of profit.[61] No doubt the market had become a lot more competitive since their father's day, but one is also left with the feeling that this second generation were nowhere near as ambitious or as driven as old John Marshall. James in particular spent a lot on buying up estates in the Lake District: in the ten years from 1836 onwards he bought over a thousand acres including several houses, a slate quarry and the fine Waterhead mansion and estate in Monk Coniston, spending £32,600 plus considerable renovation costs.[62] As soon as their father was laid in his grave the brothers felt free to be extravagant. Both employed Anthony Salvin, a notable architect, to enhance their Lake District properties. James also had a London house and became Member of Parliament for Leeds in 1847. The flax mills meanwhile went unmodernised and under-capitalised and finally closed in 1886 in the hands of the third generation Marshalls. As W.M.Thackeray observed: 'It costs a lot of money to be rich'.

Henry had already, in his role of a trustee of his elder brother John II's estate, committed a lot of time, energy and funding to Keswick in the construction of St. John's Church. John II died in 1836 having owned the eastern shore and Lord's Island a short four years. In his will he directed that the construction costs be met from his estate, and indeed lived just long enough to see the foundations laid. It was left to Henry to see the project through, and it must have kept him busy over the next two years – years in which he married and had his first-born son. John II had appointed Anthony Salvin as architect of the new church, the first of many projects Salvin would subsequently perform for the Marshall family. Initially Salvin had been approached to design a new mansion for John II and his wife Mary Ballantine Dykes, at Broomhill Point on Derwentwater. It is impossible at this remove to ascribe motives, but it is clear he was not a well man and probably knew he would not live long: witness the two complex wills he wrote.[63] Perhaps he thought a mansion would be more of a liability than an asset to Mary his wife, who in any case was comfortable

[61] W.G.Rimmer *Marshalls of Leeds, Flax-spinners* p. 256
[62] Denman, p.236
[63] Carlisle Record Office, D/MAR/2/51

in their Leeds home Cookridge Hall. Perhaps he thought a church would be a fitting memorial to his life. Or perhaps he was a genuine philanthropist who saw clearly that the burgeoning town of Keswick which had sprung up a mile from the hamlet of Crosthwaite with its ancient church needed a new church with ministers to serve the large population, now over five thousand.

Whatever his motives it is a fact that his decision to erect such a fine church provoked significant discord in the town. James Stanger, of Lairthwaite House, was a regular contributor to Keswick's life and growth and had already proposed a new church, albeit on a much less lavish scale. He had advanced far enough to have estimates of the cost and offers of funding from Joseph Pocklington, resident now at Barrow House, General Peachy, resident on Derwent Island, Mr. Spedding of Mirehouse and Robert Southey, poet laureate, of Greta Hall.[64] His letters to John Marshall II become increasingly testy over the period January 1835 – February 1836 as it becomes plain to him that John II will not agree to some sort of compromise church. It seems from the letters that one of the main principles at stake is that of the subsequent Patronage of the new church: who would have the right to appoint new vicars? It is clear that in the first instance Stanger would like to see the curate of Crosthwaite, Revd. James Bush, installed. Revd. Bush is equally keen to be appointed, though his letter to Marshall is hardly a model of self-promotion: 'I have small pretensions and a great infirmity, but I have knowledge of the people and love them, and have a delight in waiting upon them.'[65] He goes on to say his present vicarage is damp and his wife cannot live there and has decamped to Dale Head on Thirlmere. He didn't get the post.

When the church was completed in 1838 John II's remains were moved from London, where he died, and interred in the new family vault in St. John's. A slate stone in the central aisle is above the vault and simply carries his initials J.M. The Marshall family were heavily involved in the new church's life. Henry was a proxy patron for his six-year-old nephew **Reginald Dykes Marshall**, John II's first-born son, and was probably responsible for the first appointment, for The Revd. Frederick Myers had been offered his first living at the Parish Church of Leeds. He was a fiery preacher, well aware of the need for the Anglican Church to change from within. He turned down the Leeds incumbency and instead took on the brand-new St. John's – not a classic career move for a young minister. It seems fair to assume he met Henry at Leeds and was persuaded to take on his new church.

[64] CRO PR 167/7/1
[65] CRO PR 167/7/1

It was as well he did, for there he met and married Henry's younger sister **Susan Harriet Marshall.** Not however before first having married Fanny Calcroft a year after taking on the incumbency. Fanny died a mere three months after their wedding, and two years later he married Susan. They had a fine vicarage to raise their family in, for Marshall munificence stretched also to employing Anthony Salvin to design and oversee The Parsonage: what is today the Bishop of Carlisle's home and office suite. The Marshall involved this time was **Marianne**, wife of Lord Monteagle (Thomas Spring-Rice). The parsonage cost her £1630, and later she increased the endowment by a further £1800.[66] Her sister, **Cordelia Marshall** included in her will £1000 to St. John's Church and a further £2000 to the endowment of St. John's School.

Henry's next appointment was Frederick Myers' curate, The Revd. Thomas Battersby – another inspired choice. When he came in 1850 Myers was already a sick man, and from the beginning most of the parochial duties fell to his curate, so it was natural that when Frederick died in July 1851 Thomas Battersby should be offered the living. He held it for 33 years; years in which he transformed parish life, opening a Lecture Hall, a library, a 'Mechanics Institute', the Keswick Literary and Scientific Society, and beginning the Keswick Convention; surely one of the major annual events in the national and even international Evangelical Christian year.

The next refurbishment of the church was in 1889, some five years after Henry had died, but the Marshall connection continued unabated. The architect for the extension of the chancel was Henry's youngest son, William, by now a well-known and respected London architect. He it was who placed the lasting memorial to Henry's commitment to the church, bearing the words 'IN MEMORY OF HENRY COWPER MARSHALL TO WHOSE CARE AND FORETHOUGHT WORSHIPPERS OF THIS CHURCH ARE MUCH INDBTED'. At the same time stained glass windows were installed, the most magnificent being the Frederick Myers' Memorial Window – a triptych showing The Good Shepherd, The Sower and the Seed, and The Lost Piece of Silver. This last brought a flood of letters most notably from **Janet Mary Joy**, eldest daughter of John II and therefore cousin of John III who was organising the funding of the windows. By now of course **Reginald Dykes Marshall**, elder son of John II, was patron of the church, having turned 21 in 1853.

Henry and Catherine had four children when first they came to the island in 1844: Edmund (6); John III (4); Theodosia Louise (3) and Stephen (1). [John III needs his number as the Marshalls feature four Johns

[66] Margaret Armitage, *Linen and Liturgy* p. 14

who are part of the story]. Francis was born in 1847 and will have his part of the ongoing saga in Part Five: youngest was William, born in 1849. Edmund died in 1852, leaving John III to inherit the island on his father's death some forty years later in 1884. Catherine was never robust, and died after years of illness in 1853 at the age of just forty, probably finally brought low by the death of Edmund, her first-born. After her death Henry lapsed more and more into the reclusiveness that was always part of his nature. John III composed the following verse – precocious but perspicacious for a teenager:

He longs to sit in garb of sorrow
'Neath his blossoms precious sway
All night long, thus each tomorrow
Finds him sleepier than today.[67]

Once widowed Henry's melancholic temperament came more to the fore. He found it hard to take much interest in the Marshall factories and spent most of his time either abroad or on Derwent Island. After a spell of public office in his thirties, when he was first an alderman and then, in 1843 Mayor, of Leeds, he resisted any further inducements in that direction and even in Keswick was something of a recluse, metaphorically raising the drawbridge to his island. But before the sadness of 1853, losing both his wife and his eldest son, Henry doubled his stake on Derwentwater by buying the neighbouring St. Herbert's Island in 1850.

Lest we feel too deeply the melancholia suffered by Henry there is fortunately a much more upbeat account of life on the island as enjoyed by his children and grand-children: the first chapter of a book written by his youngest grand-daughter Frances Marshall, who married Ralph Partridge and published *'Memories'* in 1981. She was by then an old lady, being born in 1900, the youngest daughter of Henry's youngest son William (the architect). William himself was 51 when she was born and Derwent Island had been in the family's hands for over fifty years. John III died in 1894, his brother Stephen in 1904, and his sister Theodosia in 1892, but Frances remembers John III's widow Ernestine as 'spherical Aunt Ernie'. She tells what must have become a family legend, no doubt enhanced by time, of the three Derwent Isle brothers, having rowed up the lake to Lodore all finding themselves entranced by the mighty cataract, then in flood, and independently breaking into the 'stentorian tones they reserved for poetry'

[67] From the Marshall collection on Derwent Island, quoted in Rimmer p. 271

declaiming Robert Southey's classic poem '*How does the water come down at Lodore'*.[68]

Her Uncle Frank who built Hawes End she describes as having 'blue eyes looking mildly out from either side of an extremely crooked nose, twisted – we were warningly told – from sleeping on his face in bed.'[69] Her Aunt Theodosia, Henry's only daughter 'a mysterious, romantically named young woman, whose brilliance and charm were sometimes hinted at' she discovered eventually had died of alcoholic poisoning at the age of 51. John III's eldest son, 'Cousin Bob', she describes as 'a very strange figure. He had been dropped by his nurse, so it was said, with the result that he had a short little pair of arms barely reaching to his waist.... Short as his arms were he used his hands with consummate skill making model boats of all sizes and colours, and was exceedingly kind to us children.'

Frances herself is a fascinating character, marrying Ralph Partridge and becoming a leading figure in the Bloomsbury Set – the collection of largely bi-sexual artists and writers centred round Leonard and Virginia Woolf. The subsequent chapters of her '*Memories'* make for intriguing reading, but are sadly not relevant to a book on Derwentwater.

One of Henry's strengths was his facility with numbers, statistics – measurements of every sort. He had applied these in his early factory days but as they were beyond his older brother James' comprehension in practice they were of little use in that environment.[70] On Derwent Island he could indulge his passion freely and kept meticulous records of the height of the lake over the forty years of his life there – a practice carried on by his son John III and possibly his grandsons too. Henry determined the mean level of the lake as being 245.5 feet above O.D. – mean sea level as calculated by Ordnance Survey and gives his measurements from this level. They also installed a rain gauge. My main source for this information is a paper on the 1932 floods in Keswick and Cockermouth. published by F Hudleston: http://aquaticcommons.org/4565/1/1935_Hudl.pdf Henry installed the gauge in 1869 and Hudleston obtained records from Denis Marshall showing continuous readings at least from 1869 to 1932, and presumably they went on till 1951 (or later). The records show a mean annual rainfall of 57 inches for Derwent Island, and Keswick by extension, over the 63 years. The highest level of the lake in those records was on 28th October 1888 when the lake rose to 8 ft. above its mean level at noon. Canon Rawnsley gave a graphic description of this flood in a magazine for

[68] Frances Partridge *Memories*, p. 13
[69] Partridge, p.14
[70] Rimmer, *Marshalls*

December 1888, reprinted in his 'A Ramblers Notebook at the English Lakes' (published by MacLehose, 1902). Also available as a free download on http://tinyurl.com/leopold-ramblersnotebook00rawn .

Canon Rawnsley's photograph of the extent of the flooding up Borrowdale in 1888.

During Storm Desmond which produced such overwhelming flooding on Dec 5th 2015 the water rose far enough to remove the lowest two rows of slates on the boathouse by the boat landings, and to the bottom of the window of the present boat-hire cabin. The Environment Agency has a station beside the Lodore Landing and measured the maximum height to be 4.05 metres (13' 3") above Ordnance Datum – the same datum point Henry Marshall used in the 1888 flood. This is a mighty five feet higher! Clearly Storm Desmond was an enormous event, as shown by the devastation in the Greta valley.

Keswick readers may be interested to know that Hudleston's proposed solution in 1932 was to construct a conduit of approximately 300 square feet cross section, which is a pretty hefty 75 ft. wide channel, 4 ft deep, 'turfed at the bottom and sides to give pasturage in ordinary times' leading from High Hill corner 400 yards long in a WNW direction to re-join the Derwent.

On the other hand, opposite is a copy of an article in the fore-runner to the Keswick Reminder by John Marshall III on the drought being experienced in June 1893.

THE LOW LEVEL OF THE LAKE.

To the Editor of the Visitor and Guardian.

SIR,—The present low level of Derwentwater has given rise to so many vague statements, that it may be worth while to quote the best record obtainable of other seasons. The late Jonathan Otley, a most careful observer, wrote in 1852 as follows:—

"On the 14th of June, 1824, the water being at that time thought unusually low, a permanent notch was cut in the rock of Friar Crag, which I call 'zero.' On the 5th of July, 1826, the water was 6 inches below; but this might be in part accounted for by the state of the outlet. June 9th, 1831, it was 2¼ inches; June 1st, 1836, 1 inch; June 3rd, 1844, 4 inches; and at the present time, April 9th, 1852, it is exactly equal to it."

In 1851 my father had a mark cut to record what he judged to be an ordinary low water level of the lake, and I have a good many records of low levels since that time. Only in two years has the lake gone below Otley's "Zero" of 1824. In 1887, (the Jubilee Year) on July 9th, the water was 1 inch below Otley's mark, and again on August 29th, it was level with that mark. At the present time it is 5 inches below Otley's mark, or 1 inch above the lowest level recorded by Otley in 1826.

Yours faithfully,

JOHN MARSHALL.

June 22nd, 1893.

Eighteen months later John III was recording in his own handwriting another 'Great Storm', that of December 22nd 1894: here is the transcript.

Great Storm of Dec 22nd 1894

Greatest ~~strength~~ force on the island from N.W. between 8.30 & 9.30 am when all the trees fell.

1. Silver fir on south lawn on the S.W. path (no. 4 on page 45).

2. Silver fir on the W. side of the island on the back walk injuring laburnums and oak (no. 5) which was felled later.
3. Silver fir on N.E. side on the walk leading from front door to front landing (no. 3 page 45) injuring horse chestnut on N. lawn.
4. Beech tree on W. side of back walk adjoining the shed taking in its fall
5. N.E. beech adjoining on S.E side of path on the bank, that taking another
6. Beech SSE of last one higher up the bank (no. 4 on p.3) (damaging oak tree).
7. Large beech WSW of the greenhouse.
8. Silver fir on NE side of the path near front landing double top (no. 3 p. 45) injuring oaks on NE shore. Silver fir broken off about 20 feet up: felled later. Large branch off tulip tree, blown down NE side.

The front of the house on Derwent Island in the later 1800s. Photograph by Abraham Bros.

PART FOUR
THE EASTERN SHORES

CHAPTER ELEVEN[71]

GREENWICH HOSPITAL 1735-1832

The Royal Hospital for Seamen at Greenwich was founded by Queen Mary II, of William and Mary fame, in the 1690s as a naval counterpart to the Chelsea Hospital which existed, and still exists, as a home for ex-army servicemen. The Greenwich Hospital performed the same services for ex-seamen. It was originally funded by fines levied on merchants found guilty of smuggling. In 1735 the Hospital was granted the rents and profits, and the management, of the extensive lands acquired by the crown due to the attainder of James Radcliffe, the third Earl of Derwentwater, who was executed in 1716 for joining the Jacobite rebellion in support of the Old Pretender.

The Derwentwater Estate contained some 38,000 acres of productive land, mainly in Northumberland, but included the eastern half of Derwentwater and 1000 acres of land on the eastern shore, the old park and farm of the de Derwentwaters. In the 1770s the Hospital was granted full ownership of the estates and could buy and sell the property. The Keswick and Derwentwater parts of the huge original Earl's estates, encompassing much land in Northumberland were offered for sale in 1832 – just short of a hundred years after they were acquired – and were bought by a wealthy Leeds flax spinner, John Marshall, as a country seat for his son John Marshall II, MP for Leeds, who in turn was father of the R.D. Marshall who owned the Keswick estates in 1902 and gave permission and encouragement to the CWAAS dig.

Once the estate was under their management in 1735, the Hospital set about changes aimed at maximising annual revenue. They found that the Derwentwater Estate was encumbered with capital charges of £29,000, which took £2885 off their net revenue annually. They considered different ways of paying off those encumbrances and settled on a plan to sell the mature trees on the whole estate for felling, which might raise £10,000, half of which was in the Keswick estate, and to borrow the remainder from the Treasury.

The King's warrant for the sale of the timber was granted in 1739, but the sale was controlled by the Exchequer, in London, rather than by the

[71] Acknowledgement. My main source of information, and the basis for this chapter, is the Lancaster University doctoral thesis by Derek Denman, dated 2011. This is based on the extensive records of the Admiralty, of which the Greenwich Hospital was a part, at The National Archives, TNA/ADM. I have used information contained in this thesis, and quoted sources, with permission.

Hospital's Receivers in Gateshead. The sale was not achieved until 1747, due to the northern timber-merchants combining to offer a low and unacceptable price, the destructive effect on the Northumberland wood by the fresh Jacobite Rebellion in the 1740s, and a perverse insistence on selling all the timber in one lot.

The large value of the timber on the Keswick estate was a consequence of previous extensive cutting of timber by the German miners in the second half of the 16th Century. They did eventually manage to cut down the timber in the Keswick estate, and made extensive use of the coppices on the western shore, in Borrowdale and elsewhere. The stumps were all fenced and allowed to spring. While much of the local woodland continued as coppices, the Radcliffes developed most of the Keswick estate as timber, sessile oak and ash.

While this was commercial woodland, little was felled, resulting in a mix of mostly wood pasture, but also mature oak woods, with the trees close together to produce strong, long trunks with no low branches. Certainly, it was magnificent trees such as these in Lonning End wood, known as Crow Park locally, that Greenwich Hospital caused to be felled, plus those in the wood-pasture on the lakeshore, on their two islands, and on the higher ground. It was enduringly unfortunate for the Hospital that the harvesting of the timber on Derwentwater was in progress at just the time that Derwentwater was discovered as an area of scenic value, and its wood became considered as of great ornamental value.

J. Fisher Crosthwaite describes the felling in minute detail: I give here the gist of his record, which is inaccurate in some respects.

In 1749 the Greenwich Hospital commissioners sold the timber on Crow Park, Strands-Hagg, Cockshot Wood, Castlehead, Deer Close and Lord's Island to one Joseph Martyr[72], a joiner in Greenwich for £7,000: twelve years to be allowed for the entire clearance. Martyr employed a local man, Joseph Dawson of Brow Top, to oversee the felling. Various Whitehaven timber merchants entered an agreement with Martyr in 1748 to purchase 869 oaks, 1269 Ash trees, and 498 Birch trees from Calf Wood, Close Wood and Stable Hills Wood; and from Deer Close Wood (now known as Great Wood) a further 1045 Oaks, 2507 Ash trees, and 1429 Birch and other trees.[73] Many more are detailed, plus the information that 102 Oak and Yew trees were felled on the two islands (Lord's Island and Rampsholme). This sale amounted to £5,300 for upwards of 14,000 trees. Dawson was allowed ten years and nine months to complete this work,

---

[72] Crosthwaite and the Admiralty records name him correctly as Martyr: James Clarke sometimes calls him Marthas, or Mathews.

[73] J. Fisher Crosthwaite *'The last of the Derwentwaters'* appendix.

which equates to felling and transporting out an average of four trees per day, every day.

Crow Park, now the National Trust prime site on the northern shore of the lake perhaps demonstrates the scale of the clearance best. Fisher Crosthwaite's grandfather, the museum-founding Peter Crosthwaite, wrote of it to the Earl of Newburgh in 1800, thus:

> 'The Crow Park which will measure seventeen or eighteen acres did perhaps exceed any other park in the world for fine oak timber. The trees were in general about 27 yards high ranked close, and not one very crooked one amongst them, and many of them 12 feet in girth and not one bough on the greatest part of them until you get 16 yards high, and not even a shrub or any other kind of tree among them.' He writes a little further on that 'A Joseph Banks of 75 years of age was squaring timber here the other day with his heavy axe. Knowing he was a principal hand at cutting down the timber of the Derwentwater Estate I made much enquiry of him respecting the Island's timber, and he says that the Yew from which I took the coming piece was the largest of 21 they cut down and that there was then (50 years ago) a Willow in the middle of the house-stead (Lord's Island) which did not measure less than 11 feet in girth, and his master Joseph Dawson sold the boughs to a Cooper for half a guinea. It is about 36 or 37 years ago since Lord's Island was planted afresh.'

There is much to mull over in this letter.

- The Crow Park Oaks are consistent with an age of about 170 years, confirming that they were indeed planted around 1585, when the German miners finally managed to buy the land, fell the trees and re-plant.[74]
- There were a lot of Yew trees on Lord's Island. Interestingly there is still a copse of very ancient Yew trees just across the channel from Lord's Island, certainly dating back to before the 1700s.
- The Willow Tree growing in the middle of the house-stead gives a living clue to the date of the house's dereliction. A Willow annual tree ring is about a fifth of an inch thick, so to get to a girth of 11 feet would take it 100 years – meaning

[74] WG Collingwood, *Elizabethan Keswick,* p.180.
December 1585 – 'Bought from Lady K. Radtclieff a wood called Lonhet [Loanhead or Loning Head, now Crow Park] and Esmes [Esmess now called Isthmus] in which are oaks, ashes and birches, £24'

it was a sapling around 1650, which is when the sparse records suggest the house became derelict.

- It appears Lord's Island was deliberately replanted around 1765, which means the trees we see there now are those very trees.

I find it a rather delicious irony that Crow Park, once so admired for its beautiful oak wood is now arguably the most used open space on Derwentwater and is the chosen site for the placing of the Lake District's World Heritage Inscription plaque – a place loved by all for its sense of space and its magnificent views up Borrowdale.

In its early days, then, Greenwich Hospital ran Keswick Estate in the same business-like manner it ran the entire Derwentwater Estates, as the Earl of Derwentwater's attainted lands were called at that time. So, as we have seen, almost their first action was to try to sell all the mature timber on the entire Derwentwater Estate for £10,000 in one lot. This proved much more difficult than they anticipated. In Cumberland, John Spedding of Whitehaven was steward to Sir James Lowther and his brother Carlisle Spedding was steward of the Whitehaven coal mines. The brothers had set up a separate timber and brewing business. In effect there was so much timber on offer that it would supply all the Whitehaven merchants, so John Spedding bid only £4,100 for the wood in Cumberland knowing he could assign it to the other merchants piecemeal. Aware that they faced a cabal of the northern timber merchants the Hospital advised the Exchequer not to sell below value, and it was 1747, some thirteen years after they took on the Derwentwater Estate before they managed to get a sale they could justify. This is the background to the single sale they made to Joseph Martyr (above) and the reason for the Whitehaven merchants umbrage. Martyr paid £9,900 for all the timber in Cumberland and Northumberland.[75]

Greenwich Hospital was run very much on the lines of a modern Non-Government Agency. There was a Board of 'Receivers' in executive control, with an associated Board of Directors with a remit to oversee and ensure probity. And as with modern quangos there was no shortage of detractors ready to apportion all consequences to a distant landowner. One such was James Clarke in his 'A *Survey of the Lakes of Cumberland, Westmorland, and Lancashire* (London, 1787) who claimed the Hospital had favoured the Londoner Martyr over the local timber merchants. By 1787 the 'Lakers' movement was well under way and the Directors had had to weather much criticism on aesthetic grounds regarding their previous felling policy. West had published his famous guide to

[75] Derek Denman, p.94

picturesque touring (1778), Peter Crosthwaite had established his museum in Keswick, and Joseph Pocklington had bought Vicar's Island and was building his first Lake District Villa. Never again could the Hospital pursue simple economic considerations in its transactions regarding the Derwentwater lands: public opinion and the beauty of the scenery now had to be taken into account too.

After the first drastic clear felling in the 1750s there was no mature timber left to fell, and very little immature timber. The woods took decades to recover an acceptable appearance, even though the Hospital was allowing them to regrow and was replanting, except at Crow Park, which provided a lasting monument to the clearance. The Hospital agreed to a future programme of 'thinning' woodland, rather than clear felling, in the sensitive Derwentwater area, and to positive replanting in areas previously available for cultivation. They still had to justify their actions to the Admiralty and Parliament and tended to invent 'economic' reasons for their actions – looking for long term gain over short term finance. By 1774 a survey showed that, quite apart from the replanted woodland replacing almost all that had been clear felled, a further 187 acres had been taken into planting from previous farmland.

As a clear indication of the Hospital's intention to pursue a much more proactively 'landscape' approach to their Derwentwater woodlands they sought out advice from the great 'Capability' Brown, the foremost landscape architect of his time, and with it his endorsement of their designs.[76] As the 18th Century drew to a close the French Revolution and other European upheavals effectively put an end to the 'Grand Tour' and English noblemen instead sought out British areas to travel, the Lake District prime among them. The management of the woods around Derwentwater by the Greenwich Hospital, but not elsewhere, grew increasingly in tune with the needs of the picturesque tourists in harmony with the aesthetic model promulgated by the published guides of West and Gilpin. Across the lake Lord William Gordon had bought virtually the whole western lakeshore and was likewise replacing previous commercial coppice woodland with planting for aesthetics, and in 1786 succeeded in a quiet deal with the Hospital to rent both their islands – Lord's Island and Rampsholme – for the fairly notional sum of just two guineas per year, on a 21 year lease. This was entirely in order to preserve his view from his new villa at what is now called Derwent Bay, and not at all in order to fell any timber.

Early in the 1800s three events coincided to reinforce the policy of planting for landscape enrichment, rather than for purely economic gain for

---

[76] Denman, p.109

the Hospital. The first was Robert Southey and his extended family taking possession of Greta Hall, in Keswick, where Samuel Taylor Coleridge's family were already in residence. This may seem a diversion, but in fact Southey had both a direct and an indirect influence on the Hospital's management of its Derwentwater Estate. By 1809 he was sufficiently established as to apply to become the Hospital's Chief Receiver when the post became vacant. He thought the post would be a sinecure and, as he put it in a letter to Walter Scott: 'Being on the spot it would suit me well... and it would please me well insomuch as it would give me the power of preserving the woods and improving both the property and this beautiful place by planting'.[77]

He thought better of it when he learnt that 'The present possessor has always been employed for seventeen or eighteen hours out of twenty-four, together with his first clerk. The steward, lest his duties should leave him any time for frivolous pursuits, is in contemplation to raise up in him the seeds of controversy and quarrel, by associating him with some other person, who, under the pretence of sharing his labours, shall differ from him in all his opinions.'[78] This 'other person' was Joseph Forster, Chief Receiver, who from 1801 had tried to implement a programme of felling some of the Derwentwater woodlands.

The second event was the Napoleonic War, which pushed up prices for both land rental and for the lead produced by the Alston Mine. In these inflationary times the receipts from the entire Northern Estate showed a very healthy profit and undermined the more strident calls for profit over the picturesque. By the time of the third fortunate event for the landscape faction peace had returned to Europe and suddenly the price of lead and of rental values for land took a seriously downward turn and the calls for better returns from the Northern Estate became more insistent, with questions raised in the House of Commons. Into this hiatus strode the 'elegant, but somewhat insipid' (Wordsworth's description) figure of Edward Hawke Locker. In 1819 he was appointed Secretary to the Hospital, a position of much power over policy and its implementation. Locker was a friend of Robert Southey. Southey became his eyes and ears in the woods around Keswick and between them they held back the tide.

---

[77] Charles Cuthbert Southey, *'The life and correspondence of Robert Southey'* New York, Harper and Brothers 1851 P.258

[78] W.A. Speck *'Robert Southey: entire man of letters'* London, Yale University Press 2006. P.134

They first met in May 1815 in Carlisle, where Locker was visiting with his wife Elizabeth Boucher shortly after their marriage. Southey called her 'the beauty of Cumberland' and described her husband as 'a very accomplished, excellent and obliging man'.[79] At this time of his life Locker was producing and publishing a periodical *'The Plain Englishman'* and Southey contributed several pieces for inclusion. He was a talented artist and three of his paintings are in the Tate Gallery in London. Southey must have been delighted to find such a fellow admirer of natural beauty now in effective control over the woodlands around Derwentwater and soon after Locker's appointment he wrote (1st January, 1820) 'If your authority in the affairs of the Hospital enables you to save some part of the wood on Castled (Castlehead), you will be a great benefactor to this beautiful place. These trees are threatened and nothing could injure the immediate scenery of Keswick so much as their destruction. And in all these cases no ultimate loss would be sustained by leaving enough for beauty, instead of indiscriminately cutting everything down.'[80]

Greta Hall
An engraving by E. Francis from a drawing by W. Westall ARA

[79] W.A. Speck *ibid* p.154, quoting a letter from Southey to Grosvenor Bedford of 2nd May 1815.
[80] Speck, p.156

Castlehead is the rocky outcrop just to the South of Keswick, overlooking the eastern shore of Derwentwater. Locker confided to his wife in a letter that 'Greta Hall, Southey's home, stands on rising ground commanding a noble view of Derwentwater and looking direct upon Castlehead Wood and the lands belonging to the Hospital'. Locker restricted the felling to just 200 fully mature trees, worth £1,500 to the Hospital, which were felled over a three year period, leaving cover for the view.

Whether as a result of Southey's importuning or quite from his own sensibilities Locker actively sought to massage the Hospital's attitude to the Derwentwater Woods towards planting and felling primarily for amenity benefit. He undertook a tour of all the Northern Estates, along with Robert Brandling who had been appointed Receiver in 1821. Brandling was all that Locker was not, heavily involved in entrepreneurship and profit and keen to run the Hospital on the same lines. Locker's report on their joint tour of inspection completely side-lined Brandling, who wasn't even named in it. Instead Locker urged the Hospital to 'follow that same policy which urges the individual proprietor to forego a portion of his rents when the tenants are oppressed by the low state of the market' and that 'the Receivers may immediately be authorised to offer such relief to tenants instead of depriving them of their leases.'[81]

Locker gives special attention to the Keswick Woods, again citing a justification wider than the economic interests of the Hospital:

> 'The woods belonging to the Greenwich Hospital skirting the mountains and the Lake of Derwentwater constitute the great ornament of Keswick, and as the inhabitants derive most of their income from strangers who visit this beautiful scenery they would be seriously injured if the noble woods were cut down.'... 'A certain number of old trees may be thinned out periodically as they attain full growth without in the least impairing the beauty of the scenery, and from the stools of these trees, thus felled, new shoots would progressively supply their place.'[82]

Brandling wrote to the Receivers in damning terms about Locker's report, but was severely reprimanded for his style and deprecation of Locker.

However, despite Locker's eloquence in 1826 the local overseer marked the entire wood on Castlehead for clear felling. Southey wrote

[81] Denman Thesis P.135, quoting *ADM79/60 report 25 July 1821* p.5 Greenwich Hospital Report).

[82] Denman.

immediately to Locker, as secretary, and therefore with much power over the regional authorities:

> 'I write to you in dismay concerning the wood on Castlet. Walking there this day I saw that the trees are marked for the woodman – not for selection, but for a general fall – which more than any other possible circumstance will injure the beauty of this place. Undoubtedly there are trees there which will not be improved in value by standing: but as certainly for one that is in this condition many are marked which have not attained half their growth. The maledictions of all persons who admire this spot will be upon Greenwich Hospital if this barbarous spoliation be irrevocably decreed. I am quite certain it would be stopt if you were here.'[83]

Once again, Locker interceded and the proposed clear felling was at least postponed. It is clear, however, that Locker had a fight on his hands with the Receivers, as diminishing returns from the entire Northern Estates bit more deeply into the Hospital's ability to maintain its seamen, and questions began to be asked in the Commons. The Receivers returned to Castlehead woods in 1831, marking large swathes for clear felling. Southey wrote in despair to Locker:

> 'Our woods! Our woods! Two thirds of the trees at Castlet are marked for the axe and have been put up for auction but found no bidder, because it was a little too late in the season. Come and look at those trees from my window and judge for yourself whether Christian charity could require or enable me to forgive such a trespass as that of cutting them down. From the southern window that wood is the very nose in the face in the prospect!'[84]

What had happened? Finally the Admiralty itself, ultimate owner of Greenwich Hospital, had become impatient with protestations of scenery over profit. They had distressed seamen to provide for, a statutory duty, and they were failing in that duty and subject to increasing pressure from the two Houses of Parliament. On 6th April 1831 they sent this robust instruction: 'That the wood on the Hospital's Estates should be cut down in such manner and at such times as may yield the best revenue, without reference to the beauty of the scenery'.[85] Only changing times and fortunes saved Southey's precious woods from the axe.

---

83 W.A. Speck, p.166

84 Speck, p.170

85 Denman, p.146 quoting ADM67/82

Locker played his only card, cleverly turning the previous preservation of the woodland to his advantage. As secretary to the Receivers he wrote to the Admiralty on 19th July 1831: the Receivers considered the best pecuniary advantage would be obtained by the sale of the Derwentwater Estate, since, in its present beauty it would be likely to attract a rich purchaser prepared to pay over the odds for it. He included lots of figures demonstrating his case – and the Admiralty fell for it – or was persuaded, in more discreet language. 'Fell for it' might nevertheless be the more accurate, for Locker and the Receivers moved heaven and earth to find an appropriate mill-owner who could be relied upon to favour beauty over profit – one having quite enough funds already.

They found him in the person of John Marshall, the flax mill owner from Headingley, Leeds, whose story is amply covered in the next chapter. Keswick's infant tourist industry had much to be grateful for in the close friendship of Robert Southey and Edward Hawke Locker, and in the latter's implacable championing of the cause of landscape beauty over profit. Southey should have been relieved; indeed, I'm sure he was: but his conscience was sorely troubled by the manifest chicanery which went into the sale. The value of the timber was carefully calculated, and the value of the farmland, but the value of the land on which the timber stood was mysteriously absent from the calculations – a fact noted and commented on by Southey after the sale. On this basis the Receivers set a reserve price at the auction of £29,950. John Marshall's first, and the only bid, was for 30,000 guineas, with an obligation to buy the standing timber at an agreed valuation later. The price for this was within a hundred pounds of Locker's initial valuation: £16,768. Southey grumbled in a letter to John Rickman, the Commons' Speaker's secretary that 'You know the fate of the Greenwich property here, sold for two thirds of its estimated value.'[86]

[86] John Wood Warter, *Selections from the letters of Robert Southey,* Vol.IV, London, Longman, 1856.

CHAPTER TWELVE

THE SELF-SECLUDED POET AND THE SELF-MADE MAN.

That 'self-secluded' poet, William Wordsworth, who we saw in Part One was left a legacy of £900 in 1795 and determined to eke out the barest existence on it along with his sister Dorothy in their homely Dove Cottage, Grasmere, could hardly be more different from the self-made man of our title. We have already met some of his large family in Part Three: Henry Marshall on his Derwent Island, his brother John II with his plans for St. John's Church and their wives and children. Now it is time to meet the father of the clan: John Marshall.

Our tale begins in 1787 when a tearful six-year-old Dorothy Wordsworth, living in some style in a fine house in Cockermouth, quite suddenly lost both her doting mother (she was the only girl among four brothers) and soon after her home. Their mother Ann Cookson as was, died aged just thirty at her parents' house in Penrith after an unexplained trip to London. Their father John had never had much time for his children being tremendously busy acting as steward for the 'bad earl' Lord Lonsdale and also as coroner for Millom. Rather than employ a surrogate mother for his brood John Wordsworth packed them all off to various relatives: William to his Cookson grandparents; Dorothy to far-distant Halifax to be cared for by 'Aunt Threlkeld', her mother's cousin, already caring for her dead sister's five children. Here she went to Hipperholme School with her new best friend Jane Pollard who lived nearby. Also boarding at Hipperholme was the young John Marshall, only son among six sisters of a successful linen draper: but I doubt they knew each other then, as John was five or six years older than the girls.

No matter: Jane and John's fathers knew each other, being both cloth sellers and, more importantly, Unitarians, and in the fullness of time John and Jane were to marry – in 1795, that pivotal year in Dorothy's life when she and William her brother also decided to spend their lives together. But whereas William and Dorothy lived a life of penury, John Marshall was already well on the way to a fortune when he and Jane started married life. John's chance came at the end of 1787 when he was 22 and his father died suddenly from a stroke leaving an estate worth £9000 and John in control of the business.[87] He decided to move out of cloth-selling and into its production. It was the right moment in history, with flax-spinning machines just newly invented. In his own words:

---

[87] W.G.Rimmer, *Marshalls of Leeds, Flax Spinners*, p.22

'My attention was accidentally turned to spinning of flax by machinery, it being a thing much wished for by linen manufacturers. The immense profits which had been made by cotton spinning had attracted general attention to mechanical improvements and it might be hoped that flax spinning, if practicable, would be equally advantageous. It would be a new business, where there would be few competitors, and was much wanted for the linen manufacture of this country.'[88]

His road to success was far from straight and easy and there were many setbacks, false byways and difficult business partners to contend with, but Marshall was a classic blunt Yorkshireman intent on success and prepared to give eighteen hours a day to achieve it. Four years later, in September 1791, he opened his brand-new mill in Water Lane, Leeds – situated on the side of the Leeds-Manchester canal and initially water-powered. By the end of 1792 he had constructed a large flax warehouse, a counting house, stables, a dry house, shops for smiths and joiners, and several cottages; and converted to steam power with a 20 horse-power engine.[89]

Then in 1793 France declared war on Britain – and several other countries – bringing both threat and opportunity to Marshall's business. The threat was clear: credit was brought to a standstill, consumer buying stagnated and the banks were calling in loans. The firm lost over £3,000, and ruin was a distinct possibility. The opportunity was less obvious, but not to a wily operator like John Marshall. A time of loss is a good time to get rid of partners you don't like, and he had become hamstrung by those whose finance he had used but whose influence chafed. 'As they could neither of them be of any further use, I released them from the concern and took the whole upon myself'.[90]

Having warded off bankruptcy he was now in a position to capitalise on the war. He held large stocks of flax in an inflationary market, with very little being imported from the continent, and after the downturn in '93 people were once again buying linen cloth. The business grew rapidly and by the time of his marriage to Jane Pollard he was a wealthy man with excellent prospects.

William Wordsworth meanwhile was hovering by the bedside of young Raisley Calvert, waiting for him to die and release his £900 legacy. In war-torn France his lover Annette Vallon nursed their new-born baby Caroline, whom he had never seen and would not for several years. His

[88] John Marshall, *Life*, p.4 as quoted in Rimmer.
[89] Rimmer. p. 36
[90] Marshall, p.8

sister Dorothy had just left after the first three months they had spent together since childhood, promising to wait for him so they could set up house together in some rented place. Sojourning in Halifax, again at her aunt's house, Dorothy attended the wedding of her best of friends and her self-made man.

Dorothy and Jane kept up a lively correspondence, but it was not until 1800 that she next met John Marshall – this the first time he and William made acquaintance. John Marshall visited Dorothy and William at Dove Cottage in 1800 – without Jane, who was permanently either pregnant or nursing from 1796 to 1814 – and William and his brother John showed him around Derwentwater and Buttermere. There is a delightful sisterly touch in one of Dorothy's letters to Jane at this time: 'How fat your husband looks! If I had met him in the lane I should not have known him.'[91] The reason she did not 'meet him in the lane' was that Marshall deliberately avoided having to accept hospitality in their tiny Town End cottage, preferring to get installed in the Swan Hotel and have a hearty breakfast before announcing his presence. However, it is usually the case that opposites attract and it is clear from later correspondence that the poet and the entrepreneur found much to like and admire in the other, and to develop a mutual respect.

John Marshall and Jane née Pollard in 1802. Portraits by John Russell

[91] Alan Hill, editor, *The letters of Dorothy Wordsworth*, p.40

By 1810 Jane had borne ten of her twelve children and her health and spirits were a little fragile. They were by now a very rich couple and determined to build a summer retreat where Jane could relax and John could leave the rigours of business to his able underlings – for a season at least. He was now in his forties, immensely successful financially, and for the last few years had been keeping an eye out for a large country estate where he could be the country gentleman and Jane could regain her vigour. The Lake District was the obvious area: close enough to make travelling there tolerable; vivid in John's memory from his excursion with William and John Wordsworth; already becoming fashionable for rich Lancashire mill-owners – especially round Windermere – and, for Jane, close to her old friend Dorothy.

That summer they went for an extended stay in Watermillock, near Ullswater. 'A principal inducement was the delicate state of my wife's health, which I hoped a change of scene and air would restore; to which was added a partiality for that country and a great enjoyment of lake scenery'. [92] The holiday was a great success on all counts and by 1812 Marshall had spent over £10,000 buying an estate on the shores of Ullswater, and in 1813 began to build Hallsteads, his country retreat. A beautiful mansion, it has now long been the Ullswater Outward Bound Centre.

Hallsteads in the later 1800s, from a photograph by Abrahams of Keswick

[92] Marshall, *'Life'*, p.17

William and Dorothy Wordsworth had for many years been frequent visitors to Ullswater – cheerfully walking the twenty-odd miles from Grasmere over Grisedale Hause, down Grisedale valley and alongside the lake to Pooley Bridge and thence to Eusemere where their friends the Clarksons lived and farmed. It was on their journey home from there one spring day in 1802 that they came across the daffodils, source of William's most famous poem. Dorothy jotted down the picture in her journal that night:

> '… we saw that there was a long belt of them along the shore, about the breadth of a country turnpike road. I never saw daffodils so beautiful. They grew among the mossy stones about and about them; some rested their heads upon these stones as on a pillow for weariness; and the rest tossed and reeled and danced, and seemed as if they verily laughed with the wind; they looked so gay, ever glancing, ever changing.'[93]

It was, then, little hardship for them to visit Jane and John at Hallsteads and so to renew and refresh a friendship long sustained by letters alone.

There is a telling paragraph in FWH Myers biography of Wordsworth – the first written, in 1880 – which relates to one visit late in both men's lives around 1830:

> 'One of the houses where Mr. Wordsworth was most intimate and most welcome was that of a reforming member of parliament, who was also a manufacturer, thus belonging to the two classes for which the poet had the greatest abhorrence. But the intimacy was never for a moment shaken, and indeed in that house Mr. Wordsworth expounded the ruinous tendency of Reform and manufactures with even unusual copiousness, on account of the admiring affection with which he felt himself surrounded.'[94]

FWH Myers was the son of the first vicar of St. John's Keswick and his wife Susan née Marshall – and therefore the grandson of John

[93] Collette Clark, editor, Dorothy Wordsworth's *Grasmere Journal*, p.192

[94] Acknowledgement. My main source of information for the narrative of the Marshall purchase from the Greenwich Hospital is the Lancaster University doctoral thesis by Derek Denman, dated 2011. I have used information contained in this thesis, with permission.

Marshall, of whose house, Hallsteads, he writes here. Clearly then, by 1830 John Marshall and William Wordsworth were on very good terms.

This was to have very practical repercussions for Derwentwater and for Keswick when, as we saw in the previous chapter, the Greenwich Hospital Receivers rather desperately sought a buyer for the Derwentwater Estate in 1832. This was before John and Jane Marshall were permanently resident at Hallsteads, and it seems to have been Wordsworth who alerted them to the sale and urged Marshall to buy. After the sale of the Keswick Estate had been advertised, Wordsworth had told Sir Robert Ker Porter on 23 February, 1832 that 'this event will throw onto the market some of the finest situations for rural mansions in Great Britain. … the passing of this Beautiful Property into many hands may exceedingly disfigure a neighbourhood '[95]

Marshall was not now buying on his own behalf, but as part of a managed scheme of providing for his sons who were by now coming of age. In 1823 he had bought Patterdale Hall for his eldest son William, the only son to take no interest in the Headingley factory. He was much more interested in politics, being MP for no fewer than five different constituencies over the period 1826 -1868 – the last twenty years as Member for East Cumberland, where Patterdale Hall is situated. His second son, John II to distinguish him, was 34 by the time came for him to have his own Lake District estate. He was much more 'a chip off the old block', immersed in the manufacturing business and probably much more capable than his younger brothers turned out to be.

There were in fact two possible Derwentwater contenders for John II to seek to buy: the Greenwich Hospital Derwentwater Estate comprising most of the eastern shore, Lords' and Rampsholme Islands, and a demesne at Thornthwaite; or the western shore in the estate of Lord William Gordon, deceased. But whereas the Derwentwater Estate was full of mature and beautiful woodlands Gordon's estate had been stripped of every significant tree, leaving only unattractive scrubland. In the event no buyer was found for this estate and it remained with Lady Gordon till her death in 1841, but in 1832 it might well have been bought by Marshall.

William Wordsworth was either consulted for his opinion on which to buy – or gave it regardless. With the example of the proliferation of new housing on the shores of Windermere as a warning of what might befall Friars' Crag, Strands-Hag Bay and Crow Park he was keen that a single rich buyer who might erect one superior mansion but fend off

[95] Wordsworths, *Letters*, WW to Sir Robert Ker Porter, 23 Feb 1832, as quoted in Denman p. 263

lowlier construction should be the purchaser. John Marshall was just the man. He fired off a letter to him, beginning with a little heavy irony:

> 'I should say … that the purchase of the Derwentwater Estate, to sell out again in parcels, would be a promising speculation – provided the Purchaser did not care about disfiguring the Country when he came to divide it. … One of my neighbours, a friend, has an eye to purchase with that view … the beauty of that neighbourhood would be destroyed. Two or three Gentlemen's Houses might be erected under good taste with advantage, because it might lead to the preservation of the woods ….
>
> But if the most beautiful and commanding sites were broken up for paltry cottages, rows of lodging houses, and inns with stables etc., which would be the most likely way to make money of the thing … A house of moderate size would stand most charmingly, even magnificently, upon a field flanked by Friar's Crag on the right, with Cockshut hill and Castlet behind and on the left.
>
> … The lake never presents itself with dignity from the Gordon grounds ... but … abounds in beauty and is unannoyed by the Town. Your Son would observe that the woods upon it are much inferior in character to the other, having few trees that can be a called Timber. … I should prefer the Greenwich Hospital estate.
>
> … I agree with your Son John that the Gordon Estate is overplanted.' [96]

John junior had evidently been involved in the survey and the decision to bid for the Hospital Estate, though he left his father to navigate the tricky waters of the purchase. By the time of the auction John senior had had extensive talks with the vendors' solicitors and had negotiated various changes in the terms and conditions. In the event the Marshalls were the only bidder, and bought at their opening bid of 30,000 guineas. (£1.6 Million in today's terms). This was clearly well below its true market value and one must presume some delicate issues were skated over and the price understood before the auction began. Wordsworth was delighted to see the estate preserved intact and wrote to John Marshall senior:

---

[96] Wordsworths, *Letters*, WW to JM, late February 1832, as quoted in Denman P. 264

'It gives me much pleasure to learn that you are the Purchaser of the Derwentwater estate. ... Great mistakes can be made in valuing the wood. ... It will give me much pleasure to go over the Estate, with you...

Mr Southey will be pleased to hear that you are the Purchaser, as will all men of taste, especially when they know your chief inducement for buying the property'

He may have been over-optimistic regarding Southey's enthusiasm. In fact Southey felt the trustees of Greenwich Hospital had been sold short, as he made clear in a letter to John Rickman in December 1832. Rickman was Clerk Assistant and Speaker's Secretary in the House of Commons; John Marshall junior was the (successful) candidate for Leeds in the election of 1833...

'You know the fate of the Greenwich property here, sold for two thirds of its estimated value. Marshall, the cotton [sic] king, intends it as an appanage for his son, John, the Leeds candidate, and when that son called on me not long ago, I expressed a wish that he would ornament the unsightly and swampy ground at the foot of the lake, by planting; and I said that alders would grow well there. He answered immediately, "that alders were worth only fourpence a foot"'[97]

Southey was quite justified in his assertion, for the valuation of the Derwentwater Estates valued the timber on some 650 acres accurately enough, but neglected to value the land on which it stood. The timber valuation was £16,768 which Marshall paid soon after the auction.

Whilst my main thrust in this work is Derwentwater, I can't resist in passing that Wordsworth's help was again sought with regard to John and Jane's third son, James Garth Marshall. By 1835 it was his turn to have a Cumbrian estate bought for him – again spreading the Marshall fortune among the five sons, and Wordsworth it was who alerted John senior that Waterhead, Coniston, would be coming up for sale. He enclosed the information in a letter from his wife Mary to Jane Marshall in December 1834 in these words.

---

[97] John Wood Warter, *Selections from the letters of Robert Southey,* Vol.IV, London, Longman, 1856, Robert Southey to John Rickman, 12 Dec 1832, pp.314-5.

'The beautiful Property of the late Mr Knott of Coniston Waterhead will be offered for Sale by Advertisement early next month. The improvement which Mr K has lately made there, are very great – and it is one of the most elegant residences in the Lake District'.

It is perhaps noteworthy that all the sons who had acquired Cumbrian properties left them substantially as bought until their father died, presumably according to his wishes, but once he had passed away felt free to extend and improve them considerably. So William quickly employed the architect Anthony Salvin to extend Patterdale Hall in the late 1840s and Salvin then moved on to James Garth Marshall's Coniston property, to renovate and improve the recent Gothic style house at Waterhead. James also bought much more land and created what we now know as the Monk Coniston estate. Finally, in 1850, Salvin turned to Henry Cowper Marshall's Derwent Isle property, adding two wings and giving it an Italianate air. It is of course also true that they were all (with the exception of William) partners in the Headingley flax works and so became rich men on their own account on John senior's death. The only son we have not yet touched upon is Arthur, the youngest, born in 1814, and held to be not truly capable of running an estate. Nevertheless he was the third partner in the Leeds manufactory along with James and Henry after their father's death. He inherited the Hallsteads estate on Ullswater, already exquisitely built by his parents.

CHAPTER THIRTEEN

REGINALD DYKES MARSHALL 1832-1913

Born in 1832 Reginald was the oldest of the third-generation Marshalls to be involved in the Headingley factory. As John II's eldest son he inherited the Castlerigg Estate on the eastern shore of Derwentwater at the age of six, when John II died prematurely. As we saw in Chapter four of Part three his uncle Henry was the main trustee of John II's will inasmuch as it impinged on Derwentwater. John II was clearly in poor health for some time before his death and in 1830 wrote, without a solicitor, his first will.[98] At the time he had one daughter and no sons. When Reginald Dykes Marshall had been born, giving him a male heir, he had an official extremely complicated will drawn up comprising six sheets of parchment (January 1833) in which he left his Castlerigg Estate 'in tail' to Reginald under a Trust comprising two of his brothers – Henry and James – and his brother-in-law who rejoiced in the name Fretchville Lawson Ballentine Dykes. To be left something 'in tail' meant one had the free use of it for one's lifetime but was then obliged to leave it to the next generation's first-born male, or failing issue for the trustees to dispose of. A further complication was that the trust should rule until the last-born of his children should reach the age of 25. Since Julian, the youngest son, wasn't born until 1836, when John junior died, Reginald was unable to call the Castlerigg Estate truly his own till 1861, when he was 30, had married, and had children of his own, and moreover had lost his wife Margaret Louisa in childbirth with their second daughter.[99]

As we have seen almost all the Castlerigg Estate affairs were handled throughout this time by Henry. There was no mansion for Reginald to own and no pressing reason for him to involve himself in Keswick matters. When Reginald turned 22 in 1854 and came down from Trinity College, Cambridge, his Uncle Henry brought him into factory management – as much to relieve his own workload as to give young Reginald a purpose and a stake in the family business.[100] Indeed Reginald was soon the only Marshall regularly in the factory, for Henry and James, now both around fifty, had entirely lost interest in the business. Their sons were still teenagers; destined for somewhat reluctant factory life a decade hence, and with hefty capital inputs assuring them of good returns from the business. Reginald at first had no capital in the business, and as it was

[98] D/NT/6 in Carlisle Record Office.

[99] Inferred from the 1861 census and BMD searches.

[100] Rimmer, p.273

running at a loss, no income to show for the many hours he dedicated to it as a partner in the firm. Henry did transfer £6,000 to his account, giving him a rather paltry income of £300 per year, but wouldn't grant him any authority in the running of the business. Not surprisingly Reginald looked forward fervently to at last owning his estate when he turned 31.[101]

His cousins, Henry's boys John III and Stephen, entered the partnership in 1867 and 1871 and James' son – also James – in 1871 too, and there was really neither room nor reason for Reginald to remain. He left in 1872, taking his capital, £53,000, with him, and at the age of forty concentrated on his duties as a Justice of the Peace for West Yorkshire and took up a different business – he bought a brewery: Brunswick Brewery.

By now of course he had another wife and family. He had married Margaret Louisa Herschel in 1858 and had two daughters born, Mary and Margaret. Sadly their mother died from complications over Margaret's birth. The census record for 1861 makes sad reading. Reginald (29) and his brother Julian (24) are still living with their mother Mary Ballantine Dykes and her second husband Patrick O'Callaghan in what was his father John II's Headingley home, Cookridge Hall. Margaret Louisa has died, but still there presumably after tending her is her sister Amelia, aged just twenty. There too are his motherless girls aged just eighteen months and three months. The household supports – or is supported by – no fewer than thirteen servants aged from 14 to 40, all unmarried.

Reginald's second wife, whom he married in 1864, three years later, was Mary Jane Stewart, an altogether more robust and sturdy lady. Her mother was Mary Caroline Fitzroy and her great-uncle was Vice-Admiral Robert Fitzroy who gained fame as the captain of 'The Beagle' on Charles Darwin's expedition to the Galapagos leading to his theory of evolution and the origin of species. Fitzroy was also a pioneering meteorologist, coining the word 'forecast', and is honoured by having a sea area named after him: Fitzroy, formerly known as Finisterre. Not surprisingly, Reginald and Mary named their first-born, a boy, Fitzroy Dykes Marshall. He was to be Reginald's only son: the next seven children Mary bore were all girls.

By 1871 his mother and stepfather have moved to Clarendon Square, Leamington, Warwick and Reginald is head of the house at Cookridge, having finally come into his inheritance.[102] The servants have grown to seventeen, again all unmarried: only William Cox, the butler, is still there from the 1861 company. In the 1881 census Reginald and the family are still in residence at Cookridge, the servants have shrunk slightly to

[101] Rimmer, p. 275

[102] Census results for 1871

fourteen, including a governess for the girls. William Cox, now aged sixty, is still the faithful butler but all the rest are new again, all unmarried and generally in their twenties. He is still a JP and acknowledges on the census form that he is a 'landowner in Cumberland'.

Only by 1891 are Reginald and the family securely in Keswick, at Castlerigg Manor. There they have eleven servants plus a governess. William Cox has gone – retired or deceased. At Cookridge the only likely contender for what was called Cookridge Hall is now Cookridge Tower (not named in 1881) which is now home to a woollen and worsted manufacturer, Alfred Sykes. It would seem Reginald and family have moved permanently to Keswick.

Castlerigg Manor appears to have been built between the 1881 census when nothing of that name is shown and the 1891 census, when Reginald and family are in place. It is quite strange that for all those years between John II buying the estate in 1832 and somewhere in the 1880s decade this branch of the Marshall family had no mansion in Keswick, but they did at least have a bolthole, for there are a few references in D/NT/23 to 'The Cottage'. For instance there is a conveyance dated 27th February 1884 to Reginald (of the Tollhouse, Thornthwaite, for £25) in which he is referred to simply as Reginald Dykes Marshall of The Cottage, Keswick.[103] It seems Reginald did not build Castlerigg Manor but bought it from the Fenton family, business associates of the Marshalls, who must have constructed it and sold it on almost immediately.[104]

In the last decade of the 19th century and the first of the 20th, then, there were several families of Marshalls living around Derwentwater. Reginald and Mary were lords of the manor of Castlerigg and Derwentwater, living in some grandeur in the new Castlerigg Manor; Henry's sons and grandsons were ensconced on Derwent Island; and Henry's son Francis had renovated Hawes End over on the western shore and was frequently there with Caroline his wife and their two children, Hal and Catherine.

Boathouses

As in most families, however, there were occasional rows, and a spectacular example erupted over the Derwent Island use of Crow Park Boathouse as its landing stage on the foreshore. It belonged to Reginald Marshall. 200 yards south along the foreshore stands what is, for reasons I have been unable to determine, known as the Duke of Portland's

[103] CRO D/NT/23

[104] George Bott, *Keswick*, p. 61

Boathouse. However, there is a reference in James Clark's 'Survey of the Lakes' to the Duke, in his report on the Derwentwater Regatta, where he says 'there are also small brass guns mounted on swivels, sent here by his Grace the Duke of Portland, placed on the barges for the entertainment and amusement of travellers'.[105] The Duke was Lord of the Manor of Hutton in the Forest, some dozen miles distant.[106]

It is not the only Duke of Portland's Boathouse: a much more famous one is on the shores of Ullswater near Pooley Bridge – a picturesque and much photographed self-catering cottage now. Judging from the probable dating of these two boathouses they may well be named for the 3rd Duke, William Henry Cavendish Cavendish-Bentinck, who was very briefly Prime Minister from 2 April 1783 – 19 December 1783, and for a second term 31 March 1807 – 4 October 1809. I can find no direct connection to the Duke, other than that above, so perhaps they were simply named in his honour.

Derwentwater's Duke of Portland boathouse also belonged to Reginald. There are sixteen letters on file chronicling the progress of the row which developed between John Marshall's widow Ernestine, living on Derwent Island, and the ageing Reginald Dykes Marshall, living at Castlerigg Manor and owning the entire foreshore and both boathouses. It all begins amicably enough back in 1885 when John III (Henry's eldest son and Ernestine's husband) was still alive with a letter to his cousin Reginald:

> 'My dear Reginald,
>
> The Post Office has arranged to deliver letters to Crow Park and will deliver mine there if I put up a box. If you have no objection I should like to put it against the wall near the boat house. As the postman has to come in at the gate for Miss Gurley it would only be a few yards further for him to come to that place. But please let me know.
>
> Your affectionate cousin,
>
> John Marshall.'[107]

Clearly the Derwent Island family were using Crow Park Boathouse as their mainland terminus and as the post box was installed, Reginald was

---

[105] James Clark *Survey of the Lakes* 1787. p. 65
[106] CWAAS: ART. *XI.—Calendar of the Original Deeds at Tullie House. III.* By the Rev. C..M. Lowther Bouch. p. 140
[107] CRO, Boxes 69-72 in DB 74/2/16

content at that time. All was well for 25 years: John III died in 1894 but his widow and family, servants and tradesmen all used Crow Park Boathouse to embark and disembark for the Island. Reginald even installed a bell which they could ring to summon the boatman from the island to ferry them across. In 1909 Reginald Marshall began to grow old (he was 77 by then) and to think of his legacy and the problems there might be if he or his legatees wanted to sell land including the boathouse. In order to settle matters legally he suggests to Ernestine that she should buy the Duke of Portland boathouse in order to have her own ferry station and allow him to close down the island's use of the Crow Park boathouse, which he might wish to sell along with Crow Park Cottage beside it. He asks that she remove the post box and bell, and on Jan 24th 1909 she seems to agree, but asks that it remain till she returns from abroad. Later that year she paid £180 for the Duke of Portland boathouse. One might think that from then on the Islanders would use the Duke of Portland boathouse. Human nature being what it is, though, all tradesmen and the family preferred to use the 'desire line' cutting off the extra 200 yards walk and continued to cross from Crow Park Boathouse. By February 1910 Reginald was beginning to get crusty, though still civil, and writes – still to 'Dear Ernestine' – making clear that while he doesn't mind the continued usage of his boathouse he does require a legal agreement that such usage is 'permissive and terminable'. The letter concludes

> 'I think you will agree with me that an understanding about such matters should be come to, on my part by reason of increasing years, at all events.
>
> Yours very truly
>
> R.D.Marshall'

By early March Ernestine has apparently replied protesting that she sees no reason to change the customs of a quarter century and Reginald replies that he has no wish to make changes: only to regularise the arrangement. He reminds her that back in January of the previous year she had agreed to remove the letter box and bell as soon as she returned from abroad. His signature is simply 'Yours truly'.

Ernestine gives it a good three months before a somewhat terse quasi-response:

Dear Reginald,

In reply to your letter I shall be very glad to continue what Mr. Henry Marshall and my husband did in this matter, during their ownership of the Island.

Believe me,

Yrs truly,

E.E.Marshall

Two days later (probably on the day he receives hers) Reginald tries again, emphasising that all he requires is an acknowledgement that the use of Crow Park Landing etc. is only permissive. He ends rather plaintively

'I must have this settled, as I may die, or sell the property as I hope to do before the former event occurs.' In keeping with the emolliate tones he signs 'Reginald D. Marshall.'

Two days later Ernestine's reply falls on his doormat.

'Dear Reginald,

As you do not mention any previous agreement with the two former owners of the Island, I suppose there has been none. I do not feel inclined to pursue any different course to theirs.

Yours truly.

E.E.Marshall.'

Reginald has one last try, having given himself four weeks to calm down.

'I think you do not quite appreciate that my uncle and your husband made annual payments to me for boating rights and that you are not now doing so.

We cannot therefore go on as we were, but I am quite willing to give you a lease for the lives of your sons at a nominal rent in accordance with the terms of your letters of 27th Feb. and 8th March last.

Yours truly,

Reginald D. Marshall.'

From then on it comes down to solicitor's letters. Reginald's are Waugh & Musgrave, of Cockermouth: Ernestine's are M/s Ford & Warre. Ernestine will not budge and at some point collars Reginald's wife Mary Jane to declare vehemently that Reginald actually has no right to the Crow Park Boathouse since he never paid for it, but only for the cottage. Mary Jane is somewhat taken aback by this outburst, but writes to Ernestine a little later:

> 'Dear Ernestine,
>
> You spoke with so much certainty the other day as to Reginald's not having paid for the Crow Park Boathouse but only for the cottage when handed over to him by his uncle that knowing my memory fails me, I thought I might possibly be mistaken. However I have now seen the letter with statement of accounts in Uncle Henry's own writing dated March 3rd 1858, showing a balance to R.D.M's credit in his (H.C.M's) Trustee's account transferred to R.D.M's account with Marshall & Co. from which £500 is deducted in payment to Uncle Henry "for Crow Park Cottage and Boathouse".
>
> I thought it right to let you know.
>
> Yrs.
>
> M.J.Marshall.

And there the sorry saga limped to a halt, with Ernestine refusing to sign anything that might restrict her family's use of the Crow Park Boathouse and Reginald shying away from forcing the issue. Ernestine was clearly terribly upset by the argument and never again herself used the Boathouse, but her family and tradesmen continued unmolested. Reginald lived a further three years, Ernestine a further nineteen – just long enough to see Reginald's worst fears realised when Herbert Walker bought what he thought was a simple cottage and boathouse only to find it anything but.

CHAPTER FOURTEEN

HERBERT WILSON WALKER 1875-1934

What Henry Cowper Marshall was to 19th century Keswick Herbert Wilson Walker was to the 20th. Both came from similar backgrounds: the sons of fathers whose fortunes were made in industrial enterprises; both spent a considerable amount of that fortune in the Keswick area; and both left a lasting legacy in the preservation of the beauty of the area. Henry's father John made his fortune perfecting the industrial spinning of flax coupled with his skill in buying his raw materials cheaply during the Napoleonic wars and selling into the blossoming post-war market. Herbert's father William Walker was born into the tannery business set up in Whitehaven by his father who was already a wealthy man. William increased that wealth significantly, and when he died in 1913 was such a respected member of Whitehaven society that on the day of his funeral all the shops closed from 1 pm to 3 pm. His legacy of £410,000 – of which £52,000 had to be paid in death duty – was split equally between his wife, for her lifetime, his second son Arthur, and his first-born son Herbert who was also charged with being the trustee of his mother's share, on her death in 1931, for the benefit of his sister, Anne Elizabeth. This proved to be a long trustee-ship as Anne Elizabeth lived to 97.

Herbert was 38 when he came into his inheritance, and he used it very well indeed. He bought a lot of property in the Wasdale area, including the Lordship of the Manor, and continued his father's philanthropy in Whitehaven. He guided and significantly funded the buyers of Whitehaven Castle from the Lowther family and its conversion to a hospital to serve the town. He also considerably enlarged his tannery empire, buying and running tanneries in Workington, Maryport, Warrington, Liverpool, Leeds and London, with a number of others across Lancashire and Merseyside.

But it is his Keswick and Borrowdale connection which is our primary interest. It seems to have begun at the end of the Great War when many estates and farms were being offered for sale as the old order suffered the aftershocks of the cataclysm of that convulsion. One of the chief sellers in the area were the trustees of the estate of John Musgrave, a solicitor and businessman who had sought to link Borrowdale and Wasdale by road over Sty Head Pass. He owned Wasdale Hall and many farms and properties in Wasdale and wanted the West Coast valleys to be able to share in the rapidly growing tourism industry burgeoning in Keswick and Borrowdale towards the end of the 1800s. He bought Thorneythwaite and

Seathwaite at the head of Borrowdale in 1885 so he would own all the land over which a road might go – his Wasdale Hall Estate owned the other side of Sty Head down into Wasdale. There seemed nothing to stop his pushing ahead with his scheme, and yet he never did. Perhaps the prevailing fin-de-siècle mood of conservation, with the newly emergent National Trust persuaded him not to proceed; perhaps the expense was prohibitive; or perhaps he was just growing old, being 79 when he bought the farms.

He was 97 when he died, just before the Great War, in 1912, and his estate was held in trust for the duration. In 1919 the trustees offered his Borrowdale outlying farms for sale by auction, and this is when Herbert Walker first shows on our radar. The four farms offered were High Lodore, its neighbour Field Head, and Thorneythwaite and Seathwaite. The last two remained unsold, but Herbert bought High Lodore and Field Head, opening his account in the valley, and initiating his company 'Lodore Estates Ltd.' In the process he became owner of the lakebed in the S corner of Derwentwater. It was a year later in 1920 when the trustees offered the much larger Wasdale Hall Estate comprising 38 lots in Wasdale ranging from small cottages to huge farms, with the jewel in the crown, Wasdale Hall itself, as Lot No. 1. Tagged on to the end of the sale, as lots 39 and 40 were the unsold Borrowdale farms, Thorneythwaite and Seathwaite. Herbert was ready now to snap up another piece of this beautiful valley, adding Thorneythwaite to his 'Lodore Estates' portfolio.

His appetite for Borrowdale whetted, Herbert was a prime candidate to buy the 'Castlerigg Manor Estate' when it came up for auction in 1922. This was largely the original Derwentwater Estate sold by Greenwich Hospital back in 1832, bought then by John Marshall II, and left in trust to his son Reginald Dykes Marshall who was only six when John died in 1836. Henry Cowper Marshall was chief among the trustees who steered its course for the next 25 years. Reginald died in 1913 and rather like the Wasdale Hall Estate, and probably for the same reasons, the trustees of his legacy held it over the war years and for a short time after. Herbert was very interested in buying and engaged the firm of Wm. Heskett to produce a detailed valuation so he knew what, in strict financial terms, the estate was now worth. This entailed describing all 783 acres carefully as farmland, woodland, quarries or possible housing land. In general their opinion of the state of each aspect was favourable – except Castlerigg Manor itself, the home still of Reginald's widow, Mary Jane Marshall. Walker paid Wm. Heskett £156 6s 4d for the valuation which came to a grand total of £63,000[108] with the caveat 'As a speculative long term investment the figure might be exceeded, but we consider that that is a

[108] CRO Boxes 69-72 in DB 74/2/16.

matter for your own consideration.' In other words, the valuation assumed rents would be collected for the various farms and houses, timber would be sold as it came to maturity, stone would be quarried and sold: it did not take into account possible plot sales for speculative building. In 1922, the War over, motor transport ever increasing and the tourism industry thriving, Keswick was overdue for speculative building.

The next ten years – the last ten of Herbert Walker's life – were a whirlwind of buying, selling, gifting and negotiating that would mould and form the shape of the burgeoning town and the Eastern lakeshore. The boxes in Carlisle Record Centre tell of dozens of different sales of plots of land and larger areas sold off from his purchased Castlerigg Estate, now once again called the Derwentwater Estate in all his correspondence. They are a mixture of hard-headed business deals, peevishness at the recalcitrance of Keswick folk, and straight-forward philanthropy and care for the amenity value of the sensitive landscape he had bought.

He sold three acres on The Heads to Keswick Urban District Council for council housing and a further half-acre to a private developer, M/s Rushfirth Ltd. He sold, cheaply, land on Eskin Street to the Keswick Convention for their marquee centre. He sold a field to St. John's Church for a new graveyard. The low-lying field known as North Cockshott Bottom he sold to Sir John Randles as a car park for the very well-frequented Lakeside Tea Rooms – the car park now owned by Allerdale District Council serving visitors to the lake, the boat landings and the Theatre. He sold an orchard to a Mr. Hayes, who was a distant relative, for the establishment of a 'Garden Centre'. Like his hardy plants, Hayes' Garden Centre grew and grew, surviving and thriving on its transplanting to Ambleside.

This sale to Hayes was part of a bigger sale which Mr. Walker was keen to complete as soon as possible after his 1922 purchase of the estate – that of Castlerigg Manor House itself. Mrs. Marshall quit the tenancy in June 1924, leaving him able to sell with vacant possession. The house was in need of considerable renovation and would need a lot spending on it – not a prospect Walker relished. He had hoped to clear £12,000 for the house and 14 acres (including Hayes' orchard) when there appeared to be a willing buyer, but had to settle for little more than half that sum when he sold to Percy Hope, another Keswick worthy.

He had many dealings with Percy Hope, among them the sale of a field at Springs Road for the installation of a sewer and a gas pipe. The new sewer up part of Borrowdale Road seemed to Walker to be scarcely worth his while, connecting only a few possible housing sites, and brought forth his acid comment "I hesitate very much in paying anything to the Keswick people because they are out to take everything and give nothing, and their demands could be for the whole of the costs and maybe something more besides."[109]

On the other hand Herbert Walker's more generous and philanthropic side are shown in his many dealings with the National Trust – a growing force in the preservation and conservation of the valley and lake and many other parts of the Lake District in the 1920s and 30s. His Derwentwater Estates backed onto the eastern shoreline almost up to Barrow House and the National Trust began negotiations with him on a scheme whereby rather than actually buying the land from him they would pay some agreed figure for a covenant not to build on a large portion, for the 'preservation of the view'. This led to detailed calculations (on the unused pages of a 1920 diary!) of the value of the land as building land and an offer by Mr. Walker to the Trust to forgo any future possible building on a large number of sensitive fields for the sum of £2,500. In the event this covenant wasn't pursued, because the National Trust agreed (in 1929) to buy the much more important Stable Hills Farm plus most of the fields which would have been covered by the covenant for a final figure of £17,280. Herbert generously allowed a £2,000 donation towards this cost, and threw in Rampsholme Island for free. The other £15,000 was donated by Sir Noton and Lady Barclay.

The Trust had already bought quite a significant part of the original Castlerigg Manor Estate in the 1922 sale, as part of the Canon H. W. Rawnsley memorial, the cash being raised by public subscription in the great man's memory. This included Friar's Crag and Calf Close Bay. With the purchase of Stable Hills in 1929 and the donation of Strands Hagg in

---

[109] Letter to Mr Brown (his agent) dated 18th May 1926

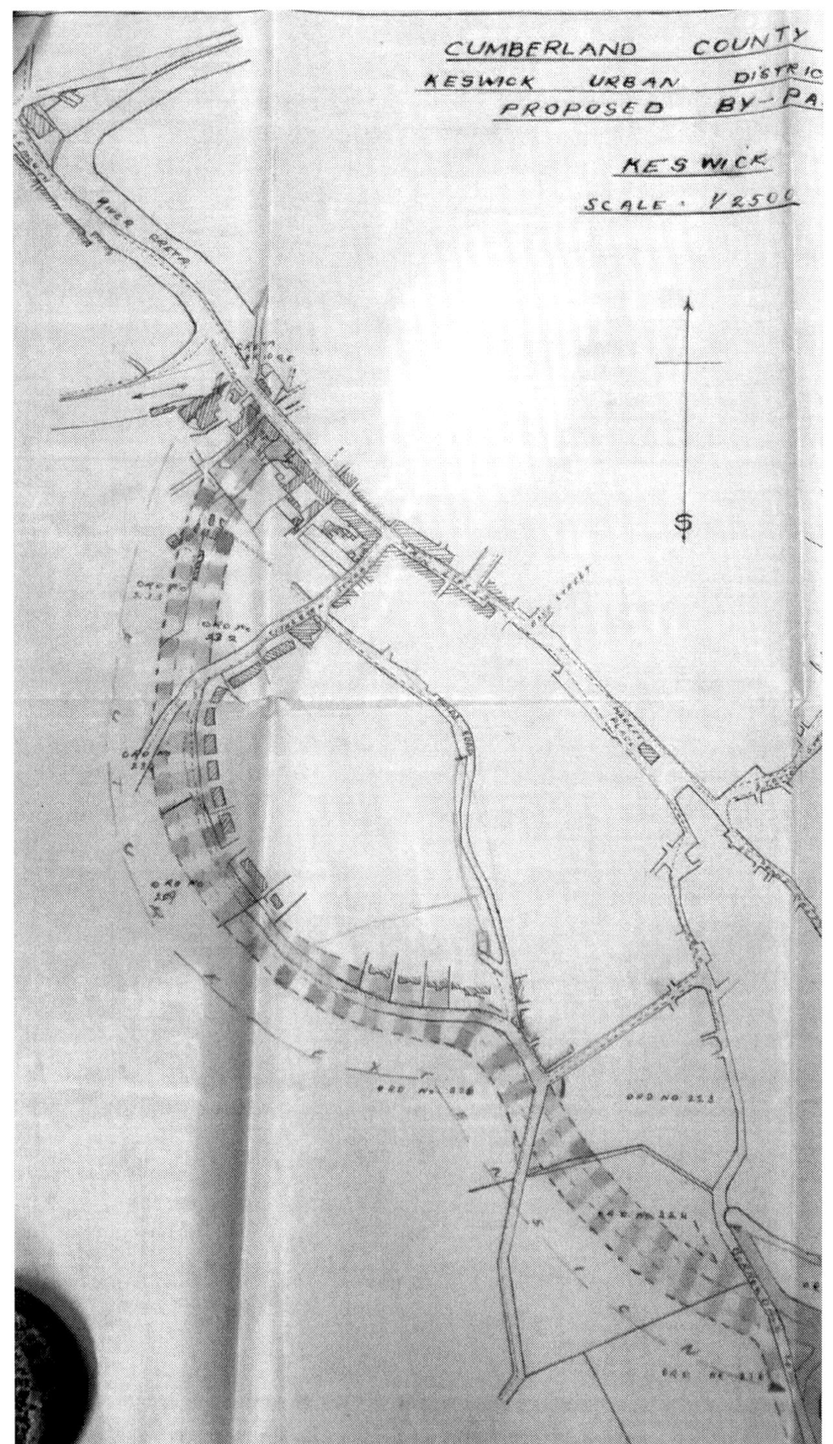
CUMBERLAND COUNTY
KESWICK URBAN DISTRIC
PROPOSED BY-PA
KESWICK
SCALE · 1/2500
RIVER GRETA
S

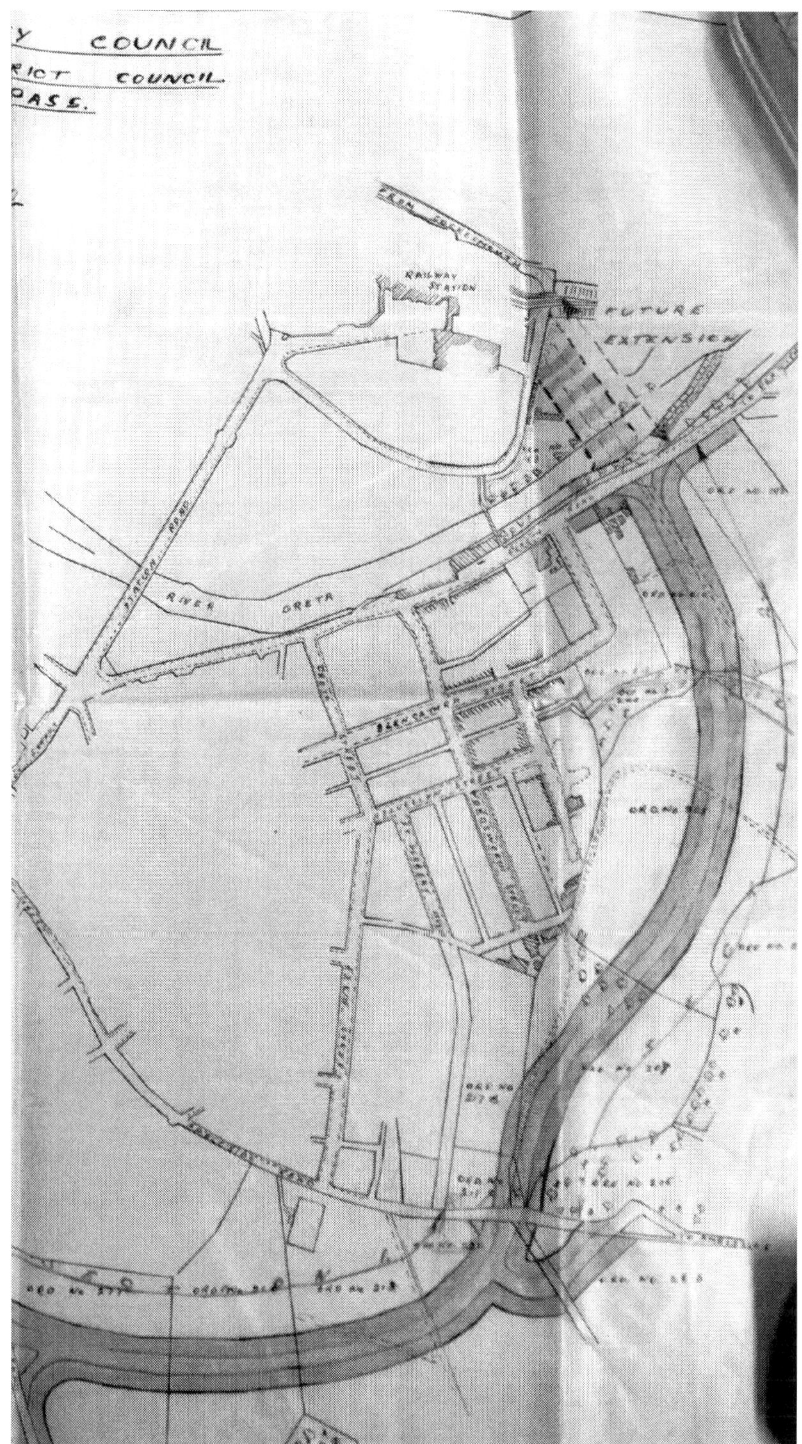
Y COUNCIL
RICT COUNCIL
ASS.
RAILWAY STATION
FUTURE
EXTENSION
RIVER GRETA
STATION ROAD

1925 their holding on the East shore of Derwentwater was now 139 acres, and stretched unbroken from Crow Park to Ashness Gate – over one and a half miles. To complete the unassailable protection from any further building on this ultra-sensitive section of Derwentwater shores H. W. Walker gave the covenants previously offered at £2,500 in 1926 for free in 1929, along with his gift of Rampsholme Island.[110]

Motor transport had evolved so quickly that by the late 1920s Keswick Urban District Council were deeply involved with the County Council over a scheme to provide a by-pass round the centre of Keswick to relieve what was already becoming serious congestion. Herbert Walker was thoroughly behind the plan, and offered free land where the road would pass through his estate and a contribution of £2,000 towards the cost. The planned road is shown on the previous double spread.

It was to begin on Penrith Road just east of the present Millfield Retirement Home; loop through the fields which are now Brandlehow Crescent; cross the Ambleside Road at the Springs Road junction; continue through what is now Castlerigg Estate and on through what is now St. John's Churchyard with a roundabout junction on the Borrowdale Road. All this land was Walker's. From the Borrowdale Road it was to loop northwards along The Headlands, behind what is now the Supermarket, emerging at Greta Bridge. It would have necessitated the compulsory purchase and demolition of three or four houses at this point, but otherwise could have been unimpeded. No doubt the negotiations were protracted, and quite soon Mr. Walker's patience was exhausted and he withdrew both his offer of free land and £2,000 contribution in a letter of 9th September 1929. This setback in no way dented the enthusiasm of KUDC for the project, and consultations continued through to 1932. Ultimately however the planned by-pass came to nought, though a version of the Borrowdale Road to Main Street section was created in the 1970s, along with the much more ambitious A66 by-pass crossing the River Greta by the magnificent concrete bridge which won the accolade 'Best concrete structure of the century'.

Herbert Wilson Walker died from a heart attack on 14th December 1934, taking his last breaths in the very hospital, Whitehaven Castle, which he had been so instrumental in providing for the town. He left well over half a million pounds in his will.

---

110 Properties of the National Trust. Out of print. p. 81

PART FIVE
THE WESTERN SHORES

CHAPTER FIFTEEN[111]

LORD WILLIAM GORDON 1758-1823

There are several lovely walks along the flanks of Catbells, with some magnificent views of Derwentwater, Keswick, Skiddaw and Blencathra to the north and the Borrowdale fells to the south. No need really to climb all the way up Catbells: the views from the upper terrace walk are as good as any in the kingdom. If you start from above Hawes End, as you would for Catbells itself, a splendid wide track leads you southwards along the flank, maybe 600 feet above the lake. You may wonder why such a fine track exists: is it leading to some quarry or mine, tramped by the feet of men hundreds of years ago going about their daily business? Certainly as you walk there are a few small spoil heaps and just over a kilometre along this stroll you come across old mine workings – the upper reaches of Brandlehow Mine. However, passing these workings and looking down the slope to the spoil heaps by the lakeshore and a bay the map tells you is Brandlehow Bay you find the track kisses the small road you could see a couple of hundred feet below the track – and then heads off again along the contour as the road falls away again. Still that wide, generous track, all of ten feet wide though somewhat grown over.

[111] Acknowledgement. My main source of information, and the basis for this chapter, is the Lancaster University doctoral thesis by Derek Denman, dated 2011, plus his article in CWAAS Transactions 'Lord William Gordon and the picturesque occupation of Derwentwater in the 1780s' TCWAAS Vol 14 (2014), pp. 207 – 230. I have used information contained in this thesis and article, and quoted sources, with permission.

You look down now on Brackenburn, home to the early-20th Century writer Sir Hugh Walpole, and to confirm it soon come across a smooth stone seat and a plaque on the craggy side of the track commemorating that creator of 'The Herries Sagas'

A little further on is a fine house atop its own hillock, with magnificent views down the valley. Once this was called Scalethorns and was a bare hill. The track curves round the wall surrounding the hill and its wood, squeezed now by boulders and debris washed down by the seemingly benign little beck that becomes a furious torrent when the mood takes it. Steeply now the track descends, broad again and in places set with a cobble base, till it reaches the little road again just short of the Manesty complex of holiday cottages.

It was no mine track, this lavish, broad, well-laid track. It was born of the hubris of yet another flamboyant 18th Century eccentric: Lord William Gordon. And not only this track, but also the lovely little tarmacked road below it that you looked down on throughout your walk. That too was a gift of Lord Gordon to a largely ungrateful world. The original carriageway, used by countless generations of Borrowdale folk on their way to Keswick via Portinscale lies far below either of these turn of the 19th Century accretions, and would be well worth your effort on your return trip to the end of Catbells. Walk back along the tarmacked road, northwards, climbing a little till you come to the entrance on your right to another tarmacked drive, with a National Trust carving of an acorn letting you know you are a part-owner of the grounds from here on. A red post box is set somewhat quizzically into the wall: whom does it serve? You will no doubt follow the road down to the little house now called 'The Warren', which means you have strayed from the original old road which cut through, but are now back on it. From here it's an easy walk through lovely woodlands till you finally rejoin the road just north-west of Hawes End Adventure Centre.

The only place you might go wrong is just after the spoil heaps that now reach right to the lake below Brandlehow mines. They cover the old track and you need to skirt them at the lakeside, then ignore the new lakeside path from the landing jetty for the Derwentwater Launches, instead striking slightly uphill on the higher path which is the old carriageway. Throughout your walk back you will never rise more than about 100 feet above the lake, whereas the terrace walk you started on rises some 600 feet, and the new road some 400 feet. You come out at Hawes End Centre, having passed all that's left of Brandlehow Farmhouse: the barn with its prominent buttress on your right.

Lord William Gordon was astonished that the local Borrowdale folk should prefer this lower carriageway when he had built them such a picturesque, broad and well-constructed upper roadway. When his solicitor Thomas Benson wrote to him that they refused to climb the extra height and were possibly afraid of the steep drops to the side he wrote back

> 'with respect to the danger of being on a hill – I think that must be a joke in a Borrowdale man. However.... I will engage to build a wall on the part of the hill where they apprehend the danger to be – close to the road if they choose it, four or five feet high... but if the road cannot be made in the highest place I will have nothing to do with it. I will not enter into any dispute with the people of Borrowdale on the subject and if they choose rather to repair the old road at their own expense than have a new one made at mine – they may indulge themselves whenever they please.'

Gordon's top road was completed in 1788 and is shown on Peter Crosthwaite's map of that year. He still failed to apprehend the mettle of the local populace and had Benson draw up an agreement dated 5th May 1789 whereby the Commoners would give up their rights on the common on the East side of Catbells, to allow him to enclose it with a wall. Once again he was thwarted – but had demonstrated why he had been so willing to build a wall under his new road, as it would have had the effect of enclosure. Ultimately he was forced to compromise: he could build a second road (the present tarmacked terrace) just above his already enclosed lower lands and the locals might just condescend to use it, thereby staying out of his domain. This one avoids the steep pull over Scalethorns and only rises some 400 feet – a fair exchange for the expense of maintaining their old lower road reckoned the Borrowdale folk. Peter Crosthwaite's revised map of 1809 shows the 'new road' – the present tarmacked road – as the only one passable by then.

Who was this upstart, this rich would-be squire? Virtually contemporary with Joseph Pocklington he had agreed to buy the small Water End estate in 1781 but didn't complete the purchase till 1784, by which time Pocklington was well established on Derwent Isle. It is tempting to compare and contrast the two men – as best we can at two and a half centuries remove. Firstly, Pocklington was by far the richer, a bachelor with his own means, his own familial home at Carlton House, Newark on Trent – which he had rebuilt – and a flair for business and the making of his own money. Lord William Gordon was almost the direct opposite: a lord in name only, he was the second son of Cosmo George Gordon, third Duke of Gordon and sixth Marquess and his wife, unfortunately another Gordon by birth, Lady Catherine Gordon, a direct

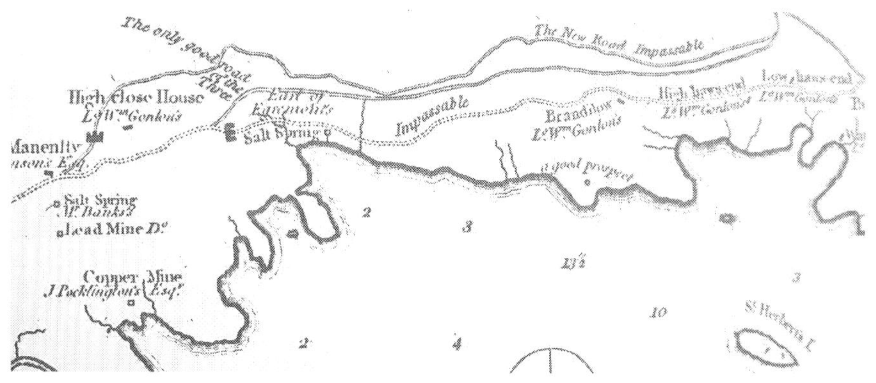

Section of Peter Crosthwaite's 1809 map showing the three roads.

cousin. Their in-bred children show distinctly idiosyncratic characteristics: the first-born, Alexander, was stable enough and carried forth the Dukedom, leaving his brothers, William and George with little wealth and no role to play. Of the two the parliamentarian Lord George Gordon is remembered as the leader of the Gordon Riots of 1780 when mob rule erupted in London as a Protestant backlash against some easing of the punitive treatment of Catholics. Ironically his followers painted a sign on Newgate Gaol proclaiming that they had freed all the prisoners 'by order of King Mob' – only for Lord George to end his days in that very jail: and that after he had converted to Judaism. Lord George's story is the basis of Charles Dickens' 'Barnaby Rudge'.

If he was a complex character his brother Lord William was even more so. Ever a ladies' man he first gained notoriety by eloping with Lady Sarah Bunbury in 1768. This was unwise on several fronts. For one thing she was his first cousin and their bloodline was already too homogenous. More importantly she was a 'favourite' of King George II and had been a candidate for marriage to King George III – not the sort of men you'd want to cross. Thirdly she was already married. Under these circumstances she brought neither dowry nor moneys into William's impoverished life. A mere year later she left with their illegitimate daughter Louisa to live for a time with her brother the Third Duke of Richmond, at Goodwood. Inevitably her real husband sued for divorce and the salacious and scandalous details filled the news-sheets for weeks and ruined Lord William's chances of any place at the court of George III.

The ensuing ostracism weighed heavily on William – a man ever seeking affirmation and royal approval, as we shall see later. He left England in 1770 vowing never to return, with nothing but a knapsack on his back and a large dog for company, and intended to walk to Rome. A man given to the fine gesture and to repenting at leisure, by 1774 he was back in London and by 1779 was MP for Elginshire, a Scottish constituency. He had, according to a contemporary account, 'a quick perception in all the modes of applicable adulation, and an intuitive sagacity in discerning the most direct and effectual roads to preferment'[112] and had clearly learnt a painful lesson from his dalliance with Lady Sarah. He had a better relationship with the Prince of Wales, George IV, and found himself a suitably rich heiress to bring him respectability and a fortune. She was Frances Ingram Shepheard, second daughter of the last Viscount Irwin and co-heir to a vast fortune as the Viscount died without a male heir. She was only 19 and although her mother thoroughly approved of her marrying Gordon the Court of Chancery intervened. This court had the power to refuse permission for the marriages of wards of court and had been specifically so empowered to prevent wildly disparate fortunes being amalgamated. Lord William existed on a mere £900 a year, and that almost entirely made up by 'an annual allowance of £500 which the said appellant had for many years past received, and continued to receive, from his brother Alexander, Duke of Gordon; the yearly sum of £100 from the appellant's Office of Deputy Ranger of the Green Park; and the yearly sum of £300 from the appellant's commission of Lieutenant Colonel of his said brother's Regiment of Northern Fencibles.'[113] In other words, William depended entirely on his brother's good will, while the 19 year-old Frances was bringing a substantial fortune and the use of the manorial house at Temple Newsham in Leeds. William's only residence was the 'tied cottage' Green Park Lodge, Piccadilly which came with the largely sinecure position of Deputy Ranger of the Royal Park.

Nevertheless, William had evidently charmed Frances' mother, the viscountess, and her relatives, and the marriage went ahead despite the Court's prohibition. In the face of public approval of the match and (limited) royal assent the Court declined to prosecute. So, in 1781 William had largely recovered his reputation and secured reasonable funds by this romantic marriage. That was the year he first expressed interest in the Western shore of Lake Derwentwater. What might have influenced such an unusual interest?

There are several factors pre-disposing Gordon towards landscape transformation – which is mainly what he sought on the Western shore of Derwentwater – and one coincidence which may have led to the site he chose to exercise his talents. For talents in landscaping he undoubtedly

---

[112] Namier, *History of Parliament* P.520

[113] House of Lords *Between the Hon. Lord William Gordon… and Frances Viscountess Irwin and others*, 9 Feb. 1781.

had. At Green Park Lodge and in Green Park itself he obtained permission to create an extensive landscaping design 'reaching from the gate of the reservoir Westward, as far as Constitution Hill Gate. The greatest part of this ground is intended to be laid out in a beautiful shrubbery and this will be an elegant addition to the Deputy Ranger's dwelling...'[114] Landscape gardening was in the family genes: his uncle, Lord Adam Gordon, was a keen and accomplished landscape gardener having laid out the gardens and grounds at Prestonhall, Midlothian a decade earlier. And after his marriage Lord William had ample opportunity to admire and perhaps emulate the greatest landscaper of them all, Capability Brown, who had completed the magnificent gardens at his new wife's home Temple Newsham, Leeds. By 1781 he had completed the transformation both of Green Park Lodge and his new gardens, much to the approval of the London chattering classes – adulation he craved and basked in.

But why choose the far distant shores of Derwentwater, 300 miles from those chattering classes and surely unlikely to be much admired by the royal circles he so sought to be a part of? Well, the Lake District and Keswick in particular were, in a sense, the novelty of that age. Thomas West and William Gilpin had done much with their guides to produce a picturesque itinerary for anyone bold enough to venture that far north and Peter Crosthwaite and others were making sure those who came were well catered for. The difficult journey to this far-flung land became part of its attraction: the horrors of the mountain landscape and the rigours of carriage rides on its steep sides were the stuff of after-dinner conversation in London drawing rooms. The same stimuli that drew Joseph Pocklington in 1778 exerted their pull on Lord William Gordon: novelty; the chance to create something in a place chosen by the rich and famous for their holidays; and a pristine area crying out to be managed by competent hands – Pocklington by his buildings, Gordon by his landscapes. Denman points out that Gilpin had practically provided a blueprint for a man like Gordon to follow, in a manuscript of around 1776 – although not actually published till 1789. In it Gilpin asserts 'A circuit round the lake (Derwentwater) naturally suggests the visionary idea of improving it. If the whole lake belonged to one person a nobler scene for improvement could not well be conceived... it might be rendered more accessible – it might be cleared of deformities – it might be planted, and it might be decorated.' Gilpin's scheme envisaged a good carriage road 'but such a road as would form both a pleasing line in itself; and shew the beauties of the lake to the best advantage.'[115]

[114] *Morning Post and Daily Advertiser*, 14th Sept 1778
[115] William Gilpin *Observations relative chiefly to picturesque beauty*

There was probably one final deciding factor in Lord William's choice of Derwentwater. Lord Egremont (George O'Brian Wyndham) lived within fifty yards of Green Park Lodge and the two were good friends. Lord Egremont was the Lord of the Manor of Derwentwater, and doubtless often regaled Gordon with tales of its beauty. He was also able to facilitate Lord William's first purchase on the shoreline and to help out in further acquisitions. That first purchase was the Water End Estate, though estate might be too fancy a word for the 77 acres which Gordon agreed in 1781 to buy from John Fletcher for £1,400. It included Water End farmhouse, beautifully situated in what we now call Derwent Bay, and had been enfranchised by Lord Egremont some years previously, leaving Lord Gordon with the responsibility for any trees. As mentioned, it was 1784 before he got round to paying for it.

He used the intervening three years to advantage, having two local surveyors draw up plans and valuations of all seven separate farms surrounding Water End, clearly intending only to proceed with his first purchase if there seemed the likelihood of his being able to buy considerably more. In the event he completed purchases giving him the entire western lakeshore from Fawe Park to Abbot's Bay by 1787. This process was, however, far from easy. Gordon found he had a serious competitor for the properties, and one with far deeper pockets than he: Joseph Pocklington. Pocklington already owned Fawe Park and was contemplating bidding for Brandlehow. The owners of these properties were quick to spot a sellers' market, and the asking price for Hawes End doubled to £500 and for Brandlehow to £1,600. Gordon cleverly opted to appeal to Joseph's vanity: at a dinner on Pocklington's Island his party far outshone the local gentry, burnishing Joseph's self-esteem. He came with his wife, her sister and her mother allowing Pocklington's butler to announce in pompous terms the presence of 'Lord and Lady Gordon, the Viscountess Lady Irwin and her daughter Miss Ingram'. These things mattered, and as the ladies admired Joseph's architectural aesthetics, exclaiming over the proportions of his mansion on his very own Isle he glowed with pride. Yes, buildings were really his forte, and he would concentrate on his planned Barrow House and Finkle Street (now Derwent Bank)

Set on this new direction for his talents to impress the coachloads of visitors Joseph now became Gordon's willing accomplice, perhaps keen to facilitate a new road along the Western shore and the beautification of the scene from his island. He sold him Fawe Park in 1787 without the intervention of his solicitor Benson, for the very reasonable £1,500, which completed Gordon's control of the entire shoreline. Control was what was needed, for the new travelling literati were a critical audience who had fixed ideas about what made for beauty: ideas which Lord Gordon was ideally situated now to satisfy. We have seen how he sought to alter the carriage-way down the Western shore to one far higher, giving better views both of the lake and of his estates. Within his grounds he created many walkways, footpaths and rides for his visitors and others to enjoy the woodlands he began to create.

At Water End itself he built a rather whimsical villa, probably intended as a small-scale homage to the Prince of Wales' new pavilion at Brighton. It comprised just three rooms, joined but not internally accessible one to the other, each having a magnificent view out over the lake.

When he took over the various estates there was scarcely a mature tree left standing, for when Lord Egremont enfranchised all the tenants in the previous twenty years their payments included a large proportion for the woods and timber on their holdings, and they needed to sell anything fully grown to reduce the loans and mortgages they had taken out. This was not the clear felling that had caused the Greenwich Hospital so much grief earlier in the 18th Century, more a sustained management, so there were lots of coppices and springing trees from axed stumps, but virtually no mature trees.

Lord William Gordon's house at Water End, watercolour by E W James, 1798. Viscount Rochdale Collection.

Lord William entirely reversed this trend: having no need to make money from his woods he preferred instead to allow them to grow so as to beautify the shoreline and his woodland paths and seats. As J. Fisher

Crosthwaite puts it: 'There was only one large forest tree on that side of the lake at that time, but Lord William planted it with oak, spruce, fir, silver fir, Weymouth pine, beeches and every variety of wood. He would not have a tree felled so that the woods in Brandelhow, Scale Thorns, Rose Trees, Silver Hill and Fawe Park added much to the picturesque beauty of the property.'[116]

Lord William Gordon ruled supreme on the Western shore of Derwentwater for forty years, dying in 1823, and his widow, Lady Frances Gordon kept it a further eleven, notching up half a century of park and woodland management purely for aesthetic value, without regard for any economic gain. In that time some of the tenant farmers were ousted from their farms the better to control the landscape. Several houses became derelict and only Derwent Bay was developed, as a new farmhouse was built adjoining the initial villa – this not completed until after Gordon's death. Parkside and Low Hawes End were no longer dwellings but Brandlehow and High Hawes End continued as farmhouses. The present-day Lingholm mansion didn't exist – only a small cottage known as Silver Hill. Old Brandlehow farmhouse remains today only as a barn with a rather interesting buttress: High Hawes End has been restored as part of the Outdoor Adventure Centre as has Low Hawes End. Fawe Park still stands proud.

By one of those strange coincidences of timing 1834 turned out to be pivotal in the ongoing story of Derwentwater and its islands, as both the entire Western shore, Lord Gordon's, and the Eastern shore belonging to Greenwich Hospital came up for sale. We have seen that John Marshall bought the Eastern shore including Lord's Island and Rampsholme; Henry his son bought Derwent Island ten years later. The Western shore remained unsold for the next seven years until, on Lady Frances Gordon's death in 1841 it was inherited by Major-General Sir John George Woodford, and it is to him we now turn.

---

[116] J. Fisher Crosthwaite, *Brief memoir of Major-General Sir John George Woodford.* A paper read to the Keswick Literary and Scientific Society, 1880

CHAPTER SIXTEEN[117]

MAJOR-GENERAL SIR JOHN GEORGE WOODFORD, KCB, 1785 – 1879

As we have seen, Lord William and Lady Frances Gordon had no son, no natural heir to the fortune they would leave. They did have a daughter, also called Frances, who would presumably have inherited but that she died, unmarried, before her mother. William also had two illegitimate children, the first as we saw in the previous chapter Louisa Bunbury, born in 1769 but long since abandoned to the care of her mother's rich relations. The second was a son, William Conway Gordon (1798–1882), born of Catherine Conway, of Brompton Row. He took responsibility for the boy, paying for his education and obtaining a commission for him, but it was inconceivable that he should inherit. By then of course Lord William had been married to Lady Frances for seventeen years, and we may well wonder what she made of this (d)alliance. The truth seems to be that, at least in the elevated circles they moved in, such behaviour was the order of the day. Lady Frances' elder sister, Lady Isabella, married the 2nd Marquess of Hertford – but that didn't stop her becoming yet another of the Prince of Wales' mistresses. It seems a fair assumption that Lady Frances herself had more than a passing friendship with the 4th Duke of Queensberry, since he left her £20,000 in his will – and a mere £2,000 to Lord William.

Into this hotbed of intrigue shuffled, somewhat embarrassedly, the young, rather callow, John George Woodford. He was Lord William's nephew, son of Lady Susan née Gordon and Lieutenant-Colonel John Woodford – their second son. He was born, by upbringing and tradition, if not perhaps by disposition, for the army, and had a distinguished and in some ways seminal career therein. As with many young budding officers of the time Woodford was packed off to the army's training ground in Brunswick, the German Duchy which had provided Great Britain with the three King Georges. It also provided the fourth George – at that time still

[117] Acknowledgement: it seems virtually all current information on Sir John's time at Water End derives from J. Fisher Crosthwaite's *'Brief memoir of Major-General Sir John George Woodford'*. Crosthwaite did have the huge advantage of knowing Sir John and clearly loved to hear him speak about his experiences at the Battle of Waterloo. Only in a few places have I referenced a different source – otherwise please take it JFC is my source.

the Prince of Wales – with his unwanted, not to say thoroughly detested, wife, Caroline of Brunswick.

When young John Woodford returned from Brunswick in 1801 he was befriended by the 76 year-old 4th Duke of Queensberry, known to all and sundry as 'Old Q'. Whether this was at Lady Frances Gordon's request or not I have been unable to discover, but it is recorded that Old Q gave the boy a racehorse from his extensive stable, and furthermore introduced him to the increasingly mad King George III. Old Q had a formidable reputation as a roué and a gambler, and was a major figure in the horse-racing world. Never married, he was notorious as a ladies' man, with many mistresses including the Marchesa Fagnani by whom he had an illegitimate daughter, Maria. Along with his bequests above he left Maria £10,000 in his will, so clearly he was a very successful horse owner and gambler. He died in 1810, a very impressive 85 years old, and also bequeathed £10,000 to the young John George Woodford.

This is his contemporary portrait, as painted by John Opie and now in the National Gallery.

A more popular caricature, again contemporary, is this gem by Thomas Rowlandson, entitled 'A worn-out debauchee'.

Exploring the connections further we come across this unexplained but intriguing nugget. Lord William's illegitimate son, William Conway, assumed the additional surname of Gordon by Royal Licence on August 13th 1839, just two years before Lady Frances died. Was this an attempt to assert his right to some of the Gordon legacy? If so, it was unsuccessful. It followed another interesting naming association: he named his fourth son, born in 1836, Woodford Conway Gordon.[118] His second son was named Francis Ingram Conway-Gordon – a clear tribute to Lady Frances (née

[118], Constance Oliver Skelton & John Malcolm Bulloch. *Gordons under arms* Aberdeen, 1912 p. 393

Ingram). Clearly he was far from being an outcast from his father's family, but it was still John George Woodford who was given the west side of Derwentwater in 1841. Young William did very well for himself, regardless of inheritance, leaving £24,000 in his will in 1882.[119]

Our Sir John Woodford, unlike William Peachy on Derwent Island, became a real Major-General, who made a career of the army and first saw active service in 1807 at the siege of Copenhagen. He was wounded in the heel by reputedly the last shot fired in the battle of Coruña in the Peninsular War the following year. This wound, though never life-threatening, did leave him with a life-long limp, and took fully eighteen months to heal. He used part of his legacy from 'Old Q' to buy the rank of Captain – rank was purchased, not merited, in those days. Not that he was unworthy of his rank – far from it. When Napoleon re-surfaced in 1815 he joined Wellington's army and was his aide-de-camp at the battle of Waterloo. J. Fisher Crosthwaite had ample opportunity to listen to the old man's stories and consequently there is a detailed section in his book regarding the battle.[120] In 1818 he took advantage of his position as Commander of the Army of Occupation to obtain leave to make a survey of the field of the battle of Agincourt (1415). He found a trove of artefacts – arrowheads, bones, lance-heads, a spur, buckles, four gold rings (one with the finger bone still in it) and over sixty coins.

A civilised and learned man he was a notable linguist and archaeologist, being fluent in German, French and Spanish – and of course having both Latin and Greek at his fingertips. He was also a humane commander, as he proved when he was given command of the third battalion of the Grenadier Guards in 1821. Promoted to Colonel in 1823 he immediately banned flogging as a punishment in the battalion, and a little later the almost equally degrading 'standing under arms'. In 1835 he published a pamphlet catchily titled *'Remarks on Military Flogging: its Causes and Effects, with some Considerations on the Propriety of its entire Abolition'*. Both his former commander the Duke of Wellington and his king, William IV, expressed the strongest disapproval, but the bans remained in place in his regiment. He also disagreed passionately with the practice of purchasing commissions – though of course he had had to purchase his first captaincy. True to his principles when he retired from the army in 1841, now a major-general, he refused to sell his commission on the open market, but redeemed it to the government for just £4,500 – half its market value.

[119] Skelton and Bulloch.

[120] Crosthwaite, pp 21 - 30

Major General Sir John George Woodford, KCB, KCH
Photographed 1875 by G P Abraham, Keswick

This then is the man who inherited the Water End estate in 1841, and retired to live the last 38 years of his life there, becoming a well-known but eccentric figure. In many ways he seems a natural successor to the hermit St. Herbert and perhaps precursor of the 20th century Millican Dalton. Like St. Herbert he loved solitude and felt in close communion with God: like Dalton he also loved to climb the surrounding mountains – often at night-time when he said the shapes were even more pleasing. It seems surprising that a man so used to the army and its ways, with the constant interaction between men, the adrenaline-fuelled battles, the perpetual need to communicate should, at the age of fifty-six be content to live in the degree of seclusion Woodhouse sought at Derwent Bay. Not that he cut himself off completely, but J. Fisher Crosthwaite tells us that no visitor was ever allowed into the house – Woodford would meet them outside and keep it that way, at least till he became very old. And very old he did become, dying in 1879 at the age of ninety-four. In 1875, not long before his death, he consented to have his photograph taken by Abrahams of Keswick – shown on the previous page.

Woodford surely cannot have been short of money, with these exceptional legacies, but he seems to have lived the life of a pauper. Although he had inherited the entire Western shore of Derwentwater he showed no inclination to make any income from it. Although he had inherited an almost new house (finished in 1824, it had scarcely had a tenant till Woodford arrived in 1841) he showed no inclination to maintain it, and it slowly sank into dereliction, mirroring the old man's decline. It seems his entire annual income was limited to the £100 disability pension he received from the army for his wounded heel, plus perhaps some rents for Fawe Park and Hawes End. Had he received the wound as a major-general the pension would have been much greater, but he was a lowly captain at the time, and 'rules is rules'. Perhaps the army would have been far more generous to a man who had given over forty years of service had he not been such a thorn in the flesh of the hierarchy with his insistence on the removal of degrading punishments and, more particularly, his leadership in the campaign to have commissions issued on merit rather than on payment. He persisted in both campaigns, writing frequent letters to MPs and army grandees, and within two years of his death flogging was formally abolished throughout the army. Buying a commission was abolished a decade earlier. Being right doesn't necessarily make friends, and being as uncompromisingly right as was Sir John Woodford makes important enemies.

He had further opportunity to espouse a cause when he took up the cudgels on behalf of the tenants and freeholders of Borrowdale over the issue of the implementation of the Tithe Commutation Act of 1836. This act removed the requirement to pay the church tithes in kind – a tenth of your hay crop, for instance – and established instead a fixed amount to be paid each year to the church for each property.

All this had been agreed before Sir John came to Water End but he took it upon himself to produce a somewhat arcane argument that the freeholders should be exempt from any payment. The township of East Borrowdale had previously been part of Fountains Abbey, West Borrowdale of Furness Abbey, and their tithes had been due to these abbeys. Woodford argued that with the dissolution of the abbeys some three centuries previously their lands had been discharged of all tithes except those in place then. He more persuasively demonstrated that the assistant commissioner for tithes, a Mr. Howard, had stated the tithes due from Borrowdale were £51 16s. 0¾, but that it was now intended to charge them £79 13s. 6d. – more than half as much again. He even took the case to law but was too late to be properly heard and the court upheld the judgement.

Having failed on the greater canvas Sir John made a stand on his own behalf, entirely out of a sense of right and fairness. In 1847 he published an answer to the Vicar's requirement of his tithe, concluding: 'I deny that the rent charge demanded by the Vicar is morally, lawfully or fairly due to him, and I refuse to pay the proportion assessed on my estate; and I look forward to a recovery of the rights of the parish according to justice and the laws'. The tithe collector was therefore obliged to seize, and in practice one particular cow was taken by the proctor (the sexton, old Isaac Hodgson.) It was then resold on the spot to Sir John for the sum demanded – and he put in an extra crown for the sexton's trouble. Each year this pantomime was re-enacted till the Vicar's cow, as Sir John christened it, grew so old it had to be shot. Woodford throughout maintained cordial relations with the vicar, the Revd. James Lynn, M.A., saying Mr. Lynn and he were good friends – he only differed with the *vicar* of Crosthwaite.

As he grew older Sir John sought solitude the more, but not at the expense of others. He disliked being seen through the windows of his home, but rather than ban visitors from landing in the lovely Derwent Bay he placed a hoarding round his house. He was aware that others found him increasingly eccentric and composed the following verses. I am not much a fan of verse but do feel that in this case Sir John expands our understanding of a hermit's motives and pleasures.

> They said his mind had wandered, his heart was ill at ease;
> He loved the lonely mountain path, he loved the mountain breeze,
> He loved the ripple on the lake, its murmur in the trees.

He loved the solemn hour of night, when night submits to morn,
When few were waking, none were near, his humble life to scorn;
And yet he was not all alone, he was not all forlorn.

To see the great Creator's works, to meditate his praise –
In that he passed his lonely hours, he passed his lonely days
Where none were near to scorn or scan his harmless childlike ways.

And yet he was not all alone – he walked with God and prayed
For that support God only gives, surpassing human aid,
Foreshadowing a future state, a promise God has made.

A future state? And what divides this life from that on high?
Can we be ever nearer God? Is God not ever nigh?
Then why not live with God on earth – on earth before we die?

Why wait for Death to spread his pall, and memory to cease,
Before we join our soul above which lives in realms of peace –
Before mortality can claim mortality's release?

Before this mortal can put on the immortal, and regain
That bliss of heaven which ensues to earthly grief and pain!
For this he prayed to God, and thought he did not pray in vain.

Oh! Let us pray that we may bear the trial and the test
Which He, our Maker, has ordained by His supreme behest,
Enjoining us to learn and own "Whatever is, is best"

What of the Western shore under Sir John's care? The truth is that for the forty years of his tenure and for twenty more before, when Lord William Gordon grew old and increasingly absent nothing was done. The paths so carefully, so artfully laid grew over. The Kelpie Bridge fell, the stone seats leant over. The woods however grew amok. Where one hundred years previously, when Lord William first set eyes on Water End, there was not one mature tree left standing now almost every tree was a century old. It was not woodland management by any stretch of the imagination, but it was most certainly mature woodland.

And what of Water End? Gordon's villa was long gone, but his house was only sixty years old. Here is a contemporary pen and ink drawing of it and old Sir John, by Mr. E. R. Grayson, done for J. Fisher Crosthwaite's book. The years have not treated it well. It's not too easy to see on this sketch, but the corner nearest to us, on old Sir John's left, has fallen out; the stones still lying where they fell. The roof of that part is gone and the rest of the house behind it looks in parlous order with big trees growing far too close, their roots no doubt undermining the foundations.

BRANDLEHOW MINES

More or less mirroring the changing fortunes of the Water End estate over the hundred years between Lord William Gordon taking it on in 1784 and Sir John Woodford's death in 1879 are the developments of mining on the edge of the estate. There had been patchy mining for lead in Brandlehow Gill for centuries, just as there had been patchy woodland management. Miners knew there was a seam of lead-bearing galena leading up from Brandlehow Bay in a North-Westerly direction, right to the top of Catbells and various surface shafts had been opened along its tracks. You can still see the small spoil heaps as you walk along the terrace walk created by Lord William. The first proper underground tunnels following the vein of copper were driven not long before he came to Water End, from 1754 to 1767, but it wasn't till 1819 when John Tebay took over the Brandlehow lease that mining for lead on an industrial scale began.[121] Tebay sank a shaft to a depth of 40 yards, or 20 fathoms as miners use as units of measurement, but then had to contend with much water threatening

[121] Ian Tyler, *Seathwaite Wad and the mines of the Borrowdale Valley, 1995*, p. 43

to drown the workings. He solved this problem by constructing a 34 feet diameter water wheel which acted both as pump and the main hauling machine to lift the tons of ore and waste out to the surface. For a while he prospered but by 1836 he was bankrupt and had to quit the mine.

Optimism is the main fuel of mining, and eleven years later the Keswick Mining Company was formed to re-open Brandlehow Mine and investment poured in to modernise the process. Water was still a problem, solved by installing a steam engine to pump out, and Tebay's derelict water wheel was replaced by a slightly smaller (30 feet diameter) wheel for crushing ore, and the shaft deepened down to 30 fathoms.

Brandlehow waterwheel circa 1880. Caldbeck Mining Museum collection.

The company laid tramways for the efficient removal of both ore and waste, and the huge pile of waste material overwhelmed the old carriageway from Borrowdale down to Portinscale at Brandlehow Bay, and now extends right to the lake shore. Fortunately by then everyone was using Gordon's new road that skirts the top of the workings. If you are persistent enough you can still find the odd heavy stone on the spoil heap which repays breaking open by revealing the bright galena inside.

By 1857 there were seventy men on the payroll and for a while the mine produced up to 270 tons of lead per year. However, water was always a major problem and pumping took most of the profits, shareholders never receiving any dividend; and just as Sir John Woodford's home slowly deteriorated under him so the mine became insolvent and closed in 1865.

Not till after Sir John's death in 1879 was there another attempt to make a fortune at Brandlehow; this time by one Henry Burrow Vercoe, scion of a mining family with a lifetime's experience behind him. In 1884 he installed a powerful steam engine to pump out water and to haul rock out of the mine, and built a variety of sheds, engine housing and a superintendent's house – which still stands as Brandlehow House on the bay. (Home to the 'teddies in the window') He built a crusher house and had a reservoir constructed to maintain a steady water supply: you can still see this historic gem if you follow a wide track down from the road just North of Brackenburn leading down to the bay. Under Vercoe's watch the mine continued to produce vast quantities of lead-bearing ore – 260 tons in 1885, for instance. By now the shaft was down to 60 fathoms, a serious depth that required serious water pumping, and the total length of the tunnels was over two miles.

Henry must have seen the writing on the wall, however, for in 1885 just as things appeared to be going well, he sold his share and withdrew from the business. He was right: production slumped almost immediately and the mine began to flood extensively and the lower levels had to be abandoned. By 1891, a mere six years after Vercoe quit at the height of its productivity, the company folded and abandoned the mine. By 1892 all the equipment had been dismantled and the shafts were sealed off, by now entirely full of water. Brandlehow was slowly taken back in hand by nature, salving the many scars left by centuries of men's search for materials.[122]

[122] Tyler, and John Adams, *Mines of the Lake District Fells,* Dalesman Books, 1988

CHAPTER SEVENTEEN

OTHER PROPERTIES ON THE WESTERN SHORE 1870 ONWARDS

LINGHOLM

Towards the end of his life, with Water End similarly being over-run by nature, Sir John did start to sell some of his estate; principally the area around Silver Hill, the semi-derelict little farmhouse between Fawe Park and Hawes End. It was bought in the 1870s by Lt. Colonel James Fenton Greenall (1834 – 1899), a member of the brewing firm which is now Greenall Whitleys. On his new estate Greenall commissioned the famous architect Alfred Waterhouse to create Lingholm, named for the little islands just off its shore.

Lingholm House, photo courtesy of Marjorie Dymock

It seems this was not the first of Sir John Woodford's sales, for the architect Waterhouse had previously designed the new Fawe Park mansion, replacing the previous simpler house.[123] These two fine new houses were to

[123] Marjorie Dymock, *Lingholm: its story and memories.* 2015, p. 1

provide inspiration and settings for one of the Lake District's greatest ambassadors – Beatrix Potter. Her parents were in the habit of taking long summer holidays at one or other of these houses in the late 1890s and early 1900s, when Beatrix was in her twenties. Here she sketched and wrote her children's tales. Squirrel Nutkin is firmly based at Lingholm, with her lovely sketch of the squirrels setting off to sail to 'Owl Island' – St. Herbert's of course. Peter Rabbit, on the other hand, is set in 'Mr McGregor's garden' – at Fawe Park.

The Potter family's extended holiday leasing of large houses – they started at Wray Castle, overlooking Windermere – is illustrative both of such rich families and of the largely absentee owners of the mansions. A quick trawl through the Census returns for 1871 – 1911for the four main houses on the Western shore, Fawe Park, Lingholm, Derwent Bay and Hawse End shows Fawe Park and Lingholm occupied by their owners only in 1881, otherwise by servants; Derwent Bay by servants only ever since Sir John Woodford died; and Hawse End by its new owners Francis Marshall and family in 1891, soon after purchase, but not in 1901 or 1911. The reason isn't hard to find: in all cases the rich owners who bought and built so assiduously were generally men of industry and of parliament, with many responsibilities. These Lake District hideaways were just that; somewhere to retreat to for rest and recuperation; somewhere to nurture for the sheer joy of creating something beautiful.

None illustrates this better than Lingholm. When James Greenall died in 1899 the driving force behind the creation and maintenance of this very large house and estate was gone, and it was put up for sale. This time the buyer was another man of industry, George Kemp, chairman of his family firm Kelsall & Kemp, woollen manufacturers in Rochdale. He was also Liberal MP for the Heywood Division of Manchester.[124] He was knighted in 1909 for political services and took the name Baron Rochdale, and for over a hundred years Lingholm was the bolthole and, in their later years, retirement home to both Baron Rochdale and, in his turn, his son John and his wife Elinor. The second Lord Rochdale, George Kemp's son John spent almost every weekend of his early working life there, travelling up in his favourite Bentley. In his turn John took on chairmanship of the family textile firm, and took his seat in the House of Lords, and after a distinguished military career in WWII traded in the Bentley for a small plane and flew up to Lingholm every Saturday afternoon, landing on a grass airstrip near Braithwaite (since bisected by the A66). His 'hangar', a corrugated iron shed, is still in the field to the south of the A66 just before it crosses Newlands Beck.

---

[124] Marjorie Dymock, *Lingholm*

The first Baron Rochdale died at the end of the Second World War, bringing to an end the era of gentlemanly pursuits the estate had hosted during his reign. The woods had been largely neglected but the new Lord Rochdale instituted five-year plans for their management as a viable forestry business. With over 400 acres of woodland this required a dedicated forestry department on the estate and the planting of thousands of conifers, but with an eye to aesthetics always with an outer band of deciduous woodland too. Most of the wood produced was processed on the estate in a wood yard just off the path from Fawe Park to Lingholm, mainly as either fence posts or logs for retail. This forestry department lasted roughly forty years, coming to its natural end when John, Lord Rochdale died in 1993.

Lord and Lady Rochdale's other enduring contribution to the life and appearance of the Western shore was the magnificent landscape garden they laid out and maintained, open to the public from 1970.These gardens grew organically from the early layouts of the first Baron, but became a major feature of Lingholm in the last quarter of the 20th Century, especially after the tearoom was opened in 1985. They were however dependent on the energy and input from Lord and Lady Rochdale, and after he died in 1993 and she in 1997 both the gardens and the tearoom were closed to the public and the Rochdale era slowly ground to a halt. A further fifteen years of limbo ensued till the main house and forty acres immediately surrounding it were sold in 2013 to the Seymour family who, in the five years since, have transformed their new home into a major business, with eleven self-catering holiday houses (including the original Silver Hill, precursor to Lingholm itself), a new walled garden, a new tearoom, and even a jetty out into Derwentwater so that visitors can come by launch. It seems appropriate that at last the main house's worth has been recognised by English Heritage awarding it Grade II listed building status.

HAWSE END & CATHERINE MARSHALL (1880-1961)

Catherine Marshall has a fair claim to be one of Keswick's most nationally important women, for her role in the Suffragist movement from 1907 till Votes for Women were legalised, along with universal suffrage, at the end of the Great War. Note that she was a suffragist, not a suffragette. The difference is one of tactics: the suffragette movement espoused all kinds of illegal manoeuvres ranging from padlocking themselves to government buildings, through various bombings, right up to Emily Davison's death on the Epsom Derby course whilst trying to bring down King George V's horse Anmer in 1913. She had already been in prison nine times and on hunger strike for seven of those periods for her many breaches of the peace. Probably the most famous suffragette was Emmeline Pankhurst, the founder of the militant Women's Political and Social Union (WPSU) in 1903.

The suffragist movement, on the other hand, saw their role as persuading the populace and coaxing the Liberal Government into an acceptance of the fundamental rightness of women's right to vote, at least those with property and taxes – as was the case with men in those days. Catherine joined the principal body of suffragists, the National Union of Women's Suffrage Societies (NUWSS or just NU) which had started in 1902. The NUWSS operated by organising rallies and meetings where women spoke and put their case; and also in 'behind the scenes' dealings with the Liberal Government, led at the time by H.H. Asquith. The complex tale of Catherine's involvement with and importance to the NWUSS is well told in Jo Vellacott's biography: *'From Liberal to Labour with Women's Suffrage'*, subtitled *'The story of Catherine Marshall'* (McGill-Queen's University Press 2016). We will just pick out some of the highlights, along with some of the tales of life at Hawse End.

Catherine's father Francis Marshall, always known as Frank, had spent much of his childhood and youth on Derwent Island. Unable to inherit it from his father Henry, as he was the third surviving son, he bought the dilapidated farmhouse Hawse End, on Derwentwater's Western shore, from Sir John Woodford's estate sometime in the 1880's as a retreat from his schoolmasterly duties at Harrow School teaching Mathematics. His wife, Caroline Colbeck, also taught at Harrow but gave up her work in 1880 on the birth of Catherine.

School holidays were long and the new railway could bring them all the way to Braithwaite Station, a short two miles from Hawse End, so Catherine and her younger brother Hal had the freedom of the woods and lake, a freedom rarely granted to Victorian children. Here, under Catherine's direction they played, with their Derwent Island cousins and any visitors, their version of 'Manhunt'. The territory was the (then bare) Swinside Hill. Two 'hares' (usually Hal was one) were released in different parts of the hill and had to find and reach each other without being caught. They were hunted down by two packs of 'hounds', each comprising a man and a woman who had to remain together. To effect a catch both man and woman hound had to be present. Somehow the game could be expanded to accommodate as many teams as required, and on occasion forty odd people would gather at Hawse End farmhouse after the afternoon's sport for tea.

I mention this because it demonstrates Catherine's flair for organisation and sense of fun: she it was who invited the participants, organised the several hunts and generally kept order. A little older, she channelled this flair into her work for the Keswick branch of the Liberal Party and into initiating, with her mother Caroline, the Keswick branch of the NUWSS, which they called the Keswick Women's Suffrage Association (KWSA) . This was in 1908 and Catherine wrote a report of their first meeting...

> 'Our Association came into being on May 18th when a few ladies known to be in favour of Women's Suffrage met at Hawse End, by invitation of Mrs. Frank Marshall, and decided to form a branch of the NUWSS in Keswick. A committee was formed, rules drawn up, and active propaganda work began at once. It was unanimously decided that our object should be votes for women on the same terms as men and that the Association should be a strictly non-party organization. We also pledged ourselves to peaceful and constitutional methods only. Our work was to consist of spreading the principles of Women's Suffrage by means of meetings, of letters to the press, of distributing literature on the subject, and of "promoting intelligent interest and a sense of responsibility among women with regard to political questions."'[125]

These meetings were hugely successful, attracting audiences of 50 – 100 regularly, both indoors and outdoors. Catherine was the main speaker and organiser and drew heavily on her school training in debate and public speaking, growing in confidence as time went on. Men usually outnumbered women at these events and there must have been some heckling, but it is significant that 'at every one a resolution in favour of votes for women on the same terms as those for men was enthusiastically carried.'[126] They were careful not to espouse universal suffrage which at that time was anathema to the politicians, and merely to require that those women who passed the same tests as there were for men – property, tax-paying, and so on – should also be able to vote.

A mere month later Catherine went to London with Ernestine Marshall, John III's widow who still lived on Derwent Island and was 65 by now, but equally passionate about votes for women. They went to join the grand procession and demonstration organised by the London Society for Women's Suffrage and their own NUWSS. Over 10,000 women took part, demonstrating to Asquith and his Liberal Government the strength of feeling in the country. Nevertheless it took another ten years and the Great War before the Labour Government gave in to the strength of feeling and granted universal suffrage – to all men and women.

---

[125] Report on 1st Quarter's work: KWSA, 18th May 1908

[126] ibid.

During those ten years Catherine worked tirelessly for the cause, taking a stall at Keswick's Saturday market giving out leaflets and selling Suffrage literature. It wasn't long before women from the KWSA were travelling to Penrith and Cockermouth helping to open stalls in their markets, and the idea was soon taken up nationally, to great effect. So great indeed that Catherine was invited to submit an article in the magazine Queen and a full report to the NUWSS annual report – the longest article therein, since there was simply so much to report on that single year's work. After a frenzy of activity throughout the summer the Marshalls were host to perhaps the most famous of the Suffragists, Millicent Fawcett, whose statue has been erected in Parliament Square (the first women there represented) to celebrate 100 years of Votes for Women. Catherine is among the fifty women named on the plinth. (Below)

For a woman so ferociously single-minded and of such tremendous organisational ability Catherine Marshall was notoriously disorganised in her private life – perhaps her thoughts were all for the cause. In her teens at Harrow her mother Caroline entrusted her with 'all the household accounts and Mother's writing work.'[127] No doubt her parents were trying to instil an appreciation of monetary management but despite having a reasonable clothing allowance (£3 -3s-4d per month) she was forever being harassed by stores for unpaid bills. This inability with money continued all her life: below is a copy of a threatening letter from Swan & Edgar, Piccadilly; a department store.

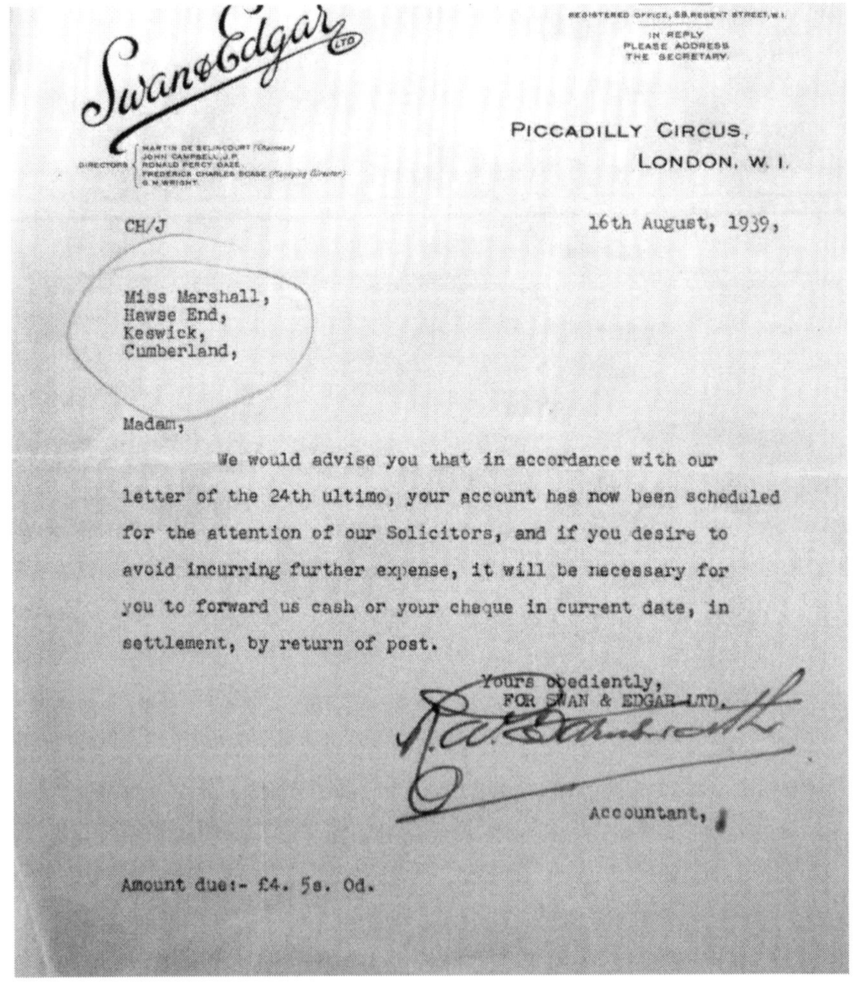

Swan & Edgar Ltd

DIRECTORS: MARTIN DE SELINCOURT (Chairman), JOHN CAMPBELL, J.P., RONALD PERCY GAZE, FREDERICK CHARLES SCASE (Managing Director), G. N. WRIGHT

REGISTERED OFFICE, 58, REGENT STREET, W.1.

IN REPLY PLEASE ADDRESS THE SECRETARY.

PICCADILLY CIRCUS,
LONDON, W. 1.

CH/J

16th August, 1939,

Miss Marshall,
Hawse End,
Keswick,
Cumberland,

Madam,

We would advise you that in accordance with our letter of the 24th ultimo, your account has now been scheduled for the attention of our Solicitors, and if you desire to avoid incurring further expense, it will be necessary for you to forward us cash or your cheque in current date, in settlement, by return of post.

Yours obediently,
FOR SWAN & EDGAR LTD.

Accountant,

Amount due:- £4. 5s. 0d.

This is typical of many, over the years, all meticulously kept by the woman constitutionally incapable of actually getting round to paying them.

We would know nothing of this aspect of Catherine's life, indeed of all the personal details that enliven her story but for an accident of history. Near

127 A letter (unsent) to her school friend Margaret Hirst.

to the end of her life Catherine and her brother Hal sold what had been her main home almost all of her eighty years to Cumberland County Council who bought Hawse End to convert into an Outdoor Pursuits Centre for the county's children. As they were clearing out one of the sheds the workmen found an old chest containing literally thousands of pieces of paper she had 'filed': a glorious mixture of letters written and received, manuscripts of speeches made, minutes of the various suffragist meetings she had attended, bus tickets, train tickets, and the many solicitor's letters threatening dire consequences if unpaid bills were not settled. They were inches from the fire that would have consumed this priceless archive when the decision was made to ask the local archivist, Bruce Jones, to come and sift through the deteriorating tangle of papers.

This was in 1962; a year after Catherine herself had died. Jones realised the value of the hoard, piled it into no fewer than forty large boxes, and took the collection off to the Carlisle Record Office.

There the boxes lay, largely untouched, till Jo Vellacott, visiting England on a Canadian Fellowship grant, asked to be allowed to sort through them – this in 1969. She was looking for sources as to the activities of the No-Conscription Fellowship (NCF) which had been active in the Great War. Catherine and the great Bertrand Russell were leading members of this organisation, and it was initially this aspect of Catherine's life that interested Vellacott. It was the NCF which provided Catherine with the only love of her life, Clifford Allen, First Baron Allen of Hurtwood.

Lord Allen was the chairman of the NCF throughout the war years, and as a leading conscientious objector was imprisoned three times. Although she wasn't a relation Catherine managed to wangle a few visits, and on the previous page is the 1916 photograph of Catherine used to allow her to visit Lord Allen in his cell. The last time he became so ill he was released on compassionate grounds and set up home with Catherine, who was by then ill herself through overwork. They spent some time together at Hawse End, recuperating. However their time together was short-lived, Allen ending their affair soon afterwards. He married Marjorie Gill, cousin of the notorious sculptor Eric Gill, late in 1921: Catherine never married. Clifford Allen suffered poor health and finally died from Tuberculosis in 1939. His widow wrote this tender reply to Catherine's letter of condolence.

> 'Dear Catherine,
>
> Please forgive the long delay in answering your kindly letter about C.A. I have had so much to do and little heart for the doing of it. You who knew C.A. so well will know how lonely & how desolate I feel. He did so long to live & he fought to the last hour with all his old courage. He suffered terribly – it was a tragic ending for him – but he died with a heavenly smile on his lips. Bob Trevelyan and I rowed out on to Lake Geneva & with great humility and heart-breaking sadness scattered his ashes on the waters. There is nothing more to say, Catherine. He has gone – and I am not the only one that weeps. Love to you.
>
> Joan.'[128] *(Marjorie was always known as Joan)*

1939 was a tremendously busy year for Catherine, in the build-up to the Second World War. She was heavily involved in the War Resisters' International movement, the League of Nations Union, the Racial Relations Group, and the Refugee Committee, working over-long hours and becoming ill as a result. Not only so, but she and her brother Hal had reluctantly agreed to sell Hawse End, the only stable place in her life, and were negotiating with the National Trust who however were unwilling to spend the £5,000 she and Hal were asking – having just had to find £75,000 for their new Pembrokeshire coastline protection scheme. Perhaps it is not surprising so many bills and invoices got over-looked this year.

In a letter to her friend Dorothy Latham, dated September 19th, 1939 Catherine says 'I have been working day and night (literally – sometimes without going to bed at all) for refugees for the last year and a half, first for

[128] Carlisle Record Office *Catherine Marshall papers*. D/MAR/2/51

Austrians and then for refugees from Czechoslovakia. I have eleven of the latter at Hawse End, plus two Austrians. I also had five evacuated children from Newcastle – such dirty little scamps!'

These refugees were at Hawse End until 1941, by which time she had found them all jobs of one kind or another, and cottages to live in. In other words, thanks to Catherine's energy and humanity a fortunate few found a new life in Cumberland and escaped the holocaust. That on its own would be justification enough for a life well-lived, but in Catherine's case is almost just a post-script. She was by now in her sixties, worn out with horrendous over-work over much of her life and suffering from chronic and incurable backache. Little wonder that she withdrew from all her political activities. She retired to the cottage in Surrey that she had owned and used frequently between the wars, and sadly was only rarely up at Hawse End for the occasional holiday.

It was a further fifteen years before she and Hal eventually sold it, in 1956, to Cumberland County Council. I'm sure she would have loved to see the huge enjoyment many generations of children have had there in the sixty years since. Do they still run a manhunt, I wonder…

Fawe Park and the Spencer-Bells

Where in the 18th and early 19th centuries the landowners we have studied seemed content to share their properties with locals and visitors alike there came a change in the second half of the 1800s. Greenwich Hospital, after their first rather wild clearance of entire forests became much more responsive to the prevailing mood, planting with an eye to beauty and enhancement. John Marshall II continued this vision – or rather, as he died just three years after buying the East shore, his wife and trustees did. On the Western shore Lord William Gordon made some enemies with his attempt to divert them from the old road to the higher one he had built, but this was more to enhance their views as they travelled. He never tried to forbid traverse on the old road, and it slipped out of use only because his new road was the better maintained. In his extensive construction of new paths and viewpoints on his estate he seems to have been happy for them to be used by any who wished to. Following him Major-General John George Woodford went out of his way to be accommodating to visitors, forbidding no-one access to any of his lands.

This easy-going attitude changed with the new generation of rich 'off-comers' who built new, large and expensive properties on the Western shore: James Fenton Greenall with his new estate of Lingholm in the 1880s; and before him one James Bell who had Fawe Park built in 1858. It is to his family and their part in the ongoing cat's cradle of life under Catbells that we now turn.

James Bell, like so many of the new land-owners, was an MP: in his case for Guildford from 1852 till 1857. 1857 was a significant year for the young James, then 39 and as yet unmarried. Firstly he lost his seat in the General Election of that year, and secondly he met his wife-to-be Mary Anne Spencer, the daughter of a Cockermouth yeoman Jeremiah Spencer. They were both Quakers and were married in the Cockermouth Friends Meeting House. Mary Anne was what would these days be called a feisty young woman, insisting the couple take on both names to become Mr. and Mrs. Spencer-Bell. This was considerably harder in those days and it took them eight years before they received the Royal licence needed and could incorporate the Spencer coat of arms in theirs.[129] As with most of the new owners, with the exception of Major-General Woodford, Fawe Park at first was simply their Derwentwater retreat. They commissioned its building as soon as they were married; employing the architect Alfred Waterhouse to design what was at first a reasonably modest house – although James was himself a qualified architect, but one who didn't need to work.

Perhaps unwisely, the Spencer-Bells situated their new mansion by the side of an ancient track from Nichol End to the woodlands beyond, used almost solely by wagons removing timber. When Spencer-Bell tried to restrict access by putting a gate across the track there was public uproar. It took the best efforts of his neighbour Sir John Woodford to persuade him to abandon his scheme and to soothe the ruffled feathers of the locals.[130] The row simmered for twenty years, but when James died his widow, Mary Anne, decided to block the track once and for all, having her gardener install gates at either end – Nichol End and by the newly-built Lingholm – and fortified by piles of timber and patches of brambles. The final straw may well have been that the newly built Cockermouth-Keswick-Penrith railway had brought in a vast influx of visitors, many of whom were seeking a lakeside walk which would naturally use this old track, as indeed we still do.

This provoked firstly intense local reaction, which steadily grew to being a national debate stimulating letters to the newspapers and debates in Parliament. It can fairly be said to have been the touch paper which ignited the whole debate regarding public access over private land: one which, had it been lost, would have deprived this land of its invaluable public footpaths. The nation should be grateful that Keswick had two men ideally

---

[129] London Gazette, 2nd February, 1866

[130] George Bott, *Henry Irwin Jenkinson* essay in Keswick Characters Vol III, published by Bookcase.

suited to lead the fight for access: Canon Hardwicke Drummond Rawnsley and Henry Irwin Jenkinson. Rawnsley gave a lecture to the Keswick Literary and Scientific Society in March 1886 in which he took no prisoners:

> 'I think of all the small, mean and wicked things a landlord can do, shutting up his footpath is the nastiest. Is England to become a land where, from a public road, a visitor can pause at look-out stations and pay a small charge to catch a glimpse of a field of corn or a bank of wild flowers?'

Brave words from a clergyman whose living depended on the patronage of the very landowners he berated thus. Prime among these was John James Spedding, chairman of the local magistrates and of the family whose seat for centuries had been, and still is, Mirehouse, on the shores of Bassenthwaite Lake. Rawnsley offered him the Presidency of the newly-formed Keswick and District Footpath Preservation Society. Not surprisingly, he refused, for he would have had severely conflicting interests. J.J. Spedding's sister Jane had inherited the ownership of Latrigg – as an absentee landlord – and it was to be access to Latrigg that stoked the embers of the row that had almost subsided over Fawe Park.

Rawnsley's plaque on the path to Friars' Crag

It was at Fawe Park that the fledgling KDFPS learnt to fly. For a year the new secretary, Henry Irwin Jenkinson, sought to negotiate a settlement with Mrs. Spencer-Bell – to no avail. On 30th August 1887 he led a party to remove the sundry impediments – gates, felled trees, fences and thorns – and to confront Mrs. Spencer-Bell. She gave a long, impassioned and sympathy-seeking speech, reminding the crowd arrayed on the other side of the first gate that she was recently widowed and that, just a year ago, her son James Frederick Spencer-Bell, had drowned aged but twenty-three in Derwentwater. She went on to claim her husband had been a great benefactor putting some £40,000 (well over £2M in today's money) into the local economy. Then rather bizarrely she claimed "I am the attraction! I bring lots of people by the railway. The railway gains, everybody gains by having resident gentry, people with money to spend. If you drive people away you will have nothing but what you get from the tourists!"[131]

She might have been better advised to go to the law, for in fact the disputed track might well never have been a public road. James Bell, when he signed the contract for Fawe Park, had to accept a 'right of access' clause allowing the vendor to use the road through the property. Had it been an acknowledged public right of way there would have been no need for such a clause (although it might have been inserted in a 'belt and braces' fashion).[132] She might also have been better to end her harangue there, but she went on to accuse the Keswick people of being hungry sharks, led on by firebrands. Canon Rawnsley should stick to his preaching and not play the politician. Whatever sympathy she had engendered melted away; the barriers were breached and the horse and carriage, followed by several hundred on foot, surged along the disputed track.

When it came to Latrigg, as it did in that same year, 1887, both sides were more inclined to go to the law. Jane Spedding had inherited the fell in 1850, but handed over its running to her brother John James. For many years local people had ascended by the Terrace Road which starts at Calvert Bridge near Old Windebrowe on a track installed and maintained by the man who had enclosed Latrigg from being common land in 1814, William Calvert, of Greta Bank. This continued unimpeded, indeed actively encouraged, until the coming of the railway, and with it Station Road Bridge. Locals and visitors alike took to using the easier Spooney Green lane to access Latrigg and J.J. Spedding unilaterally closed the Terrace Road access. When he also covered the whole hillside with young conifers, planting over the footpaths the Footpath Preservation Association, fearing the Spooney Green access would also be closed, decided on action. For a while they tried to negotiate, but Spedding the magistrate was determined to have the matter settled in a court of law.

He challenged Henry Jenkinson to organise an official trespass via the Terrace Road which he had very effectively blocked up. Rather than mobilise a troupe of trespassers twice over Jenkinson and the Society

---

[131] George Bott, *Keswick*

[132] Letter to 'The Spectator' 26th November 1887.

unblocked the Fawe Park track on the morning of 30th August then moved on to Latrigg in the afternoon. Spedding's barriers were more formidable than Mrs. Spencer-Bell's: an iron gate with a heavy chain, piles of timber, a rusty old plough – the lot covered liberally in sticky tar. Undeterred, Jenkinson and his protesters cleared all away and marched triumphantly to the top of Latrigg. This was but the opening salvo: Spedding restored his barricades, throwing down the gauntlet. This time the Footpath Preservation Association mustered some 2,000 followers, largely Keswick people, to undertake the clearance and march to the top – all under the leadership and organisation of Henry Jenkinson. The date was 1st October 1887, a date that should be celebrated annually by all who treasure our nation's footpaths. On the way up the crowd – never a mob – sang 'Rule Britannia', and on the top joined in lustily with 'God save the Queen'.

Mr. Spedding then carried out his stated intention of bringing the whole argument to court, and on 6th July 1888 Canon Rawnsley, Henry Jenkinson and six other Keswick worthies appeared in Carlisle to defend the Society against the charge of trespass. Their case rested on usage, and they produced many witnesses who confirmed they had used the Terrace Road unimpeded for many years. Ever the diplomat the judge, Mr. Justice Graham, suggested that both sides should meet again and try to reach an agreement. In time-honoured British fashion a compromise was reached: the Footpath Association gave up its claim to the Terrace Road path, and in return Mr. Spedding recognised the public right of way to the top of Latrigg by the Spooney Green lane and zigzag path still used by thousands today. It seems a rather tame end to such a bitter struggle, but the ruling set the precedent which freed all legitimate footpaths for the next century and led finally to the 'Right to Roam' legislation of the early years of this.

Henry Jenkinson's legacy to the nation is incalculable in the freedom to walk the acknowledged footpaths unimpeded. His memorial, fittingly, is in Keswick itself: the fine memorial gates to Upper Fitz Park. They are there in recognition of his pivotal role in finding the funding for Fitz Park and were erected before the Battle for Latrigg, on 21st June 1887 – a busy year in the life of a very busy gentleman. (See overleaf.)

What of Mrs. Spencer-Bell? In the 1891 census she is shown still at Fawe Park with two of her daughters, Helen and Juliet, both in their twenties; seven servants, and a German lady listed as a companion – Henriette Schunck – some ten years her junior. Unable to prevent the increasing numbers of tourists passing by her house and kitchen gardens she had a high stone wall erected to protect the house from view and an equally high wooden palisade for the garden. When Beatrix Potter dreamt up Mr. McGregor, Peter Rabbit and his siblings in the garden in 1903 she could do so in privacy.

She was justified in reminding the crowd seeking to remove her barriers about the death of her son, for it was an extremely well-publicised accident that took him from her. James was a spirited 23 year-old and an excellent swimmer who, like young men the world over, loved a challenge. Thursday 16th September 1866 was a squally afternoon with white horses on the surface of the lake: just the kind of testing time for sailing that James loved. He persuaded his friend Edward Rathbone to join him, but Fitzroy Marshall, son of Reginald of Castlerigg Manor, thought better of the idea, seeing the violent state of the water.

The pair were seen enjoying the speed such a day produces for some time, but were then spotted capsized about 70 yards out from Lingholm. Two rowing boats put out from Lingholm and rowed to the capsized dinghy, but no bodies were visible. Boats tried draglines but found nothing, so next day a diving crew came from Liverpool to search for the young men, and after several hours searching found them both, no more than 60 yards from the shore, in about 20 feet of water. It became clear that James Spencer-Bell, who might have been expected to save both himself and his companion, being a strong swimmer, had been knocked senseless by the boom suddenly swinging across the boat in a freak wind. Without his help Edward Rathbone stood little chance in the stormy waters. [133]

Henry Jenkinson's memorial on Fitz Park gate.

[133] Keswick Museum, English Lakes Visitor 18th Sept 1866.

CHAPTER EIGHTEEN

THE STEPHENSON CONNECTION TO THE SOUTH SHORE OF DERWENTWATER

On 28th July 1785 a travelling gentleman, intent on making a complete survey of the Lake District, took his mid-day meal at a 'neat and commodious little inn' where his boat had landed him on his tour round Derwentwater. Here he was joined by the house's cat and dog and most of his survey of this particular nook of Borrowdale is taken up by his tale of how the pair of them conspired to share in the scraps from the rich man's table. The gentleman was James Clarke, one of the less dependable of the early travellers, and the inn was the 'Low Door' – somewhat less imposing than it is now, with its vast new spa building. It has been an Inn ever since, and for an unknown length of time before Clarke's visit, and at the time he notes that 'this house and the lands from Barrow Beck to above High Low Door belong to Rowland Stephenson esq., now MP for Carlisle, and are freehold'.

Peter Crosthwaite's map of Derwentwater, first published in 1783, but updated here in 1808, clearly shows the extent of Stephenson's properties on the East and South of the lake.

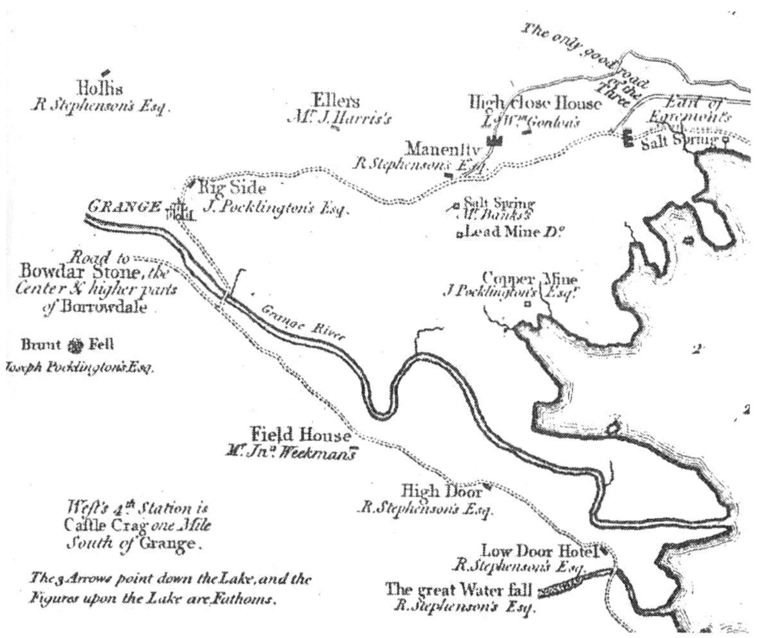

His three farms, Manesty, Hollins and High Lodore, plus his Low Door Hotel, occupy a lot of the land at the South end of the lake and abut Lord William Gordon's extensive estates. This simple mention on a map and Clarke's throwaway comment are tantalising clues to a cornucopia of 18th century intrigue, derring-do, enterprise, respectability, fraud and embezzlement. The Grand Old Man of the family, Edward I – there are going to be four Edwards – was a gentleman and entrepreneur in the simple little market town of Keswick in the latter half of the 17th Century. Let's start with a brief introduction to the main players over four generations.

Edward I: Born around 1660, Edward married into money and may well have been reasonably rich in his own right. He married Rebecca Winder of Lorton: the Winders were a well-off family as can be seen in the still existing Winder Hall, a fine house in Low Lorton, recently a first-class hotel, and now a self-catering house. They had four children: Mary, born in 1665; Barbarie born 1687; Edward II born 1691 and John born 1700.[134]

Edward II: Born 1691 as we have seen, Edward is a major character in the story. He married late, in 1741 but had no children and was widowed in 1744[135]. He left a vast estate, worth £32 million pounds in today's money, largely to Rowland I, of whom more later.

John I: Edward II's brother, born 1700. Married into a fortune to the daughter of a convict transporter to America. Had one son, another Edward who seems to have been rather simple or otherwise disabled and who died unwed and without issue at 44.

John II: In the next generation, and son of a cousin of Edward II and John I. Another enterprising man who made good in America but opted to return in 1782 as the War of Independence ground to its climax. His third child, Rowland II, was born on the voyage home.

Rowland I: In the same generation, the only son of Henry and hence a first cousin of John II. This is the Rowland who owned the south shores of Derwentwater in the 1780s.

Rowland II: A son of John II, born 1882, who followed the family tradition of banking on Lombard Street but who came spectacularly unstuck once he became a partner in the bank and started embezzling. Married to Mary Eliza, grand-daughter of Rowland I.

---

[134] Crosthwaite Church registers

[135]CWAAS: Brigadier J W Kaye, *Governor's House, Keswick* vol 66 p.344

Here's a pared-down family tree of the relevant players, to the best of my ability. It's not possible to be sure of the antecedents at nearly four centuries removed.

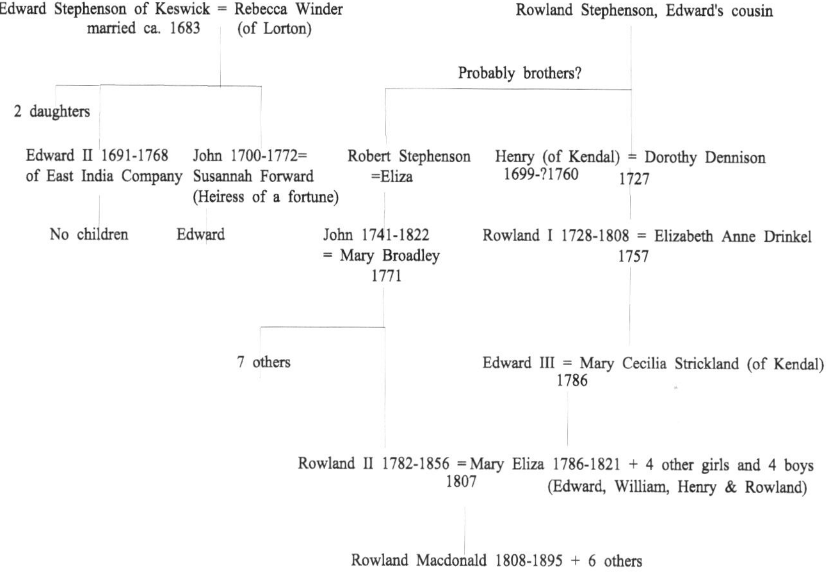

Having introduced the main players let's now take a closer look at their roles in the ongoing story of the southern shores of Derwentwater.

Edward I spent his life in Keswick and was responsible for opening at least one of the inns and hotels which still ply their trade in the town. This of course was after the great influx of German miners in the later 1500s and before the smaller influx of tourists and visitors who started to make the pilgrimage to the Lakes in the later 1700s, but nevertheless Edward made a decent living. Crosthwaite registers point up the main events in Edward and Rebecca's lives. As in most families in those days a baby was born more or less every two years. The first two were girls, and at least reached baptism in church: Mary in 1685; Barbarie in 1687. The next two were boys, both hopefully called Edward after their father, but both buried at Crosthwaite; one in October 1688 and the next in November 1689. At last, in October 1691 the third baby Edward survived to baptism – and thrived, as we shall see. Rebecca must have found some form of contraception then, for no more children were born or died till 1700 when younger brother John was baptised in May. Staying with the registers we find old Edward I survived and prospered till 1728/9, being buried in church – the first in the Stephenson vault – on March 3rd.

Probate for Edward I's will lists all his goods and chattels and show him to have been a rich man, owning £1,102 worth of goods but telling us nothing of any property he may have had. However, since £14 worth of goods were in the Royal Oak it seems reasonable to assume he owned that historic inn in Keswick.[136] The Borrowdale properties are not mentioned but it is likely that Edward I bought them, rather than Edward II. Edward I spent his entire life in Keswick and was rich enough to buy property, and experienced in inns and hotels and so may well have made Low Door into a public house. Edward II on the other hand spent very little time in Keswick and was prone to grand gestures rather than tin pot investments, as we shall see. On balance I reckon he inherited Manesty, Hollins and High and Low Door from his father, but I have been unable to prove this one way or the other.

Edward II had an exotic history culminating in becoming Governor of Bengal in 1728 – for 35 hours! He was one of the most successful employees of the East India Company, that part trader, part coloniser, part suppressor of the Indian Sub-continent. He was born in Keswick in 1691 and first went to India as a young man in 1708. While most emigres died within the first few years abroad Edward, made of sterner stuff, not only survived but 'made good'. He rose up the company hierarchy step by step till in 1728 when the governor suddenly died he was the obvious choice to take over, at least transitionally. The transition proved to be very short, as the genuine successor arrived the next day. Edward graciously handed over the keys to the Residence, and the whole of Bengal, and stayed a further year before at last returning to his native Cumberland – by now a very wealthy man.

In the short time he sojourned in Keswick he built a new house which he whimsically named 'Governor's House'. It is now the Derwent Club in St. John's Street. In the 1960s Fink's Greengrocers in Lake Road was called 'Governor's House' and was presumably built in the garden of the original house.[137] Brigadier Kaye's treatise for the Cumberland and Westmorland Antiquarian and Archaeological Society puts forward the theory that the fields known as 'The Howrahs' between Keswick and Portinscale may well derive their name from this Edward Stephenson, Howrah being a city in Bengal, where Stephenson was governor for a day.

However, 'The Governor' found provincial Keswick not even up to being provisional and moved out as soon as his house was built. A man of his wealth and personality needed a London house and a house in the country, and before long he had bought 41, Queen's Square, Bloomsbury

---

[136] CRO: PROB/1729/AINVX8

[137] Brigadier J W Kaye, *Governor's House, Keswick*. CWAAS (1966)

and an estate in Essex: Bardfield Lodge. Not long after (in 1738) he bought Dawley, near Uxbridge, from Lord Bolingbroke for £26,000. Nor was he quiescent in Cumberland: in 1732, just two years after his return from India, he bought the extensive Holme Cultram estate for £11,000, and offered his new-found friend Richard Gilpin a mortgage of £7,000 secured on Gilpin's pile, Scaleby Castle, close to Carlisle. The Governor was a rich man, intent on a position in society and a portfolio of property that might return a decent interest: the rate for his friend Gilpin was 4½%.

The next logical step, it appeared to Edward, was to become a Member of Parliament. Sudbury was but twenty miles from his new home, Bardfield Lodge and he was rich enough to ensure he was returned as its MP in 1734, thereby starting what became rather a tradition for the Stephensons: that of spending a great deal of money to become an MP, rarely if ever attending the House, never voting or speaking, and refraining to stand for a second term.[138]

As is often the way of loans and mortgages between friends the Governor's £7,000 connection to Scaleby Castle slowly festered. Richard Gilpin was an artist – many of his family were too – but he was no business-man. He never paid any of the interest owing to Stephenson, and slowly the debt mounted: surprisingly to me only as simple interest, not compound. That is to say Edward never demanded interest on the interest owing, but simply £280 per year, so that by 1748 when Richard's world was beginning to implode he owed seven years and seven months interest - £2,120.[139]

Nor was this the limit of Richard Gilpin's troubles. His wife, Mary, had been married before and had two teenage daughters, Sarah and Eleanor Dove. Sarah remained a spinster all her life, but Eleanor married a clergyman from Whitehaven, Curwen Hudleston. Richard 'borrowed' £500 from each of the Dove girls: but was it a mortgage or not? The question came to matter as Richard neared bankruptcy and death in the 1740s, and Curwen's brother Andrew Hudleston, a famous lawyer of the time, struggled hard firstly to sell the Castle and then, when there were no takers, to persuade Edward 'the Governor' Stephenson to buy it and pay off Curwen and Sarah. To cut a very long series of letters to a quick synopsis Stephenson did buy/foreclose being by then owed £11,100 but declined to pay off any debt Gilpin owed to others. Curwen and Sarah had eventually to swallow their losses.[140].

[138] R Sedgewick, editor, *The History of Parliament: 1715-1754*

[139] CRO: DHUD/8/21

[140] Ibid.

Edward did marry in 1741 but had no children and was widowed in 1744.[141] He died in his Queen's Square house in 1768, childless and reputedly intestate[142], and administration was granted to his brother John Stephenson, of Tottenham High Cross, London. He is however buried and commemorated in Crosthwaite Church where a large stone slab below the chancel steps reads:

EDWARD STEPHENSON ESQ.
LATE GOVERNOR OF BENGAL. OBIIT 7 SEPT 1768
AETATE SUO 77

A brass inset to the slab carries his armorial bearings.

When Edward died he left over £500,000; worth around £32,000,000 today! Clearly the Borrowdale properties formed part of this estate. I have been unable to determine whether he bought them or inherited from his father, but as I observed they seem rather parochial for the Governor's tastes, so I suspect he inherited them.

Rowland I, the owner in 1785, was a nephew of Edward II's as already stated, but he was not administrator John's son (that was another Edward). Nevertheless, he appears to be the chief beneficiary. John died just three years after his brother Edward and left an intricate will, but one which certainly doesn't account for the bulk of old Edward's fortune. He does instruct that his body be buried in the family vault at Crosthwaite, alongside Edward's, and the will contains the following instruction, among many others; 'To Anthony Askew of Queen's Square, London, doctor of physic, and my cousin Rowland Stephenson, of Lombard Street, London, Banker, my two executors £500 each.' Our Rowland I is this banker (cousin could often mean nephew then): and certainly he himself was also a banker in Lombard Street. It's time to gather together the several loose strands above, to take stock of our Rowland's standing, and that of Anthony Askew.

- Anthony Askew is probably the ancestor of the Askew family who built and owned the Borrowdale Hotel and ran the first bus service up the valley. They in turn are part of the Leyland family, current owners of Manesty.
- Anthony lived in Queen's Square as did Edward. Was he a relative, living in the same house?

141 Kaye, p.343
142 Kaye,. p. 345.

- Our Rowland Stephenson owned a lot of the land at the South end of Derwentwater by 1780, soon after Edward and John's deaths.
- He also owned Scaleby Castle at least in 1786 and probably before, from where he launched his bid to be MP for Carlisle – see later.
- Rowland Stephenson also lived in 41, Queen's Square in 1780, from which address he granted a mortgage of £3,200 in 1780 to Dr. William Brownrigg, of Ormathwaite, Underskiddaw, and a later top-up of £1,400.[143] Presumably he inherited this house from Uncle Edward too.
- By 1806 Rowland is described as 'Lord of the manor of Holme Cultram' in a document seeking the enclosure of common land around Abbeytown.[144] It seems safe to assume he also inherited that from Uncle Edward.
- Edward rented Stable Hills (opposite Lord's Island) from Greenwich Hospital on a 21 year lease from 1766. By the time for renewal of the lease it was in Rowland's hands, but he failed to secure another lease: further proof that he was principal inheritor of Edward's estate.[145]
- We can say then that he was chief beneficiary of Edward's legacy, but if Edward died intestate it is difficult to see why. He was Edward's cousin Henry's son[146] – a little tenuous for 'next of kin' inheritance if there was no will.
- In fact, looking at the family tree given earlier, it becomes clear that Rowland I was the only male relative Edward II could leave the bulk of his fortune to. When he died in 1768 he had no children: his only brother John I only had a disabled and probably simple son (Edward) who was unfitted to deal with a fortune. Neither of his sisters appears to have married – at least there is no record of a marriage in Crosthwaite register. That leaves his cousins' children, John II and Rowland I. At the time John II was in America and likely to stay there forever. Only Rowland I was a suitable and dependable male relative to take on the mantle and the

143 CRO *DX 448/19.*

144 CWAAS: Professor John Glaister, M.D., F.R.S.E Vol 20 (1920). p. 225

145 Derek Denman: *Lord William Gordon and The Occupation Of Derwentwater In The 1780s* CWAAS (2014) p. 224

146 Hansard reference volume 1754-1790.

fortune, and to him it was left, either by will or by brother John I's administration.

So who was this Rowland Stephenson? From parliamentary records covering his brief position as MP for Carlisle 1787-1790 we learn that he was born around 1728, the son of Henry Stephenson of Docker Garth, Westmorland, and his wife Dorothy Dennison of Whinfell, Westmorland. In 1757 he married Elizabeth Anne Drinkel, of Kendal, though they married in London, and had one son, Edward III. From the same source we learn he apparently began his career with Martins of Lombard Street, and by 1766 was a partner in the firm of Batson, Stephenson, and Hoggart, with which he was associated till his death. It seems likely that his father Henry was cousin to Edward the Governor and also John, his administrator. It also seems likely that Governor Edward, in the absence of an heir apparent, took Rowland under his wing and paved his way in London society.

What then of Edward's brother John who was his administrator and presumably oversaw the transfer of the bulk of Edward's fortune to Rowland? He himself married into money for his wife Susannah Forward was a joint heiress of the estate of Jonathon Forward, who also made a large fortune. It has to be said that neither of these fortunes (Governor Edward's and Jonathon's) were honourable. Edward grafted shamelessly in India, purloining much of the last of the Moghul money there; Jonathon ran two ships to America bringing back tobacco – but going out they were the first to transport convicts to the Americas, a highly lucrative but intensely cruel and barbarous trade.[147]

Paul Bangay in his book *The Dapper Little Banker* claims the fortunes of both old Edward and Jonathon Forward ended up in Rowland I's hands: if so, he was a very rich man indeed.

I have alluded to Rowland's brief career as MP for Carlisle and to his ownership of Scaleby Castle, eight miles NE of Carlisle. His bid for election was a classic example of 18th century skull-duggery on the part of his opponent, none other than Lord Lonsdale, the Bad Earl who refused to pay his dues to the Wordsworth family. The series of elections there from 1784-1803 are known as the 'Mushroom Elections' because of the way Lonsdale chose to gerrymander the result. At that time Carlisle was what was known as a freeman borough – only 'freemen' could vote. There were about 750 of them out of a population of 7,000. There were only two ways to become a freeman: either be the son of a freeman; or be apprenticed for seven years to a freeman and then be 'brothered' into one of the cities'

[147] Paul Bangay *The dapper little banker* 2011 ch.2

eight guilds.[148] Lonsdale effectively removed this latter criterion, proclaiming that Carlisle Corporation had the power to create honorary freemen and in 1785 it conferred the freedom of the city on 1,477 men, unsurprisingly largely drawn from lists made out by Lonsdale's stewards consisting of miners from his Whitehaven collieries and his Westmorland estates. All guaranteed to vote as instructed. As they had suddenly appeared overnight, they were known as 'mushroom voters'.

The guilds of course launched a legal objection to this attack on their privileges but the case had not been heard and judged by the time Edward Norton, the 'Yellow' MP for Carlisle, died in March 1786, triggering a by-election. (The two parties at the time were designated Yellow and Blue: Lonsdale's was Yellow. Blue were Whigs; yellow were Tories.) Lonsdale's candidate, his cousin John Lowther, won because of the mushroom voters, but a later judgement overturned the result but without finally settling the legality of the mushroom voters. Later that year the other Carlisle MP, Charles Howard, Earl of Surrey, (of the Blue party), was elevated to the House of Lords on the death of his father, the Duke of Norfolk. This triggered yet another by-election, and Lord Lonsdale had every intention of using his mushroom voters again.

This time Rowland Stephenson stood as the Blue candidate, giving his residence as Scaleby Castle though he was still a banker in London, and of course was initially beaten by the Yellow candidate Edward Knubley, supported by all those mushroom votes. The Blues duly objected and a select committee of MPs overturned the result and Rowland became one of Carlisle's two MPs. Strangely the select committee still didn't rule the use of mushroom voters illegal, and Lonsdale was able to use them again in 1790. Again, Yellow at first won but the poll was overturned on objection and by the 1796 general election Lonsdale was forbidden to use his mushroom voters.

He was a very bad loser and after his setback in 1876 when Rowland Stephenson was returned as MP he used his influence to deny licences to five publicans who had voted for Stephenson and the case reverberated for the next four years. After all this kerfuffle one might have thought Rowland would be a meticulous MP, especially as he mainly lived in London, but in fact his only recorded votes were with the Opposition over the Regency, 1788-9, and he is not reported to have spoken in the House. Interestingly, in terms of colours, the Yellow party were basically Tories, the Blue party Whigs, who morphed slowly into the Liberal party – a reversal of current colours. Though in the USA blue represents the

[148] M J Smith, *The mushroom elections in Carlisle 1784-1803*. CWAAS: (1981). pp. 113 - 121

Democrats, closest to our Liberals, while the conservative Republicans sport red.

Rowland I died in 1808 leaving his bank, Remington, Stephenson and Company in very good shape. His nephew Rowland Stephenson II managed to destroy the company utterly at the end of 1828, a mere twenty years later. With this catastrophe all Stephenson connection to the Manesty lands and the South shore of Derwentwater was ended, abruptly and finally.

This **Rowland II** was born in 1782 and became the subject of a great scandal. He was the son of John Stephenson of Kendal, Cumberland who, on his return from an America ill-disposed to Englishmen joined his uncle Rowland Stephenson's Lombard Street bank: Stephenson, Remington and Company. Young Rowland Stephenson himself joined them from Eton College, and succeeded his father as a partner in 1822.Young Rowland II shared many of his great-uncle's interests: banking, the arts – and a desire to enter Parliament. He tried in Carlisle in 1816, unsuccessfully, and spent a small fortune over the next decade till, again like his great-uncle, he was elected in Leominster after a legal challenge disqualified his opponent. This was in 1826. He also made no speeches in the house, and precious few votes. But time was running out for young Rowland. In one of those strange coincidences when Rowland II was unceremoniously unseated in 1828 he was replaced by none other than William Marshall, of Patterdale Hall, a scion of the Marshall family who played such a part in shaping Derwentwater.

As can be seen from the family tree above Rowland II married his cousin Mary Eliza, a grand-daughter of Rowland I in 1807. This was a happy, productive marriage. Both were highly musical; Mary Eliza an accomplished singer and a private scholar of Sir George Smart, a prominent coach.[149] In 1816 they bought a mansion in Romford, north of the Thames, named – again somewhat coincidentally in the context of this book – Marshalls, and entertained there lavishly. Mary Eliza however was not constitutionally strong and seven pregnancies wore her down.

She died soon after her only daughter, Emma Louise, was born in 1821 (Her memorial tablet in All Hallows churchyard, Tottenham says 1820). Until then Rowland II had been the very model of decorum, a meticulous banker, a patron of the arts, a collector of beautiful objets d'art – a 'dapper little banker'.

He seems to have gone to pieces almost immediately after Mary Eliza's death; not in any sense obvious to his friends and family, but in terms of finance. His lifestyle if anything grew ever more lavish.

---

[149] Paul Bangay, *The dapper little banker*

Significantly his father John II also died, aged 81, the year after Mary Eliza, and Rowland II replaced him, becoming a full partner and the 'Stephenson' in the Lombard Street Bank, Messrs. Remington, Stephenson, Remington, Toulmin and Co., commonly known as 'Remington'. This was a big mistake.

Rowland spent a fortune trying to become an MP, firstly in West Looe in 1822 then in Newport in 1823: both were Cornwall 'rotten boroughs' and he had no realistic chance of winning against landowners who had most of the electorate dependent on their good will. When he eventually won in Leominster his answer to a friend who asked why on earth he wanted to be an MP anyway was 'MPs get free postage'. By this time, 1826, Rowland was mired in financial trouble all of his own making. He authorised the Bank's backing of a wildly extravagant scheme to build the huge domed 'Coliseum' in Regent's Park which was intended to house a panorama of all London on its hemispherical ceiling. The entrepreneur was one Thomas Hornor, a skilled architect and draughtsman. It was the complexity of this ever increasing debt which finally precipitated Rowland's downfall, but for some years (ever since being made a partner in 1822) he had been using the bank as his personal money box. He would take money out just before the close of the day's business, leaving a promissory note, and re-instate it next morning after some shady deal. His unwilling accomplice was his callow young nephew Henry Stephenson, brother of Mary Eliza and therefore also brother-in-law to Rowland. Aged 29 he seems to have been over-awed by Rowland. His duty was to 'cash-up' each night and so he knew what Rowland was up to; but in the way of these things the embezzlement grew from petty beginnings and Henry found himself embroiled.

By Boxing Day, 1828, the game was up. The Bank discovered a black hole of £58,000 owing to the Bank of England and hundreds of thousands of pounds worth of other discrepancies and was forced to close its doors at 1.30 on Saturday 27th December. A day later an earthquake killed 30,000 in Japan. There wasn't room in most London newspapers to report this disaster: all eyes were on Rowland II and his bankrupt bank. Having unsuccessfully tried to blow his head off Rowland escaped to America with his long time clerk and accomplice James Harwood Lloyd and successfully resisted attempts to extradite him. The case reverberated in the press for many weeks.

The Times Newspaper on 23rd June 1829 gave notice of the sale by auction of Marshalls and all the properties around Romford... and numerous lands, residences, inns, public houses, dwelling houses, shops, tenements and the manor of Cockermouth, to go ahead on July 2nd 1829'. NOTE The manor of Cockermouth has nothing to do with the Cumbrian town of Cockermouth: it is part of Dagenham! So passed the Stephenson connection to Manesty, Hollins Farm, High Lodore and the Lodore Hotel. His eldest son Rowland Macdonald Stephenson (1808-95) visited him in the summer of 1829 and afterwards paid 15,000 dollars for Dr. William Shippen's 170-acre estate, Farley, on the Delaware River, in Bensalem township, near Bristol, Pennsylvania, where Stephenson settled in October 1829. He died there in July 1856 and was buried in the churchyard of St. James's Episcopal Church.

Back in London, the memorial to Rowland I in All Hallows Church yard, Tottenham, is shown below; where thirteen years later his grand-daughter was to join him.

The text reads
IN MEM:
ROWLANDI STEPHENSON A.R.M.
DEFUNCT NOV 30 1807
AT 70
HOC MONUMENTUM FILIUS EJUS
MOERENS POSUIT

The last lines translate as 'This monument was placed here by his grieving son'. Given that Rowland I's grand-daughter Mary Eliza is buried there too and has the memorial on the next page we can assume that 'grieving son' was Edward III, Mary Eliza's father. It is surely significant that Rowland II should have chosen to place his wife's body beside her grandfather rather than at home in Romford. They were a close family by all accounts, which may explain it: or did Rowland II already know he was sailing close to the wind and might have to flee Romford and the country?

From the memorial we can also see that Edward III inherited Scaleby Castle from his father Rowland I.

THE SALT WATER SPRING UNDER MANESTY

We can't leave a section on the southern shores of Derwentwater without a brief visit to two of the natural wonders which have fascinated people down the centuries. The first is the salt water spring in the field below Manesty Farmhouse. This has been known and used for centuries, though is sadly neglected nowadays – and indeed has been so for over a century. My main source for this section is the excellent paper by Charlotte Kipling of the Freshwater Biological Association (somewhat contradictorily) published in CWAAS as Article VIII, Vol 61 (1961) pp. 57-70.

The Salt Well below Manesty.
The walls are the remains of 'Woodford's' building.

There is no mention of the salt well in the records of the Furness monks who held the land from its sale to them in 1210 by Alice de Rumilly so it was presumably either unknown or of no use in those days. Since the usual method of extracting salt from brine in those days was by evaporation in open shallow pans this is hardly surprising: in Borrowdale such pans are more likely to overflow from the rainfall than to evaporate.

The first mention of possible interest in the commercial possibilities of the well is in a commission appointed in 1555 'to enquire as to minerals in the manor of Borrowdale'. This is the preliminary enquiry which resulted in the influx of German miners in the 1560s to extract copper from the nearby Copperplate mine at Manesty and Goldscope in Newlands. The enquiry found that a rent of two shillings a year might be reasonable for the salt well. This doesn't sound much, but at the same time the commission recommended that an annual rent of fourteen shillings might be expected for the wad mines at Seathwaite. This can have been the only time the salt well was worth a seventh of the wad mines!

By 1614 and the 'Great Deed of Borrowdale' when Whitmore and Verdon asset stripped Borrowdale and sold all the non-attributable rights to the commoners they thought so little of the salt well that it was thrown in with the deal, whereas the wad mines were carefully reserved to the pair above. At that time Manesty was bought by the sitting tenants, 'John Lambert and Richard Hyne of Manesty'.[150] Sixty years had seen the wad mines profit exceedingly, and the salt well languish. By 1783 Peter Crosthwaite's map shows the salt well owned by 'Mr. Banks.' By this time there was great interest in the country for spa water as a curative for rheumatism and skin diseases and it seems the spring had been walled about and the floor flagged by 1816 when T H Horne was writing his guide.[151] This is partly borne out by John Postlethwaite's book 'Mines and Mining in the Lake District', published in 1877 where he says 'About sixty-five years ago a well was dug by the proprietor, Major General Sir John Woodford, KCB, and a house built over it for the convenience of bathers and this was opened to the public free of charge: but the public did not appreciate the privilege and the house was allowed to fall into decay.' I say 'partly' because the dates really don't tally. Sir John didn't come to Water End till 1841, a mere 36 years before Postlethwaite's book – a lot less than the 65 years claimed. In any case, Lord William Gordon never owned Manesty and nor did his heir Woodford, so we must conclude that the well was housed around the early 1800s, but not by Sir John Woodford.

It remains, secluded in its isolation in the middle of the rough field, unnoticed by the many walkers who pass within a hundred yards on the main 'Cumbria Way' path to the east of the well, one of the few tourist attractions in this valley not to have made good.

---

[150] CRO, *Great deed of Borrowdale*, 1614

[151] T H Horne, *The Lakes of Lancashire, Westmorland and Cumberland* (London 1816) p. 44 as quoted in Kipling.

THE FLOATING ISLAND

While the Salt Well stands visible but little-regarded the second natural phenomenon at the south end of Derwentwater tantalises by its fleeting appearances and problematic pedigree. The geologist John Postlethwaite referred to above claims to have stood on this fleeting floating island when his parents went there for a picnic. This is not impossible, though pretty risky, and there is a photograph probably from the early 1930s which a quote in F. J. Carruthers' book *Lore of the Lake Country* describes as "a girl guide planting a Union Flag on it and claiming it for England".

Photo courtesy of Brian Wilkinson

The standard text on the 'island' was first published in 1888 by George James Symons and is a masterclass in amateur Victorian curiosity and satisfaction. Its slightly ponderous title is *'The Floating Island in Derwentwater: its history and mystery, with notes of other dissimilar islands…'* You can buy the original from Abe Books at £150 or a perfectly usable photo-copy reprint also from them at £8.11. Other booksellers also advertise the copy. Symons was alerted that the island had once again floated to the surface on August 25th 1884, late in the afternoon. He immediately hired a boat and rowed the two-and-a-half miles up the lake to see for himself this phenomenon he had previously written off as 'boatmen's hyperbole'. 'Where usually the water is about six feet deep we found the island up, and about twenty feet in diameter…'(p.9)

With huge enthusiasm Symons spent the next day amassing implements of all sorts which he hoped would help his research and early on the 27th set out by boat with three like-minded friends to 'get to the bottom' of the mysterious irruption. His most technical instrument was a Casella-Galton pocket altazimuth – he is so proud of it he includes a photograph:

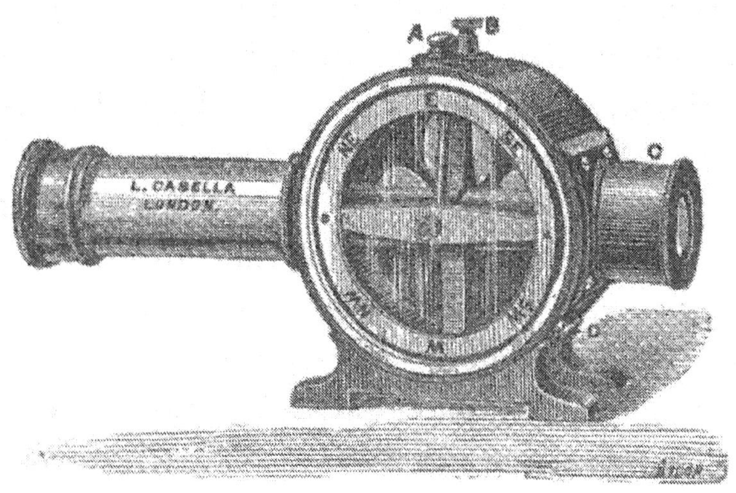

Other gear included a simple depth sounder – an empty bottle suspended on a cord marked off in feet; and two ingenious systems for collecting whatever gas might be present. One was a ten-foot long tube, complete with a stopper in the end to prevent it bunging up when he thrust it through the island and another ten-foot rod to dislodge the stopper when through to the lake floor – this to see if there was a store of gas beneath the island forcing it up, as one theory held. The other was to collect the gas bubbles he had observed coming up to the surface sporadically. He obtained from a chemist in Keswick some large stoppered glass bottles and a five-inch funnel. To collect the bubbles he filled a bottle with water, upended it under water and inserted the funnel. Catching gas bubbles displaced the water in the bottle, and when it was empty of water and full of gas he removed the funnel and inserted the stopper – all under water to prevent any gas escaping or air intruding.

This was a great success, yielding a bottle of gas per day for analysis. The tube however produced no gas whatsoever, leading him to conclude that the island wasn't forced up by gas building beneath it, but that it genuinely floated up because the prolific growth of Littorella lacustris (shore-weed) and the peat it was growing in produces so much marsh gas (for such were the bubbles he caught) that the whole becomes less dense than water and so detaches from the lake bottom and does indeed float to the surface.

This is not to suggest that the island is a detached floating body, but that while the middle floats up the edges are still firmly fixed to the lake floor. This he inferred from the fact that (a) it never floats away, but stays put whatever the wind and surface conditions, and (b) there is visible a large tear, or rift, where the peat has parted to allow for the greater surface area when the mass has become an underwater hillock. He produces the following block-prints to illustrate what is happening.

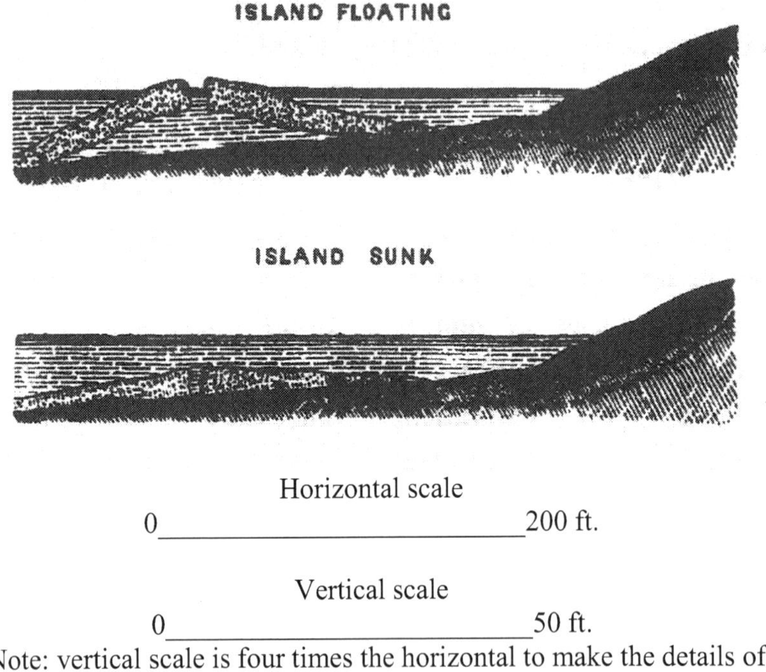

Horizontal scale

0______________________________200 ft.

Vertical scale

0______________________________50 ft.

(Note: vertical scale is four times the horizontal to make the details of formation clear.)

With his trusty altazimuth Symons calculated the position of his island precisely, and produced the following map of the three visible parts of the island on August 27th 1884.

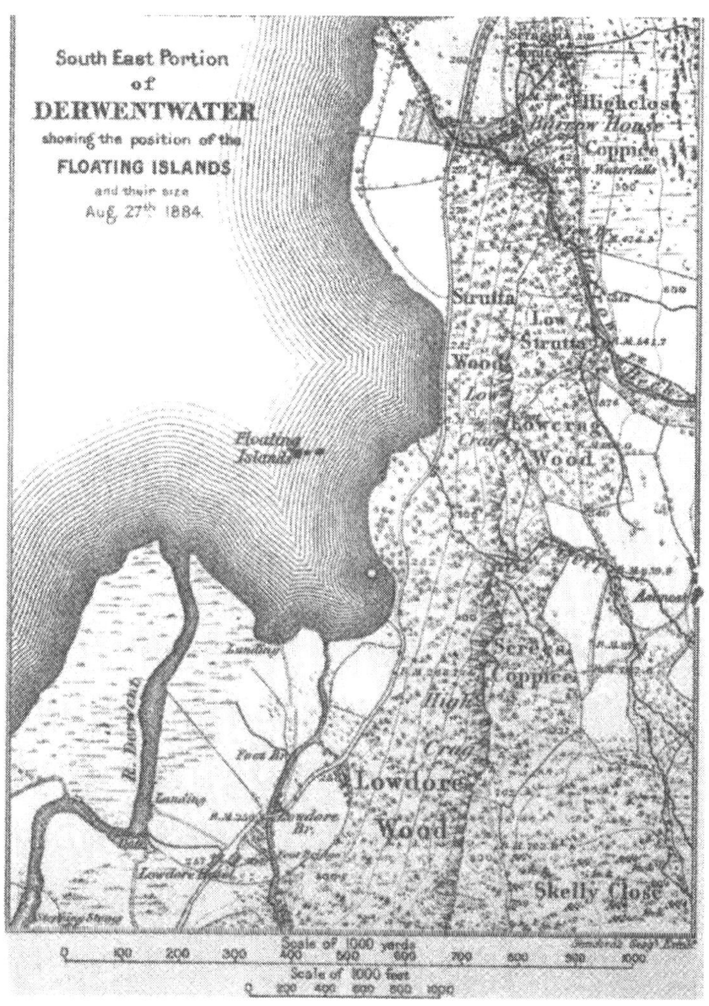

Symons records that it was possible to stand on the island and that with a plank on top all four of the intrepid party stood there together. He also produces tables to show which years (from 1753 to 1888) the island(s) have been observed, which show meticulous noting from 1753 to 1780. It failed to rise till 1773 but then rose several times in the next decade. The next twenty years are poorly recorded except for 1797 and 1798 when it was over a hundred yards long. Records are then well-kept till 1847 when it rose in seventeen different years and failed to rise in 32 different years. These were the Otley years, when Jonathan Otley, polymath of Keswick, was keeping records on many aspects of town and lake life. Otley also collected the gas from the island and had it analysed by the eminent chemist John Dalton in Cockermouth, coming to the same conclusion –

that it is largely marsh gas. Subsequent records are sparser, recording many occasions when the island rose but keeping silent in the years when it probably didn't. It is recorded as rising in ten of the years 1846 to 1888.

My wife Jennifer and I have canoed over the site shown by Symons many times each year from 2005 and never found an island as such. However we are each summer finding ourselves pushing through a strong growth of weed, with the apparent lake floor just a foot or so under water, so it would seem the island does float to some extent each year, inasmuch as it rises from the lake floor, but not with enough buoyancy to produce the rift needed to allow it actually to surface. The staff at Platty+, the boat hire station nearby, say they have never seen an island fully formed this millennium. We wait in eager anticipation for an opportunity to stand on 'the floating island'.

SOME DROWNINGS ON DERWENTWATER

Long before Platty+ began trading Lodore pier was the site of a disastrous outing, more due to the drunkenness of the boaters than the vagaries of the weather. One Sunday in August 1885 six young men from Keswick hired a boat at the Lakeside Boat Landings and rowed the three miles up to Lodore. They spent the afternoon drinking in both the Lodore and the Borrowdale hotels and were less than sober when they returned to their boat. Four of them put out, leaving the two stragglers still making their way down – only to manoeuvre their way back when cursed from the shore. When all six were unsafely aboard they pushed off again, weaving an erratic course which ended in the reed bed not fifty yards from the start. One of the less able rowers grabbed the oars and pushed them out successfully, only to run them aground on a sand bar some distance out from shore. Getting off this obstacle they lost an oar and in the melee which ensued managed to capsize. Three of them drowned, two were rescued clinging to the upturned hull and the last was picked up, exhausted, trying to swim to the shore.

The young Beatrix Potter, nineteen at the time and holidaying at Lingholm, was particularly scathing about the poor drowned men, writing of them in her journal as 'those drowned belonged to the lowest set in the town, and will not be missed...'[152] She was clearly upset by the drunkenness in the town, and in her journal goes on to claim 'There have been many drownings on this lake, but invariably caused by drink' and gives as examples 'the landlord of the Derwentwater Hotel at Portinscale went out with another man, both drunk, and both drowned. Twenty two

[152] The journal of Beatrix Potter. 1966

years later to the very day his son and one of the others went out in a similar condition...the son drowned...' Keen to make her point – that Keswick was a drink-crazed town – she recounts a story of another three drunken youths drowning rowing up to Lodore. Then 'there was a cheap tripper on a Saturday, but the list is endless.' As if to make that very point she goes on to rail at the drunkenness 'on the fourth Saturday, when the miners are paid all their earnings and go to the gin shop'. With a foretaste of her later literary ability she continues:

> 'Westward the thunder clouds came rolling across the fire; yet under such a sky and amidst such peace and calm one hears shouting and drunken voices singing 'hold the fort' in a variety of discords. Next morning the boatmen are trolling up and down with fishhooks fast to a board, and down below the water lilies, among the greedy pike, there is a man, the highest and the lowest in the scale of creation. The last body was caught on the Sunday, when was also half a pig's head, stolen from the inn. The parents of one of the men were both drunk at the funeral.'[153]

Potter makes a cogent case, but she is exaggerating: not all the drownings on Derwentwater are the fault of drunkenness. We have already seen that James Spencer-Bell and his friend Edward Rathbone died from youthful over-confidence, and that several workers died from over-loading their boats. Saddest of all, perhaps, was the case of the five young women from Nelson, in Lancashire, who were drowned when their overloaded boat took on water and was sunk near St. Herbert's Island. This was, admittedly, thirteen years later, on 12th August 1898. Drink was certainly not a factor in this case, but perhaps poor judgement was; poor judgement and the vagaries of this lake which can change from a calm and placid millpond to a maelstrom in a few minutes, and where conditions out in the middle can be much different from those on a sheltered shoreline.

The ladies were part of a Cooperative Holiday Association party which took over The Towers at Portinscale for their annual week's holiday from their work as weavers in the one of the Nelson mills. They were all Methodists and also taught in the Sunday School there. On their last full day they were due to walk to Watendlath with a big party, some of whom went by coach to Calf Close Bay to join those who opted to be rowed across from Nichol End. They had hired two boatmen, John Reed and his son Edward, but the boat the ladies were in was to be rowed by two men of their party. Initially there were to be only those seven in the boat, but just

---

[153] Beatrix Potter, Journal.

before they were pushed off an older man, a Mr. Radcliffe, asked if he could join them. Young Edward Reed said the boat was registered for eight, so it was permissible. Radcliffe sat in the bow, the five ladies arrayed themselves around the stern, and the two amateur oarsmen, John James and John Lane took their positions as bow and stroke.

The lake at first, in the lea of Lingholm promontory, was calm, but became increasingly choppy as they approached Derwent Island. At this point the first boat, under the experienced John Reed, had opted to abandon the course and pulled off to beach at the lakeside landings, but wasn't spotted by either the ladies' boat or by the third, under Edward Reed, who was following close behind them. Reed shouted to Mr. Radcliffe to move from the bow towards the centre of the boat, as he could see a lot of water breaking over the bow. When this tricky manoeuvre was completed their boat was back-heavy, with the bow breaking out of the surface.

At this point one of the ladies lost her lunch-box over the side and the oarsmen back-pedalled to retrieve it. This caused the stern to sink further and water gushed over it. Inexorably the boat sank, stern first, and all eight were struggling for their lives. All three of the men could swim, but were hard pressed to tread water, and unable to save any of the women, none of whom could swim, and all five were drowned, even though Edward's boat was quickly on the scene.

The inquest established that their boat was something of an unknown quantity, having been borrowed for the occasion by the boatmen and not one of their own. John Reed had registered it himself as being suitable for up to eight, though its registration when used from the Keswick boat landings was for six. The coroner made a recommendation that all boats used on the lake should be independently registered as to their capacity – a recommendation that was swiftly put into force.

Their story is well told in Ray Greenhow's book 'The Derwentwater Disaster'.

The week following the accident Mr. Mumberson, who was foreman of the inquest jury, wrote to the Keswick Guardian, forerunner of the Reminder, listing all the known drowning incidents on Derwentwater since 1814. He listed 17 separate incidents resulting in the loss of life of 35 people. All were men until this tragedy at the end of the century, and he was making the point that, in the main, the accidents had all been as a result of male hubris, drunkenness, or failure to listen to advice. Derwentwater, he was at pains to point out, was not inherently an unsafe lake, and visitors could be confident that if they hired a boat from a bone fide launch-man they would be safe. Dead visitors are a poor advert for a tourist town.

Part Six
External Agencies

CHAPTER NINETEEN

THE NATIONAL TRUST YEARS: 1902 ONWARDS

If you walk along Lord William Gordon's lakeside path starting at Hawes End Youth Centre you will soon descend to the lake shore beneath what was High Hawes End Farm, now also part of the Youth Centre. Here lies an ancient fallen tree which has been artfully carved (by a chainsaw) into a memorial of one of the most significant events in Derwentwater's history. It was carved in 2002 and is now showing its age, but it commemorates the first Lake District purchase by the fledgling National Trust of Brandlehow Woods, the area you will walk through as you carry on along the lakeside path.

Half a mile further on, past Low Brandlehow landing stage, you will come across a much more detailed wood carving depicting the pair of cupped hands shown – now too sadly suffering from the elements. These, as the plaque shown on the next page says, commemorate the Millennium and the National Trust's mission statement to own land and buildings "for ever, for everyone". It is perhaps naughty of me to perceive a secondary meaning in these cupped hands: that of hands open to receive gifts and alms, covenants and legacies, buildings, castles, land aplenty. However one looks at it the Trust has been phenomenally successful over the 20th century in acquiring land in particular in the Lake District. Although it wasn't started here – the first property bought was Alfriston Clergy House for the princely sum of £10 – one of its three founders was the indomitable Canon Hardwicke Drummond Rawnsley, vicar of Crosthwaite.

He knew well the history of philanthropic protectionism that had marked the various owners of the shores and islands of Derwentwater throughout the 19th century, and could see how it might all break down in the 20th with free-for-all development likely to spoil the beauty and harmony of the 'Vale of Elysium' as Thomas Gray had described it in 1769, and Camden long before him. He actively sought to bring as much land into National Trust hands and as quickly as possible.

Rawnsley already had history as a conservationist and adversary of schemes which he thought would ruin the beauty and peace of the area. In 1883 he led the campaign to prevent the building of a railway which would have run down the Borrowdale valley from Honister quarry, through the Hawes End gap, and so on to Braithwaite to join the Penrith-Keswick-Cockermouth railway. He enlisted the help of the other two founders-to-be of the National Trust, Octavia Hill and the lawyer Robert Hunter, along with the much-respected John Ruskin, already well established at Brantwood, overlooking Coniston Water. With this significant victory under his belt Canon Rawnsley went on to found the Lake District Defence Society (later to become The Friends of the Lake District), with an impressive list of luminaries on its board including the poet Robert Browning, the Duke of Westminster, John Ruskin and even Alfred, Lord

Tennyson. In 1888 he was elected as a member of the new Cumberland County Council and became chairman of its Highways Committee, a position he used to oppose the construction of roads over Lakeland passes. (This may well be why John Musgrave's scheme to forge a road over Sty Head Pass failed).

Rawnsley first met Beatrix Potter as a young girl when she holidayed at Wray Castle with her parents in 1882, when he was vicar of Wray. His views on preserving the natural beauty of the Lake District had a lasting effect on young Beatrix, who was already taken with the area. He was the first published author she had met, and he took a great interest in her drawings, later encouraging her to publish her first book, The Tale of Peter Rabbit. It was a friendship which was to have important repercussions for the Trust in the Lake District: when she died in 1943 she bequeathed it fourteen hill farms, all committed to breeding the native Herdwick sheep, plus almost all the original illustrations for her books. The ongoing annual income from visitors to Hill Top Farm (which she bought in 1903) and their Beatrix Potter Gallery in Hawkshead is still a significant factor in the Trust's success. In total the Trust now owns 91 fell farms.

Actual land acquisition however was slow in Rawnsley's lifetime. After the heady purchase of the 108 acres of Brandlehow in 1902 it wasn't until after the Great War that other land began to be bought or donated – the summit of Castle Crag in Borrowdale for instance by Dr W H Hamer & family as a memorial to 2nd Lieutenant John Hamer and the men of Borrowdale who died in the First World War. This was in 1920, the year of Canon Rawnsley's death. He had moved into Allan Banks, Grasmere, (one of Wordsworth's homes) in 1915 on his retirement, where Edith, his wife of 38 years, sadly died a mere year later. Briefly married again, to his long-standing secretary Nellie Simpson, Rawnsley himself died in May 1920. True to his principles he bequeathed Allan Banks to his National Trust, requiring only that Nellie might live there till her death – which wasn't in fact till 1959. In its obituary The Times said of him "It is no exaggeration to say – and it is much to say of anyone – that England would be a much duller and less healthy and happy country if he had not lived and worked."

His death seems to have opened the floodgates. The National Trust opened a public fund in his memory and were able to buy Friar's Crag, Calf Close Bay and Lord's Island in his honour by 1922: Lord and Lady Randles gave Cockshott Wood and North Strands Hagg in 1925; Stable Hills, Broomhill Point and other land were bought for £15,000 from Herbert Walker, the purchase price given by Sir Noton and Lady Barclay in 1929. Mr. Walker threw in Rampsholme Island as a further gesture of good will, and entered a covenant freely to prevent any building on 52 acres of sensitive land between Cockshott Wood and the Keswick to Borrowdale road. Crow Park, now the site of the World Heritage

Map showing National Trust owned land around Derwentwater in 2018

monument, was given by Sir John and Lady Randles in 1925 and it can fairly be said that in the single decade from Hardwicke Rawnsley's death in 1920 the Trust gained control of all the sensitive East shoreline of Derwentwater.

Succeeding decades have all brought purchases and donations large and small; perhaps the most significant from this book's point of view being the gift in 1951 by Denis Marshall of Derwent Island and St. Herbert's Island, and the purchase of the western half of the lakebed in 1958. This now meant all the islands were in single ownership for the first time in recorded history. The steady accretion over the last 120 years now leaves the National Trust in charge of over half the lake and most of its shores and of every farm in the Borrowdale Valley save Chapel Farm in Stonethwaite. The map of the region reminds one of the old World maps of the Victorian period where half the globe seemed to be coloured red. Overleaf is the map of Borrowdale with Trust land shown grey: the new (2016) Thorneythwaite lands shown a darker grey.

And yet Lake Derwentwater itself defies unification. The old boundary line, there ever since 1100 and probably longer, still holds sway.

CHAPTER TWENTY

THE LAST SEVENTY YEARS

1949 is a landmark year in the ongoing story of Derwentwater. It marks the beginning of a different sort of regime ruling over the lake, the islands, and the surrounding shorelines: a move from private landowners to a more public kind of ownership. In 1949 the Labour Government of the day passed an Act of Parliament to establish National Parks throughout Britain, and the Lake District National Park was one of the earliest to come into existence. Over a ten year period the oversight of Derwentwater underwent a profound change. In 1951 Denis Marshall gave Derwent Island and St. Herbert's Island to the National Trust, making them the first ever owner of all four major islands. Also in 1951 the Lake District National Park was established, marking the beginning of tight planning control, in particular the almost unassailable assumption that no development would be allowed between the lakeshore and any of the surrounding roads. In 1958 the National Trust bought the western half of the lake bed from the Leconfield Estate. They already owned virtually all the western shores and hinterland. On the eastern side of the lake the National Trust had acquired most of the lands, but still do not own the eastern lakebed itself. That is split between two/three owners along ancient lines. The heirs of Herbert William Walker own what used to be the Greenwich Hospital section – the North-East part; his 'Lodore Estates' company own the South-East section, and almost the only area of shoreline not in NT hands; and Allerdale Borough Council seem to own somewhat ill-defined small sections which are sometimes covered by water, sometimes not: all as shown on the map on the following page. The East/West boundary line opposite Barrow House is of ancient lineage: it separated Greenwich Hospital water from old Edward Stephenson's water in the 18th century and in the 19th separated the manors of Castlerigg and Borrowdale.

Since 1949 many other government agencies and quasi-autonomous non-government agencies (Quangos) have also become involved in the care and administration of the lake and shores. The Environment Agency was established in 1995 and increasingly monitors and legislates on all matters involving rivers, lakes and the agricultural, business and sewage activities which may have an impact on water quality. Before that the National Rivers Authority ruled with a lighter touch. English Nature, a quango under the auspices of the Department for Environment, Food and Rural Affairs (DEFRA), was formed in 1990 and had a huge impact on fell

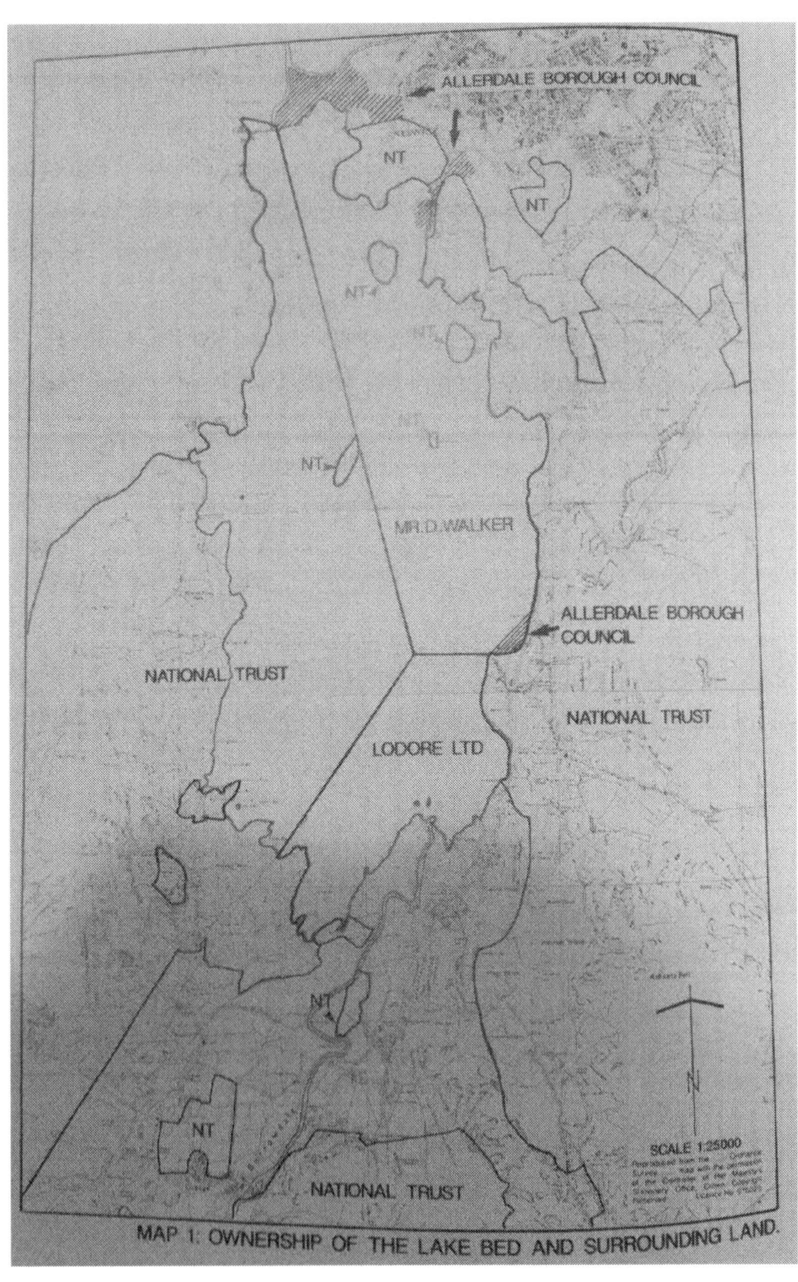

Map in the LDNP Derwentwater Management Plan of 1995

farming and the economics of hill sheep production (among many other things). It morphed into Natural England in 2006 and continues to have a big say in the way farming takes place in the Borrowdale valley – as elsewhere. English Nature was responsible for designating the entire lake a Site of Special Scientific Interest (SSSI) in the late 1990s. Cumbria Wildlife Trust maintains twenty sites in and around the lake which it considers special.

It is probably as well that so many official bodies are involved in the ongoing care of the lake and water quality, for it is certainly true that visitor numbers have increased exponentially over the last seventy years, along with cars, lorries, bicycles, coaches and minibuses on the roads and parking; and craft of almost every variety on the lake itself. The only transport to have disappeared is the railway, the Cockermouth to Keswick section closing in 1966 and the Keswick to Penrith section in 1972. There is no longer a closed or quiet season for tourism: most businesses are open all year round and find plenty of customers. Almost the only exception is rowing boat hire from the Keswick Foreshore, but it a rare day when some craft or other isn't to be seen braving the elements.

These responsible bodies have gone a long way towards mitigating the harm done by countless booted feet trampling every shoreline, but still there are large areas where erosion is all too plain to see. Calf Close Bay is a prime example. My wife, Jennifer, brought up in Keswick from the age of one vividly remembers grassy banks right down to the lakeshore where families put up tents for the afternoon and enjoyed ball games on the sward. Now there is nothing but a stony shoreline all round the bay, with even the tree-roots well back from the normal water-line undercut and exposed, leading to many falling.

Thanks to the National Trust we now have an excellent footpath from Fawe Park in Portinscale, past Lingholm and through its woods to Derwent Bay and Hawse End, along the lakeside right along to Brandlehow Bay and across the splendid wetlands at the southern end of the lake frequently on sturdy plastic duckboards which show little sign of deterioration, over the Chinese bridge and so to the Borrowdale road near the Lodore Hotel. The entire length is accessible by wheelchair. The path on the eastern shore is not as good, but is much better than it ever was, and is almost entirely off-road. These paths take a tremendous amount of wear with only reasonably light maintenance.

Off the path many areas have been fenced to isolate the wetlands and their breeding colonies of birds, to keep cattle and agricultural machinery away from the river-banks, and in many places to dissuade walkers from trampling on the vulnerable hydrosere (the delicate flora and soil which is sometimes exposed, sometimes underwater). Current Natural England subsidies and the Common Agricultural Policy have led to much reduced use of agricultural fertilisers and consequent improvement in water quality. The 'Vale of Elysium' is now a national treasure, a national venue for leisure, recreation and adventure and can only be tended by national bodies with national resources.

On the water itself there has been a very noticeable increase in various craft, some of which have come and gone with fashion. There used to be a considerable number of cabin cruisers and windsurfers: now there are very few. On the other hand the number of dinghies, canoes, kayaks and paddle-boards has increased dramatically. Much of the change is probably due to the much improved facilities for rental at Derwentwater Marina and Nichol End in Portinscale and at Platty+ at Lodore. The National Park Derwentwater surveys of 1982 and 1993 found an overall increase of almost 60% of craft on the water on summer days, and I'm sure there are many more now. Here is their table for those interested in such statistics.

TABLE 1: AVERAGE NUMBER OF CRAFT ON DERWENTWATER SUMMER 1982

Based on 6 days	People on the shore	Motor boat or cruiser	Small open motor boat	Sail dinghy or cruiser	Sail board (wind-surfer)	Canoe	Rowing boat	Launch	Other	Total
Summer average	524	14 17%	2 2%	20 25%	12 15%	8 10%	17 21%	1 1%	8 10%	82 100%
Min - Max	156 - 870	1 - 30	0 - 8	8 - 59	0 - 41	2 - 15	3 - 30	0 - 1	2 - 16	32 - 178

TABLE 2: AVERAGE NUMBER OF CRAFT ON DERWENTWATER SUMMER 1993

Based on 5 days	People on the shore	Speed boat	Motor cruiser	Small open motor boat	Sail dinghy or cruiser	Sail board (wind-surfer)	Canoe	Rowing boat	Launch	Other	Total
Summer average	665	5 4%	1 <1%	11 8%	19 23%	16 12%	42 33%	21 16%	3 2%	2 2%	129 100%
Min - Max	422 - 1,072	1 - 10	0 - 1	2 - 29	8 - 55	5 - 26	31 - 66	8 - 29	2 - 4	0 - 5	62 - 171

Shoreline footpath users have also increased by 21% in the same eleven year period. Again, our experience in frequently walking round the lake suggests these numbers are far greater now. There is a well-established public right of navigation on the lake, and several launching places (only Kettlewell Bay is free), but there is a 10 mile an hour speed restriction which is generally obeyed. Derwentwater is smaller than Windermere, Ullswater and Coniston which makes speed-boating much less attractive. This restriction was made a binding bye-law on 23rd January

1975 and removed any attempts at water-skiing which in any case had practically ceased because of the danger of the submerged rocks and shallow water which are a feature of this generally shallow lake.

THE WEIR AND LOW LAKE LEVELS

In the late 1990s the very low levels of water in the lake became the subject of much debate. There had long been an unofficial weir at the mouth of the lake near Derwentwater Marina, built of large stones and the accumulation of debris and weed collected on them which provided an effective but unsanctioned minimum lowest level to the lake. Not long before 1995 the National Rivers Authority, forerunner to the Environment Agency, removed this barrier – and, local opinion had it, some of the river bed too, and the lake level dropped nine inches in the next two days.[154] The drought of 1995, (which saw Haweswater reservoir so low as to reveal the old Mardale village), coupled with the removal of the dam, led to Derwentwater falling to its lowest ever recorded level. There is a long tradition, going back to 1887 and mayor W. Bromley, whereby mayors of Keswick fix slate plaques below Friar's Crag to show particularly low levels. 1893 saw an all-time low marked with a plaque which stood as a record till the 1940 plaque, which in turn gave way to the plaque of 20th September 1959, which modestly reads simply 'KUDC September 1959', that mayor apparently shyer than most. Martin Jordan, mayor in 1983 and currently still a councillor, marked that year's record low, and in 1989 Robert Welsh was able to mark yet another.

Since the removal of the dam, however, these records have regularly been beaten, as the lake continues to drop. The proposal to construct an official weir, or sill as it was described, ebbed and flowed throughout the latter years of the 1990s. Eventually almost everyone was in favour. The National Park Authority led the argument for a sill, after the various boating companies had set the ball rolling, as they were significantly affected by low water: the launches couldn't reach Lodore landing stage, boats putting out from Derwentwater Marina and Nichol End had great difficulty; and many hired boats were going aground on unsuspected rocks just below the surface. The first problem was that of funding. The Environment Agency wouldn't spend the £25,000 needed for a thorough assessment of lake levels and the impact of a sill unless it could be assured the bodies pressing for a change would be able to afford the estimated £50,000 an official sill would cost. The Dept. of the Environment

[154] Keswick Museum, Derwentwater files.

unexpectedly came up with £15,000 towards this assessment, which then went ahead.

In brief the assessment confirmed that over the preceding 100 years the lake's lowest level had been steadily falling, and that the natural sill level at the mouth of the River Derwent was eroding, partly naturally and partly as a result of human activity. It recommended a proper built sill, a short distance down river, which would keep the minimum lake level 23 centimetres (nine inches) higher than it was then. The National Park Authority put out a consultation paper seeking the views of the public and concerned organisations to the plan in 1998/9, and on receiving confirmation that most at least were in favour began to organise the raising of the £50,000 expected cost. Then the management of the Derwentwater Hotel in Portinscale, who owned one of the banks which the new sill would have to be attached to, objected and would not allow the construction.[155]

There is, therefore, no sill, and successive mayors can regularly claim yet another record low and place another plaque below Friars' Crag.

One of the original proponents of the sill was Peter Sorton, a forensic scientist who, with his wife Vanessa, took the tenancy of Derwent Isle from the National Trust in that pivotal summer of 1995. They accepted a 21 year lease from the Trust, but, somewhat ironically, were obliged to give it up after only four years because the frequent high water levels sometimes made it impossible to cross to the foreshore. When this led to Mr. Sorton having to miss a session at Carlisle Courts where he should have been an expert witness in the enquiry into a road traffic accident he and his wife judged it time to move on.

THE VARIOUS BOAT LANDINGS AND HIRING OUTLETS

The 'Derwentwater files' held in Keswick Museum contain a great deal of information on the boat landings on Keswick Foreshore – by far the oldest boat-hire venue. Walter Walker became secretary of the Derwentwater Launch Co. but was earlier a tout for one of the fourteen independent boat hirers operating on the site, each with their own landing stage and among them no fewer than 17 motorised boats and 94 rowing boats. Touts sold tickets for individual owners to visitors arriving by train and at busy times there were booths at intervals all the way from the railway station to the landings, much to the annoyance of the very visitors they hoped to attract. Walker tells how these fourteen opted, in 1933, to combine into one company, the Derwentwater Launch Co. Amalgamation led to some rationalisation, and by the mid-1960s there were five larger

[155] National Park: Derwentwater Management Plan, 1995

launches, 18 slow motor boats and 68 rowing boats. Rather surprisingly the price of a trip round the lake on a launch was still the two shillings it had been back in 1920, though the rates payable for the foreshore had risen from £230 per annum to £1,000.[156]

George Bott gives the history of some of the launches in a letter to a 'Miss Day'[157]. "Lady Derwentwater" still plies her trade today and was originally built in Windermere as a houseboat for Sir George Mellor. The Launch Company bought her in 1947 and had to undertake a major overhaul and refit, at a cost of £25,000. Replacement ribs were made from oak trees felled in Cockshot Wood. The old "Iris" belonged originally to the Lodore Hotel and was built in 1904 with a narrow keel to allow her to reach the landing stage there. She was used by the hotel to ferry guests to and from Keswick and was battery operated. In this millennium the company bought a twin-hulled iron built ferry boat which was used on the lake for a couple of seasons. It was horrendously loud, ugly and unloved and was sensibly sold on after a mercifully short period of operation.

Two other companies compete for the trade at the northern end of Derwentwater, on the western shore at Portinscale. Nichol End has been a launching site since mediaeval days, at first for freight and passengers to Keswick. Its more recent incarnation as a boat hiring and tuition venue was started in the 1970s by Nick Newby who operated from a tin shed and a few workshops where he maintained and built boats. The current café and tuition building date from the 1980s when the business expanded into the many areas of hire, maintenance and tuition still available today. The Museum papers bear witness to a few battles with the National Park Planning Board, as it was then – inevitable perhaps given their policy of resisting any development between the road and the shore. Fiercest of these came when Mr. Newby brought in twenty or more lorry loads of gravel to make his foreshore better for the launching of canoes, sailing dinghies and cruisers. Eventually he was obliged to dig the gravel out and remove it all. Nichol End, with its main building close to the lake, perhaps suffered more than any of the other marinas in Storm Desmond, 5/6th December 2015, when the café was flooded almost to ceiling height. The business continues today under the management of Mr. Newby's son Roger and his wife Natasha.

Derwentwater Marina, the other boating site on this NW corner of the lake, grew from a boating club which many years ago used this handy little bay to launch and store its boats. This club aspect is still visible here, with the West Cumbria Canoe Club storing its canoes on site, and with

[156] Derwentwater files.

[157] Derwentwater files.

sailing dinghies available for training towards RYA certification. All the usual activities are here, canoeing, kayaking, sailing, paddle-boarding and wind-surfing, plus group activities such as raft building and other team building exercises. The recently formed Lake District Rowing Club started here with a couple of four man skiffs, but has proved so popular and moved on to full eight man skiffs that there was no longer enough room, so they have taken up residence on the opposite shore at the Isthmus and now can often be seen skimming across the lake.

At the south end of the lake, using the Lodore Pier and the gently shelving shoreline, a new company was set up in the mid-80s initially to provide training in canoeing and kayaking. John and Sarah Platt capitalised on their surname to launch 'Platty+' which has gradually expanded over the years to provide a wider range of watersports hire. The disadvantage of being a distance from Keswick and the hub of the boat hiring business is perhaps outweighed by being able to use the much quieter south end of the lake for their fleet of paddle-boards, canoes, kayaks and the fearsome 'dragon-boats' – very large canoes with up to twenty oarsmen. The 1995 annual Dragon-boat race round Derwentwater could have ended in disaster when stormy waters overwhelmed two of the four boats and in all 58 contestants had to be rescued. A timely reminder that this generally benign little lake can sometimes develop large waves almost in the blink of an eye.

My title is 'Derwentwater – in the lap of the Gods.' In general I have portrayed the Gods as the influential men and women who have owned the land around the lake and the poets and visionaries who have opened our eyes to the beauty all around us here, and have sought to influence those influential men. But there are other Gods at work here too: Gods who have punished those who venture unprepared or insolent upon the waters, the Gods of wind and weather; Gods who have moulded the valley and the lake, either by ice and glacier, over millennia, or by flood or drought almost overnight.

The Gods of profit and gain have ever sought to take more than they give; from the miners who plundered the mountain sides leaving gross spoil-heaps that nature slowly heals to the entrepreneurs who would string vast cables across these lakes and mountain for the delight of those for whom the beauty of the surroundings is secondary to their visit.

The main pressure now must be that of tourism. The lap of the Gods is crowded; the Vale of Elysium thronged with souls seeking peace and spiritual refreshment. And excitement, adventure, adrenaline-fuelled thrills. The skies are spangled with multi-coloured paragliders, helicopters, gyroplanes and the thunder of passing tornado jets on manoeuvres. The forests are home to mountain bikes careering downhill and there is currently a plan to install a cable car to ease the uphill section. The fells are scarred by wide footpaths worn by countless pilgrims 'doing the Wainwrights' or just bagging the odd peak. The narrow roads groan under the weight of passing 'Chelsea Tractors' – and the all-too-genuine immense tractors and trailers ferrying sheep, cattle and forage from the upland farms to their newly bought lower lands. Keswick Town Centre, fortunately pedestrianised, regularly resembles Mecca at Hajj-time, but with the added entertainment of hundreds of dogs on hundreds of intertwining leads.

Many different organisations seek to impose some sort of order on the increasing chaos. The Lake District National Park Authority has the statutory duty, now reinforced by World Heritage status, to regulate development by strict planning control. The National Trust is by far the biggest landowner and has its own protocols and agendas. Pressure groups such as the Friends of the Lake District and the Wildfowl and Wetlands Trust actively seek to restrict developments that threaten the peace.

Are we in danger of killing the goose that lays the golden egg? It is the case that very few geese now lay eggs on St. Herbert's Island – overwhelmed by the number of would-be hermits for a day. Those humans seeking peace are increasingly like the geese; pushed out to the quieter islands of calm. Keswick now styles itself 'the Adventure Capital of Britain' and is home to many enterprises offering activities such as 'gully-bashing', various water-borne craft, cycling – especially now on electric bikes – Via Ferrata, tree-top scramble nets, zip-wires, rock-climbing and so on. It's a far cry from the original tourists with their viewing stations, Claude glasses and delight in the picturesque. Fortunately the valley and its lake have shown themselves robust and resilient: the scars of mining and forestry heal over as Nature re-establishes herself. If we, the present generation of minor gods, can only follow the examples of Marshall, Gordon and Walker – all entrepreneurs in their own way – then all will be well.

ACKNOWLEDGEMENTS

Thanks first and foremost to Dr Derek Denman whose thesis, published online to read freely, provided a stimulus and some waymarks for my research. Derek kindly agreed to meet, bringing lots of literature, ideas and encouragement. He has given permission to use much of his material from the thesis. The way in which it is used and presented is my own, as are any conclusions which I make.

The National Trust's archaeologist, Jamie Lund, also made time for me, providing copies of otherwise unavailable leaflets and sections of NT records, including his original 1999 archaeological 'digs' on St. Herbert's Island and Rampsholme.

As ever the staff at Carlisle Record Office were unfailingly helpful, bringing box after box of files, papers, letters and maps and suggesting other avenues for study that would otherwise have remained unknown to me. Thanks too to Keswick Museum, and especially Ros Roberts, for making available their impressive collection of papers on Derwentwater comprising many ancient newspaper clippings, some jottings of Jonathon Otley and J. Fisher Crosthwaite, and more recently George Bott.

My interest in Cornet Robert Phillipson was initially piqued by a single reference in a paper by Susan Johnson in the Transactions of the Cumberland and Westmorland Antiquarian and Archaeological Society, but without the additional online promptings of Pauline Wharton's blog I may never have filled in the huge gaps in my knowledge of him and his part in the Civil War activities on St. Herbert's Island.

Lastly, as always, my thanks to my wife Jennifer for her interest in the convoluted stories of Derwentwater's past which I regularly inflict on her on our walks through the very history I was writing about. Without her criticisms, encouragement and suggestions the text would have been much more impenetrable than I hope it now is.

BIBLIOGRAPHY

Armstrong, Margaret *Linen and Liturgy*. Peel Wyke Publications, 2002

Bangay, Paul *The dapper little banker* 2011

Bott, George Keswick, *The Story of a Lake District Town* Cumbria County Library 1984

Bouch, C.M.L. & Jones, G.P. *The LakeCounties 1500-1830*. Manchester University Press 1961

Brown, M.E. *A man of no taste whatsoever: Joseph Pocklington 1736-1817* Author House 2010

Clark, Colette (Editor) *Home at Grasmere, Dorothy Wordsworth Journal*. Penguin 1960

Collingwood W.G. *Elizabethan Keswick* Whitehaven, Michael Moon, 1987

Collingwood, W. G. *'The home of the Derwentwaters'* TCWAAS 1902

Crosthwaite J. Fisher *'The last of the Derwentwaters'* Keswick Literary Society,1874

Crosthwaite, J. Fisher *Brief Memoir of Major-Gen. Sir John Geo. Woodford* Keswick Literary & Scientific Society 1880

Crosthwaite, J. Fisher *Old Borrowdale* CWAAS 1875-6

Crosthwaite, Peter *A series of accurate maps of the principal lakes of Cumberland, Westmorland and Lancashire. 1783-1794*

Davies, Hunter *William Wordsworth*. Frances Lincoln Ltd. 1980

De Quincey, Thomas *Recollections of the Lakes and Lake Poets*. Penguin 1970

Denman, Derek *Materialising Cultural Value in the English Lakes, 1735-1845: A Study of the responses of new landowners to representations of place and people,* Lancaster University thesis, 2011.

Published as a Lancaster University Eprint at http://eprints.lancs.ac.uk/61596/1/DenmanThesisEprint.pdf

Denman, Derek, 'Lord William Gordon and the picturesque occupation of Derwentwater in the 1780s' TCWAAS Vol 14 (2014), pp. 207 – 230.

Donald, M.B. *Elizabethan Copper*, Michael Moon

Dymock, Marjorie Lingholm, *Its Story and Memories*. McKanes, Keswick, 2015

Farrer, William and Clay, Charles Travis. Editors, *Early Yorkshire Charters*,

Gell, William *A tour in the Lakes 1797* Edited by William Rollinson, Smith Settle Ltd, 2000

Gilpin, William *Observations relative chiefly to picturesque beauty* 1776

Glaister, Professor John, M.D., F.R.S.E., CWAAS: *The Glaisters of Scotland and Cumberland* Vol 20 (1920).

Gray, Thomas *A tour of the English lakes 1769*

Greenhow, Ray, *The Derwentwater Disaster, 12th August 1898*

Hankinson, Alan *The Regatta Men*. Cicerone Press 1988

Hill, Alan (editor) *The letters of William and Dorothy Wordsworth,* 8 vols, ed. de Selincourt, 2nd edition, Oxford, Clarendon Press, 1967-1993

Hill, Alan G. (Editor) *The letters of Dorothy Wordsworth* Oxford Letters and memoirs1981

Hutchinson '*Cumberland' Vol 2,* Carlisle: F. Jollie. 1794

Jones, Kathleen *A Passionate Sisterhood* Virago 1998

Kaye, Brigadier J W *Governor's House, Keswick* CWAAS:, vol 66

Keswick Historical Society & The Friends of Keswick Museum & Art Gallery *Keswick Characters, vols.1 and 3* Bookcase 2006 onwards.

Ladyman, Samuel: ''*Thoughts and Recollections of Keswick and its Inhabitants during Sixty Years* (1885), Keswick, available online at http://archive.org/details/thoughtsandreco00ladygoog

Lees, Rev. Thomas Article XXXII of the *Transactions of the Cumberland and Westmorland Antiquarian &Archaeological Society* .

Lefebure, Molly *'Cumberland Heritage'* London, Gollanz, 1970

Myers, F.W.H *Wordsworth*, London, MacMillan, 1880, [Project Gutenburg etext 8747]

Nicolson, Joseph and Burn, Robert *The history and antiquities of the counties of Westmorland and Cumberland* 1777

Otley, Jonathan *A Description of the English Lakes*, published by the author, Keswick, Cumberland, by J Richardson, London, and by Arthur Foster, Kirkby Lonsdale, Cumbria, 1823 onwards.

Partridge, Frances *Memories* Phoenix 1981

Potter, Beatrix *The journal of Beatrix Potter 1881-1897.*

Rawnsley, H.D. *A Rambler's Note-book at the English Lakes* James MacLehose & Sons 1902

Rimmer, W.G. *Marshalls of Leeds, Flax-spinners 1788-1886.* Cambridge University Press 1960

Scott, Walter & Lake J. W. *The Poetical Works [of Sir Walter Scott]: With a Sketch of His Life.* Edinburgh: Adam and Charles Black, 1853

Skelton, Constance Oliver & Bulloch, John Malcolm. *Gordons under arms* Aberdeen, 1912

Smith, M. J. *The mushroom elections in Carlisle 1784-1803.* CWAAS: Vol 81 (1981).

Southey, Charles Cuthbert, *'The life and correspondence of Robert Southey'* New York, Harper and Brothers 1851

Speck, W.A. '*Robert Southey: entire man of letters*' London, Yale University Press 2006

Symons, G. W. '*The Floating Island in Derwentwater: its history and mystery, with notes of other dissimilar islands...*'

Thomason, David & Woof, Robert *Derwentwater: the Vale of Elysium*, Trustees of Dove Cottage 1986

Tyler, Ian *Seathwaite Wad & The Mines of the Borrowdale Valley* Blue Rock Publications 1995

Vellacourt, Jo *From Liberal to Labour with Women's Suffrage.* McGill-Queens University Press 2016

Warter, John Wood (editor), *Selections from the Letters of Robert Southey*, (London, 1856)

West, Thomas '*Guide to the Lake District*' . W. Richardson et al., London, 1796

Wilson, Frances *The Ballad of Dorothy Wordsworth* Faber & Faber 2008

Woof, Pamela *Dorothy Wordsworth, writer,* Grasmere, Wordsworth Trust, 1988

Ian and Jennifer (née Wake) were brought up in the Keswick area and both went to Keswick School 1960-1967. They farmed in Eskdale for most of their working lives, and their time there is the background for Ian's first book 'Fisherground – living the dream'. Not one to waste experiences Ian then wrote a history of his own teenage years on his parents' farm in Borrowdale, mixing their experiences with the long history of that farm, Thorneythwaite, from its earliest existence as an Iron Age settlement through all its recorded history from 1552 onwards. Titled 'Thorneythwaite Farm, Borrowdale', it is available at various outlets in Keswick and online at Amazon.

Ian and Jennifer have two daughters. Catherine, the elder, lives in London and is a novelist with three titles to her name while Sally, the younger, is the founder and director of Sally's Cottages, a well-known Lakeland holiday letting agency.

22932392R00113

Printed in Great Britain
by Amazon